I0824592

ADVANCE PRAISE

"*The Permission Mission* is a powerful invitation to stop waiting and start living. With warmth, clarity, and real-world insight, Dr. Cindy McGovern helps readers recognize the invisible rules holding them back—and shows them how to confidently give themselves permission to speak up, set boundaries, and step into the spotlight of their own lives. This book is both deeply affirming and decisively practical, reminding us that the courage we're waiting for isn't external—it's already within us."

—DR. MARSHALL GOLDSMITH is the *Thinkers 50* #1 Executive Coach and *New York Times* bestselling author of *The Earned Life*, *Triggers*, and *What Got You Here Won't Get You There*

"*The Permission Mission* is a powerful reminder that the permission we're waiting for rarely comes from the outside. Cindy McGovern shows readers how to trust their own voice, quiet the doubts that hold them back, and take meaningful steps toward the life they actually want. Thoughtful, encouraging, and deeply practical."

—DORIE CLARK, *Wall Street Journal* & *USA Today* bestselling author of *The Long Game*

"*The Permission Mission* is the mic drop we all need. Dr. Cindy McGovern has written more than a book; she has sparked a movement. One that reminds us we never needed to wait for a seat at the table. Our seat has been there all along, and we are the ones who set the agenda.

"With warmth, humor, and zero fluff, Dr. Cindy shows us how to stop seeking approval and start giving ourselves permission to lead, speak up, and shine. She delivers practical tools to unlock confidence, embrace authenticity, and create meaningful change in our own lives and in the lives of others.

"As someone who has spent a career closing the gender gap and building spaces where all voices are seen and heard, I believe this book is essential reading for every woman and every leader. When you give yourself permission to show up fully, you do not just transform your own life; you elevate everyone around you. And that is how real impact happens.

"Read it. Share it. Live it. The world is waiting for your voice."

—SHELLEY ZALIS, CEO, The Female Quotient, Chief Troublemaker and Champion for Women in Business

"Let me be very clear: No one is coming to give you permission. And if you're waiting, you're wasting time. Dr. Cindy McGovern says what too many people are afraid to: You're not stuck because you're not capable… you're stuck because you're waiting for validation. *The Permission Mission* blows that door wide open. Dr Cindy doesn't coddle. She challenges. She pushes you to stop second-guessing yourself, trust your instincts, and step into rooms like you belong there (because you do). This book isn't a book on motivation. It's about owning your value, betting on yourself, and taking bold action. Read it, apply it, and stop waiting for permission to become the person you already are."

—HEATHER MONAHAN, Top 50 keynote speaker and bestselling author of *Overcoming Your Villains* and *Confidence Creator*

"Dr. Cindy McGovern's new book, *The Permission Mission,* is a must-read for any high-achieving woman who needs a permission slip to advocate for herself. As women, we're so often over-functioning and endlessly giving, yet somehow still waiting for approval to rest, pivot, dream bigger, or choose ourselves. Dr. Cindy doesn't just give you permission to put yourself first- she teaches you how to claim it unapologetically.

"Cindy and I met as two professional women who instantly recognized the fire in each other. We bonded over our shared belief that women don't need to be fixed; they need to be freed. Freed from guilt, from expectations, and from the idea that your worth is the sum of your achievements. If you've ever felt the quiet pull to live more authentically but hesitated because you were waiting for the 'right time' or someone else's approval, this book is your sign. Read it, absorb it, and give yourself the permission you've always deserved."

—TIFFANY MOON, MD, *USA Today* bestselling author of *Joy Prescriptions*

"This book is a powerful guide for women who feel the pull to step forward, speak up, and make their mark—yet too often hold back. If you've ever let doubt call the shots, this is a must-read. Our world needs more brave women willing to make the difference their difference makes, and this book helps you do exactly that."

—DR. MARGIE WARRELL, global leadership speaker and bestselling author of *The Courage Gap*

"As someone who's spent a career helping people connect through trust and storytelling, I believe the most powerful sale any of us ever make is the one we make to ourselves. In *The Permission Mission,* Dr. Cindy McGovern delivers a message that's as timely as it is timeless: We don't need to wait for anyone else to give us permission to step into our greatness; we already have everything we need. This book is part guide, part coach, and all heart. Dr. Cindy has a gift for helping people uncover their authentic voice and use it boldly, not to impress others, but to fully own their worth. She combines practical strategies with real-life vulnerability. *The Permission Mission* isn't theory but lived experience. And she walks you through the process of reclaiming your power, one courageous choice at a time. I highly recommend this book to anyone ready to stop playing small and start showing up in life, in business, and most importantly, for themselves."

—**MIKE BOSWORTH,** bestselling author of *Solution Selling, Customer Centric Selling,* and *What Great Salespeople Do*

"Permission granted….yes you can! We're all inhibited by things in past that subconsciously holds us back. This book is the one we all should have read years ago, thankfully we can today. Even if you don't feel you need this book you need to read it. It is time you unlock your potential because no one will do it for you!"

—**MARK HUNTER,** "The Sales Hunter," author of *Integrity First Selling*

"We are not just supposed to survive through life, we are supposed to thrive in it. But that won't happen by accident; it will happen by choice. *The Permission Mission*, by Dr. Cindy McGovern, is a powerful reminder that you cannot truly thrive while waiting for permission—permission to speak up, step forward, trust yourself, or claim the success you've earned. Dr. Cindy challenges the unseen silent limits we place on ourselves, the secret doubts that we have about ourselves, and shows us how to move from hesitation to execution. This is about reclaiming your own power and choosing to lead your life and career from a place of confidence rather than caution. If you are ready to release the need for external validation, and fully THRIVE in your work, your leadership, and your life, this book is your map."

—**MERIDITH ELLIOTT POWELL,** Hall of Fame speaker, award-winning author

"If you've ever failed, felt like an imposter, not known when to let go, or when to ask for help, this is the invitation you've been waiting for—the key to any door. Though Dr. Cindy McGovern offers it to you here from her experience as a woman, this book will provoke and help any of your friends, family, or team members. I'm thankful for it."

—ETHAN BEUTE, ***Wall Street Journal*** **bestselling author of** ***Human-Centered Communication*** **and** ***Rehumanize Your Business***

"In *The Permission Mission*, Dr. Cindy McGovern gives you permission to trust what you already carry inside of you—your own story. She helps you replace borrowed confidence with self-belief and shows how owning your voice transforms the way you connect, communicate, and lead. Dr. Cindy turns lived experiences into clarity and conviction. If you've ever questioned whether your story truly matters (and by the way it does), this book will give you the clarity needed to flourish with your best self."

—LARRY LEVINE, author of ***Selling from the Heart*** **and** ***Selling in a Post-Trust World***

"At the heart of everything I teach and believe is one simple fact: connection matters. Our confidence, leadership, opportunities, and impact grow in direct proportion to how well we connect with others and with ourselves. That's why *The Permission Mission* by Dr. Cindy McGovern resonates so deeply with me. This book is a powerful reminder that before we can truly connect outwardly, we must first give ourselves permission inwardly. We must give ourselves permission to be seen, to be heard, and to lead with our full humanity. Dr. Cindy masterfully bridges communication and connection, showing us that permission isn't about waiting for validation from others; it's about aligning with who we are and how we choose to engage with the world.

"*The Permission Mission* is about more than building relationships rooted in trust. It's about understanding, the most important connection is with yourself. This is the kind of book that shapes your daily habits, your mindset, and the conversations you carry forward. If you're ready to deepen your connections, amplify your voice, and step fully into the impact you're meant to have, this book is for you."

—MICHELLE TILLIS LEDERMAN, author, ***The Connector's Advantage*** **and** ***The 11 Laws of Likability***

"*The Permission Mission* alone doesn't dismantle systems, but it does shape how women move within them. It invites readers to examine the internal barriers that influence their voice, visibility, and choices, and to begin choosing themselves with greater awareness and agency."

—ERICA ROONEY, founder of HER Collective, author of *Glass Ceilings and Sticky Floors*

"Women are often taught to avoid risk, be responsible, and wait for the right moment. Over time, that conditioning can turn trusting our own voice into something that feels risky rather than necessary. In *The Permission Mission,* Dr. Cindy McGovern thoughtfully examines the many ways women learn to second-guess themselves, particularly when it comes to their own judgment and success. This book is a clear and timely reminder that the permission we are waiting for has always been our own."

—LAURA CASSELMAN, CEO and Co-Owner, JVZoo, *Wall Street Journal* bestselling author of *Trust Your Increments*

"Voila! Another masterpiece in Dr. Cindy McGovern's conversational and enthralling style that blends supportive encouragement with research-based grounding––this time to steer women's increased self-esteem, self-confidence, and self-expression towards empowerment and goal attainment. Dr. Cindy is like a Michelin Star Master Chef who serves up wholesome morsels of wisdom through her celebrated wit and engaging examples from personal experience, authors, composers, movies, TV, books, politicians, historical figures, and world leaders. The "edu-taining" McGovern weaves in enough mini-references to proven psychology principles and research to lend credence to her prescriptions, but without any theoretical heaviness.

"*The Permission Mission* isn't just for women, since men will find applications for themelves, especially if they view themselves as allies and advocates for the women in their lives. Who among us couldn't use a personal life coach, workshop teacher, counselor, therapist, and social activist all wrapped up in a fun, quick page-turner?"

—DR. RICK BRANDON, president of Brandon Partners and author of *Wall Street Journal* bestseller *Survival of the Savvy: Political Tactics for Career and Company Success*

"Dr. McGovern delivers a powerful truth: The permission we seek from others is really ours to give ourselves. *The Permission Mission* is a wake-up call for anyone who has ever blamed circumstances—or other people—for their lack of success. This book will guide you through powerful insights and practical steps to stop waiting for permission from others and trust your own voice to step into the spotlight of your own life."

–LINDA GALINDO, author of *The 85% Solution: How Personal Accountability Guarantees Success, No Nonsense, No Excuses*

"Reading *The Permission Mission* feels like having a wise, steady voice remind you that you already have what you need. You have simply forgotten to trust it. As a professional speaker and social media strategist, I spend my days helping people find the confidence to show up, speak up, and be visible, online and in real life. Over and over, I see the same challenge: People hold themselves back—whether that's advocating for themselves at work, sharing their ideas on social media, or stepping into leadership. Dr. Cindy helps readers quiet the "backup singers," reclaim their confidence, and take meaningful steps toward the spotlight of their own lives. And as a proud girl dad, this message resonates with me on an even deeper level. I want the next generation to grow up knowing they don't need anyone's approval to speak up, take up space, or pursue what matters to them. This is a book people will not just read. They will return to it when they need courage."

–COREY PERLMAN, keynote speaker, author of *Authentically Social*

"Fantastic read for any woman who feels the weight of expectations and has been waiting for permission to break the rules and fully own her story. *The Permission Mission* will inspire you to trust yourself, take action (even when fear is trying to pull you back!), and live your life with passion and purpose."

–HEATHER WHELPLEY, keynote speaker and award-winning author of *Grounded Wildness* and *An Overachiever's Guide to Breaking the Rules*

"*The Permission Mission* is a powerful reminder that the most important trust we build isn't with others. It's with ourselves. Dr. Cindy challenges the quiet rules and voices that hold us back and gives readers permission to step forward, speak up, and own their voice. This book is thoughtful, practical, and deeply human."

–JOEL GOLDBERG, baseball broadcaster, keynote speaker, and podcast host

"*The Permission Mission* is the road map we didn't know we needed, until now. Dr. Cindy McGovern has given us a powerful reminder that the life we want doesn't come from waiting for approval. It comes from choosing ourselves, unapologetically and without delay. As a transformational coach, I've worked with so many high achievers who are stuck in the cycle of overthinking, people-pleasing, and putting themselves last on their to-do list. This book offers the antidote. Dr. Cindy writes with clarity, compassion, and just the right amount of tough love. She doesn't just inspire, she equips the reader with actionable tools and relatable stories to create a roadmap to the life they really want. *The Permission Mission* guides you to do the one thing that changes everything: Give yourself permission to live boldly, speak freely, and own your worth. This isn't just a book. It's a mission worth joining and a movement I fully support."

—MAKI MOUSSAVI, transformational coach, speaker, and author of *The High Achiever's Guide*

"One of my favorite quotes is 'Quiet the mind, and free up the soul.' Dr Cindy has provided us with a step-by-step guide to hearing and trusting your inner voice, lowering your need for the approval of others, and eliminating the practice of giving away your power. Even better, she gives real world examples and inspires the reader at each stage of the journey."

—MARTY SELDMAN PhD, co-author of *A Woman's Guide to Power, Presence and Protection*

"*The Permission Mission* encourages readers to find their voice, overcome self-doubt, and embrace their true potential. Through relatable anecdotes and actionable steps, this book provides a roadmap to challenge societal norms and take steps toward living authentically. If you're ready to step into the spotlight of your life, learn to set boundaries, pursue your dreams, or simply say 'yes' to yourself, this book is for you."

—LIZ CASSELMAN, attorney and author of *Not Just a Title*

"There are moments when a manuscript does more than inform or inspire. It mirrors something the reader has felt but never fully named. *The Permission Mission* is one of those rare works.

"As I read these pages, I did not feel like I was being taught. I felt like I was being accompanied. That distinction matters. Dr. Cindy McGovern does not stand above the reader with instructions. She walks beside them with honesty, humility, and an uncommon respect for the interior life of human beings. This book does not shout. It invites. It listens. It waits—then gently asks the question most of us have been avoiding: Whose permission are you still waiting for?

"What struck me most is how deeply personal this work is without becoming self-indulgent. The stories are not included to impress. They are included to liberate. Every reflection, every metaphor, every carefully chosen example serves one purpose—to help the reader trust their own voice more than the inherited voices that have governed them for far too long. That is not motivational rhetoric. That is transformational leadership at its most human level.

"The concept of "backup singers" is deceptively simple and profoundly accurate. Anyone who has spent time studying leadership, psychology, or organizational behavior knows how powerfully the past narrates the present. Dr. McGovern gives language to that phenomenon in an accessible, compassionate, and actionable way. She does not demonize those voices. She honors them, then teaches the reader how to right-size their influence. That balance is rare and deeply responsible.

"This book also carries courage. It speaks directly to women without excluding men. It names cultural realities without bitterness. It acknowledges systemic barriers while refusing to let them define the story's ending. The message is clear and steady: Worthiness is not earned, permission is not granted, and power does not arrive from the outside. It is reclaimed.

"From a leadership perspective, this book belongs in boardrooms, classrooms, therapy offices, and kitchen tables alike. It is as relevant to a young professional learning to speak up as it is to a seasoned leader who has achieved success yet feels strangely constrained. The through-line is trust—trust in intuition, trust in lived experience, and trust in one's right to step fully into the spotlight of their own life.

"I am grateful for this work. Grateful for its clarity. Grateful for its kindness. Grateful for the way it refuses to rush the reader while still refusing to let them remain stuck. *The Permission Mission* is not a call to rebellion. It is a call to alignment.

"That is where real leadership always begins."

—**DON BARDEN, PhD, economist and bestselling author**

The Permission Mission

The Permission Mission

RECLAIMING THE POWER TO TRUST YOUR OWN VOICE

DR. CINDY MCGOVERN

IDEAPRESS PUBLISHING
WASHINGTON, DC

Ideapress Publishing | www.ideapresspublishing.com

Interior Design: Jessica Angerstein
Author photo: Living Notes Photography

Cataloging-in-Publication Data is on file with the Library of Congress.

Hardcover ISBN: 978-1-64687-241-1

Special Sales
Ideapress books are available at a special discount for bulk purchases for sales promotions and premiums, or for use in corporate training programs. Special editions, including personalized covers, a custom foreword, corporate imprints, and bonus content, are also available.

1 2 3 4 5 6 7 8 9 10

Hi!

I'm so glad you're here.

I knew you'd show up when you were ready.

When you were done second-guessing yourself...

When you were tired of ignoring your instincts..

When you could no longer deny the feeling

that there is something more for you...

Welcome.

I wrote this book for you.

Dr. Cindy

Contents

PART FIVE

Part One

Your Personal Permission Mission

G ive yourself permission rather than asking or waiting for permission from someone else.

R ealize that your passion for what you want, need, and deserve is greater than the fear of trying.

I n-power yourself to trust your own voice more than the voices of the past.

T ake a step forward into the spotlight on the stage of your own life.

Chapter 1

I Wish I Had Said Something. *Anything.*

> You are not an extra in somebody else's film. You are the star in your own life.
>
> **—Faye Dunaway**

I had been kicking myself all day.

"Hey, frizz-bomb." It was a classmate I barely knew, poking some good-natured fun at my long, naturally curly hair in front of everyone at the lockers a few minutes before first period.

"Jealous much?" was my clever retort.

Wait. I didn't say that. I didn't say anything. I was embarrassed.

I wish I had rolled my eyes at her. I wish I had told her to mind her own business. I wish I had asked her why she needed to pick on me just because my curly hair was different from her thick, straight coif. I had all of these comebacks in my head, but I didn't say them.

I wish I had said something. *Anything.* It wouldn't have been snarky or hurtful, even though that's what her comment seemed like to me. As feisty as my very opinionated grandmother was, she taught me better than that.

But I didn't say anything at all, and I had been kicking myself all day.

Looking back now, I realize that I did that a lot. Someone would make a comment that I didn't agree with, but I would nod my head and smile or do nothing. My dad would ask me to run an errand for him, and running it would mean I had to miss the trip to the mall I had planned with my besties. I ran the errand without complaining. Another time, I asked a smart girl in science class to be my lab partner, and she brushed me off as if she didn't hear me. So I pretended that she didn't hear me. And once, I couldn't even muster up the courage to audition for a solo in the holiday concert, and I wound up settling for a role in the chorus even though I really wanted the lead.

Sometimes, I felt like I was stuck in the chorus of my own life instead of standing in the center of the stage under the spotlight where I wanted to be. I was raised to be so polite that I became reluctant to ask for, let alone insist, that I get what I really wanted or felt I deserved.

As an adult, there was a time when, during a job interview, I was offered less money than I wanted. Instead of speaking up and articulating my value, I expressed my gratitude. Why did I do that? Many other times, I accepted invitations to parties that I really didn't want to go to. And on more than one occasion, when a neighbor volunteered me to help plan a fundraiser, and I knew I didn't have time, I went along with it anyway so I wouldn't upset her. I didn't speak up because I didn't want to make anyone uncomfortable, even though others were making me feel that way. I didn't want to inconvenience anyone, but they were inconveniencing me.

In every case, I wish I had said *something.* Anything. I wish I had the courage to object. I wish I had the words to make my case. Instead, I said nothing, because that's what good girls do.

Granny taught me that, too, and her voice was loud and clear. It still is. Come to think of it, almost everyone who helped raise me reinforced that's what good girls do. Who made these rules anyway? Who invented the good girl guidelines?

What I didn't realize then was that guidelines aren't exactly laws. I had a right to defend myself, to speak up on my own behalf and to set my own boundaries instead of staying inside the lines Granny and others had drawn for me, both for how much I was willing to take and what I was willing to do about it. I didn't quite grasp the fact that I deserved the respect of that classmate, and that it would have been OK if I told Dad I had already made other plans or negotiated with him so I could both keep my shopping date and run his errand afterward. I didn't consider that most of these rules aren't even real. They're definitely not one-size-fits-all. In fact, a lot of people make them up as they go along. I learned much later in life that negotiating the rules—or even bending them—is totally OK. I found out over the years that it's even OK to reject the rules and decide not to follow them when they don't seem to benefit anyone except the rule-maker.

What imaginary rules are you following? Where did they come from? Who introduced you to the good girl guidelines?

What's nagging at you? What's holding you back? Do you wish you could speak up? Do you regret it when you say "yes" even when, deep down, you'd rather say "no"? Do you kick yourself for staying quiet when someone has crossed the line? Have you ever silently beaten yourself up after you felt too timid to make a really important point at a meeting that nobody else had thought of, and then somebody else said it and everyone was impressed?

If you know what you want, why don't you go for it? Is there a mental obstacle in front of you? A velvet rope you cannot cross?

Are you waiting for someone to give you permission to say and do what your gut is telling you to go for but your parents or grandmother or someone else you trusted has taught you not to? If so, let me ask you this: Whose permission are you waiting for, and why?

I know that I'm never going to get Granny's permission to say the things I wish I had said. And if you're waiting for some wise voice from your past to give you permission to finally say or do what she told you, probably as a child, that you shouldn't—you might be waiting forever.

Are you waiting for someone to tell you it's OK to speak up? Are you waiting for the rules to change?

Why don't you give *yourself* permission to say and do what you want to, instead of waiting for someone else to grant it? Why don't you change the rules if they don't make sense? It's your life, after all.

Aren't you tired of waiting? Are you searching for a solution that will help you give yourself permission to say and do what your instincts already feel is right?

That may be why you picked up this book. If so, you've come to the right place. This book will help you take a step forward—and then another and another—until you're standing in the spotlight of your own life.

Chapter 2

Meet Your Backup Singers

> You are not a single self, but a chorus of voices. Wisdom is learning which one to hand the microphone to.
>
> —**Anonymous**

I can admit that standing in the shadow of the spotlight instead of directly under it can be pretty comfortable.

I can also admit that there were times in my past when that spotlight was shining on the very tips of my toes—just enough to let me know that stepping forward onto center stage was possible but not happening yet—and that made me feel equal parts excited and scared to death.

Chances are good that if you feel the same way, your go-to choice is to stand still. You choose comfort and familiarity. After all, it's easy and comfortable.

But are you truly happy there? Are you happy standing in the shadow of the spotlight on the stage that is a metaphor for your life? If you are, that's absolutely a valid choice. But I'm going to guess that you wouldn't have picked up this book if you were already completely happy there. I would imagine that you created space in your very busy schedule and diverted your attention away from work and your family to read these pages because you're searching for tools that will help you take that step forward toward whatever your next goal is.

Maybe you don't even know what your destination is, but you know there's more—or better.

I want to help you, nudge you—maybe even propel you—toward the happiness, success, and abundance that you want and deserve in your life. But first, let's take a look at why you're not already giving yourself permission to step, run, leap, or rush into the spotlight.

Let's go back to your parents, grandparents, teachers, coaches, neighbors, childhood friends, old bosses, and others who taught you, along the way, to be cautious and humble. They managed your expectations so you wouldn't get in over your head in life. They shared the wisdom that worked for them, fully believing it would work for you, too. Their voices helped to shape you. Their lessons were most likely valuable at the time you learned them.

But you have carried those lessons into adulthood with you, and if you're like most people—especially women—you at least occasionally stop yourself from moving forward because you know they wouldn't approve. Or you remember that they warned you not to take risks. Or you've become so used to doing what they said that you have never really appreciated or trusted in your own ability to make decisions for yourself.

In a way, we want them to give us permission to do the very things they warned us against. The problem is, they never will. Many of them aren't even part of our lives anymore because they have passed away or we've lost touch.

I call these well-intentioned people, the ones who teach and mold us into compliance from the time we're children, the "backup singers." Their voices constantly sing in the background of our consciousness, reminding us of the important lessons ("Look both ways before crossing a street," for example) to the oppressive ("You're not smart enough to earn a degree." "You're not witty enough to keep up in the conversation." "You're not talented enough to sell your art.").

They withhold their permission, at least in our memories of the wisdom (was it?) they imparted, and we obey the rules we have never really bought into because we were conditioned to accept them.

Frankly, we're probably afraid to *not* obey those rules. And they were probably afraid as well.

We've constructed an imaginary rulebook for ourselves, full of the dos and don'ts these backup singers prescribed for us from the time we were toddlers. And even after all this time, we're still afraid to break their rules—along with society's cultural norms, customs, traditions, and doctrines shaped by a society that historically has valued men over women, youth over maturity, and the majority over minority. Those unwritten rules are keeping us trapped in boxes that are too small for us.

We want out of those confining boxes, but we don't have the permission of those influential role models—past and present—who could set us free. And we know, somewhere in the back of our minds, that the truth is that we'll never get it from them.

Take a breath here so you can fully absorb what's next: *You don't need their permission*. The only permission you need is your own.

Trust me, this reluctance to disobey people who have no authority over you—at least not anymore—is not uncommon. In fact, it's deeply rooted in psychology, socialization, and even neurology.

Psychological studies suggest that reflecting on our past allows us to understand our own personal narrative and how we relate to the world. Retaining a connection to those voices gives us a sense of continuity in our lives and a framework for understanding our past and present as well as planning our future. Researchers call this "narrative identity."

The key word here is *narrative* identity, not *actual* identity. Are those inner voices narrating your life story, writing the script you live by? By this time in your life, shouldn't you be doing that for yourself?

Shouldn't you be drawing your own boundaries instead of remaining boxed in by theirs?

Even if you believe you're writing your own story, do you base it on other people's ideas of who you are and what you bring to the table? Think about it: Who is the star of your story? It should be you, not what others said about you or what they insisted you are supposed to be. We have been conditioned and convinced to believe the version of *our* story that was told to us by our role models.

Is that the narrative you're still living? Who wrote that narrative? You, or someone else? Who is holding the pen?

And again, are you happy with that life?

Those people had no idea then who you would be today, with your experience, your wisdom, your beliefs, and your talents. You are the only one who truly knows that.

And you're the only one who truly knows what you want. You're the only one who can accurately identify what your personal mission—or missions—are. What are you really here to do? What is the mark you want to make on the world? Or at least on today?

What are you waiting for?

Something is holding you back—and chances are it's the story you're telling yourself *about* yourself. It's the box that your backup singers tucked you into long ago. It's the labels they have stamped on you year after year.

I love the 2013 documentary *20 Feet from Stardom* by director Morgan Neville, a story about the real-life backup singers who stood behind the superstars who were singing on center stage. Some of them were completely satisfied and filled with joy just to be singing. Others were aching for their turn in the spotlight but held back by a tough industry, image expectations, cultural obstacles, and their own limitations.

They weren't happy. They wanted their time in the spotlight. They wanted their solos.

Now it's time for your solo. It's time to snatch the microphone away from whichever backup singers from your past are still narrating your story.

It's time to have the confidence of this kid I recently saw wearing a cute T-shirt that said: "Whatever you do today, do it with the confidence of a 4-year-old in a Batman cape."

Chapter 3

I Was Raised This Way

> Many of us were raised with unspoken rules: Be nice. Don't rock the boat. Keep the peace. Work hard. Don't ask for too much. Smile more.
>
> **—Megan Dalla-Camina**

About that four-year-old. He got that T-shirt because he asked for it.

In my book *Every Job Is a Sales Job: How to Use the Art of Selling to Win at Work,* I wrote that children are born with excellent sales skills and they use them to get what they want. They know what they want and they're not afraid to ask for it. They usually can figure out how to talk their parents into giving it to them. And their timing is pretty good: They wait for an opportunity to catch Mom in a good mood or Dad feeling generous.

Then, as they experience "no" for the first time, and the second, and the third, or they're told asking for stuff makes them look greedy, or they're reminded that money doesn't grow on trees, they stop asking. They begin to believe that they don't deserve to have everything they want. They start asking for permission instead of asking for what they want.

That lesson, which probably started with trusted parents, teachers, and older siblings—the original backup singers—stays in the back of the child's mind and surfaces every time she wants something as an adult. She is conflicted: Do I deserve it? Am I inconveniencing anyone by going after it? Can I afford it? Do I really need it?

Those are great questions. But if the answer to all of them is "no" because that's what you remember your parents telling you so many times, it's time to bring your notions of what you want, need, and deserve into harmony with the lessons from your past that convinced you to say "no" to yourself way too often. It's time to let your intuition overrule the advice or criticism you absorbed as a child.

Your backup singers are not just figments of your imagination. They're the ones who said "no" and changed you from confident to complacent. They're the ones who taught you that you don't deserve to have everything you want.

It's the way we were socialized, the way we were raised. We didn't do this to ourselves. It's part of our identity. It's part of our personal history.

It's also part of our shared history.

Psychological and sociocultural studies about self-worth point to five reasons why women in particular feel they don't deserve certain things:

1. **Gender stereotypes.** Many of us were raised to believe we should be self-sacrificing, humble, and not overtly assertive. Studies suggest that women are often socialized to downplay their achievements, desires, and needs, leading to the feeling that we don't deserve them.

2. **Imposter syndrome.** Certainly not exclusive to women, imposter syndrome describes the feeling that you are a fraud or not good

enough. When you have the chance to take on a job or another role that's outside of your comfort zone, you ask: "How did I get here? When are they going to figure out that I don't belong here? When are they going to take all of this away from me?" You might feel that you don't deserve to have what you have achieved, despite the evidence that you earned it.

3. **Good girl syndrome.** William Fezler and Eleanor Field coined the term in their 1985 book, *The Good Girl Syndrome: How Women Are Programmed to Fail in a Man's World—and How to Stop It.* Their premise: Women are raised to be caretakers and put others' needs before their own. That kind of social conditioning can lead to a diminished sense of self-worth and an inability to advocate for ourselves or go after what we want and need.
4. **Social backlash.** Research has shown that women can face backlash when they assert themselves or pursue success in the workplace or in life, reinforcing feelings of unworthiness and guilt when they step out of traditional gender roles. No wonder so many women believe they do not deserve success or recognition.
5. **Wage gap.** The fact that women were paid 85 percent of what men earned in 2024 (95 percent for women aged 25 to 34) is a deafening cultural statement affirming that women are considered less worthy than men. That leads to an internalized belief that women are not entitled to the same rewards or recognition as men.

This is the hand we've been dealt as women. Overcoming the feeling that we are undeserving is no small task. But once we understand that the cards are often stacked against us, we can begin to realize that it's just a house of cards—not meant to be permanent and susceptible to being knocked over. You just have to give yourself permission to knock it over.

You're not imagining these barriers. They're real, and you're definitely not the only one who struggles with them every time you try to step out of your comfort zone—or the comfort zone of your backup singers.

Chapter 4

The Rules Aren't Real

> Some rules are nothing but old habits that people are afraid to change.

—Therese Anne Fowler

You're not imagining that society's rules exist, but I call them imaginary rules.

The fact is that the norms of society and culture, and the traditions of our family or community, are simply expectations. We're not talking about breaking any laws here. If you give yourself permission to ignore those expectations, your only penalty will be sideways glances from those who want to keep them in place.

In some cultures, of course, those norms are actual law, and there are severe punishments for breaking them. That's a different conversation.

Still, some outdated laws linger on the books even in the US, but the fact that the police do not enforce them speaks volumes about the truth that rules are sometimes optional. A 1963 law in Carmel-by-the-Sea, California, for example, requires anyone who wants to walk in public wearing heels higher than two inches to get a city permit. I've broken that law! The city's reasoning: Someone who trips while wearing them on a public sidewalk might sue the city. What would Carrie Bradshaw say about that?

That's a fun example, but being boxed in by rules you don't agree with and did not agree to is anything but fun.

In *An Overachiever's Guide to Breaking the Rules*, author and leadership consultant Heather Whelpley explains that those boxes lead many women to feel they need to constantly prove their worth and intelligence, often by overworking or being perfectionists. The syndrome, she suggests, stems from—you guessed it—societal expectations. And it's reinforced by parents and others who lavish praise on their children for overachieving, who then grow up believing that is the path toward success and acceptance.

That can negatively affect a woman's identity and happiness.

Do you identify with that? Did you learn at a young age that these are virtues and are more important than going after what you truly want or what makes you happy?

Consider this: If the rules aren't laws but rather just expectations, yet you're still following them as an adult, then you're the one actually enforcing them. That means that somewhere along the way to adulthood, you bought into these rules, even though you may not have agreed with them. But they were reinforced by the trusted adults in your life, and today, you're still respecting them.

So, what are you getting out of that? Have you really thought about it? Or more importantly, are those rules holding you back? If you could change or omit any of them, which ones would you give yourself permission to overrule? At this point in your life, does it make sense to continue to follow rules created by people who lived in a different time and probably even in a different place?

In the South, I grew up saying, "Yes, ma'am" and "No, sir." I was taught that it was disrespectful to call adults by their first names, so I never did. Not long after I moved to California, my neighbors told me that I sounded so formal that when they first met me, they thought I was snooty. I'm neither of those things; I was just being polite. I was raised that way. Now, I had to learn the new rules and let go of the old ones.

Let's pause here to talk about whether we have any right to break these imaginary rules—to give ourselves permission to aspire, to ask for, to take, or even to have the things we want, need, and deserve.

When we talk about permission, it's usually framed as if someone else must grant it—an external authority or gatekeeper deciding whether we deserve something. But at its core, permission is deeply personal. It's about recognizing your own inherent right to pursue what you want, to have what you deserve, and to be who you truly are.

For women, especially, this is profound. Society has long imposed limits and rules—both explicit and subtle—on what women can or should do and say or even become. These constraints can make it feel like the right to dream, to succeed, or to simply prioritize your own joy and fulfillment is something to be earned, negotiated, or even borrowed. But the truth is, every woman already has the right—by virtue of being herself—to claim her goals, ambitions, and happiness.

So as we wade through life, we constantly need to rewrite the rulebook—until it's ours. As a woman in business, I quickly observed that most of the women executives I met wore pant suits. I enjoy wearing them, too, thank goodness, but I also really like skirts and dresses. For a while, I complied with the unwritten pant suit rule, but I gradually unveiled my more feminine wardrobe. I felt like I was breaking the rules, but guess what? There was no hall monitor sending me home to change into a more appropriate outfit.

That imaginary rule never existed. I've come to believe that most of the rules we follow truly are not rules at all. They're simply the preferences or expectations of others who would like you to do as they do rather than to express yourself authentically.

Sometimes, you have to follow the rules that others make for you. For instance, if you break a rule at work, you could be reprimanded or fired. If you break a law, you could be arrested. But for many of the rules that you blindly follow—just like the rest of us—simply because someone, at some time, said you have to, it's worth asking: "Do I really have to?" You might be surprised at how many "rules" are really just suggestions or preferences.

Sit with this for a moment: You don't have to follow those rules.

Chapter 5

Permission Is Power

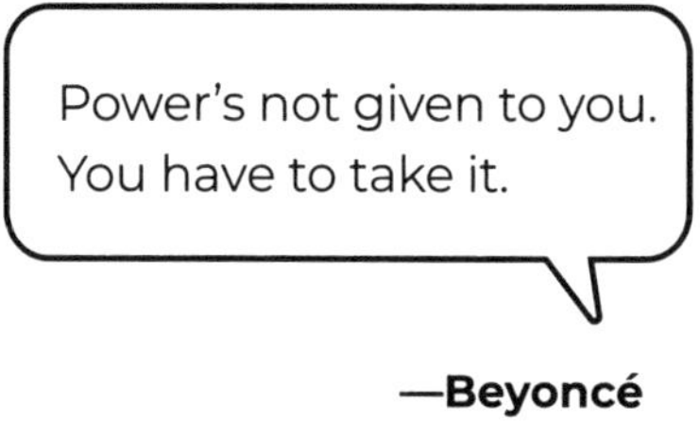

—Beyoncé

Once you have identified which backup singers are not singing in harmony with your best interests, dreams, and goals, and that the rulebook they wrote for you is far out of date, you may have another hurdle to navigate: Weaning yourself off of your reliance on both the rules and the rule-makers.

If you have relied on the ingrained wisdom of those who raised you and guided you rather than on your own instincts and experiences, relying on yourself and choosing your own path can be a difficult and emotional experience.

Your backup singers—including the people who have had influence over you, the social and cultural norms, and even your own imposter syndrome—have been your constant sidekicks since you were a kid. Your own inner critic, fashioned after those who once ridiculed or berated or censored you, is likely part of the foundation of your belief system. You believed the criticism. You believed these trusted adults who told you that you would never amount to anything or that you weren't smart enough to ever be more successful than they were.

Unbelieving that is a very hard thing to do. As we'll explore in a later chapter, a good place to start building trust in yourself is to identify each one of your backup singers. Give them names, like Mom, Dad, Big Sis, or Mrs. Thompson, and acknowledge the role each one plays when you're debating the pros and cons of your next move.

That way, you will know who's singing in harmony with your goals and who is way off-key. In the process, you will be able to silence the ones who are holding you back, to tone down those with the loudest voices (the critics are always louder than the cheerleaders), and to elevate the most positive backup singers to soloists.

The funny thing about backup singers, though, is that most of them, even your critics, probably taught you some valuable lessons and offered solid advice alongside their harsh assessments of your abilities and potential. My grandmother, for instance, taught me not to touch a hot stove, and she also taught me not to question authority. So sometimes I want to hear her voice loud and clear, and other times, I want to turn the volume way down or off altogether.

The key to taming your chorus of backup singers is learning to consider their advice without believing it is a hard-and-fast rule. It's to make sure that your own voice, and not any of theirs, is the loudest one in the chorus.

Over time, as we'll explore a bit later, you will grow into trusting your own voice more than you trust any of theirs. Only then will you be able to concentrate on naming exactly what you want—for right now and for the future—and what you are willing to do to get it.

That's when you will experience that magic moment when your mission—what you want—is greater than the fear of doing what's necessary to achieve it. That's when you will *in-power* yourself to go for it; that is, you will realize that nobody can empower you except you.

Yes, I just invented a word. But it's perfect: Nobody can empower you to go after what you want. Only you can do that. I call that *in-powering.*

It's when you will finally feel confident enough and trust yourself enough to give yourself permission to do and say what you need to do and say to achieve your goals. And *that*, my friends, is the moment when you will achieve your personal permission mission.

I hope the pages that follow will convince you that permission is power:

Permission comes from you, and only you. Give yourself permission to live your dreams.

Only you have the final say when it comes to decisions about your life. This is your story in your voice.

We don't do this life alone. Ask for help when you need it.

Empowerment comes from within; in-power yourself to give yourself permission.

Rely on your intuition. Trust yourself to do what's right for you.

Chapter 6

Make Grit Your Guide

> Grit is living life like it's a marathon, not a sprint.
>
> **—Angela Duckworth**

By now, you're getting an idea of why you don't always give yourself permission to go after what you want. You're also thinking about what it is, exactly, that you do want, need, or deserve. You're formulating your own *personal permission mission.*

The next step is taking small steps toward achieving it.

The women and men who achieve their personal permission missions have one very unique quality in common: They have grit.

Unlike so many of the characteristics we share that prevent us from going after what we want, need, and deserve, grit isn't something you learn; you already have it. But you might not be using it to get you where you want to go.

Grit is your ability to power through, to do what you never imagined you could—and what your backup singers may have convinced you was impossible. It's your firm resolve that you deserve to have what you want and need. It's your unyielding passion to go after it. It's your persistence in the face of naysayers. It's what drives you to say "Move out of my way" when your backup singers are standing right in it.

It's your moxie, your backbone, your courage, and your resilience to navigate change and recover from failure. It's the part of you that sticks up for yourself when nobody else will and that scoffs at the rules that others would have you follow but that you know do not serve you.

It's in you, and in all of us, even if we rarely call on it. Start calling on it. In fact, make grit your lead backup singer. Make it the voice that sings louder than your childhood mentors, the boss who fired you, the snooty aunt who made fun of you—in front of everyone at the party you were helping her with—because you sliced the lemons instead of cutting them into wedges. Put your grit in charge of the chorus and consult it first before you decide to settle for something safe and familiar—take the chance that will move you closer to stepping into the spotlight.

Grit is your guide to achieving your personal permission mission. Calling on it will help you find the courage to walk onto a stage and give a speech, if that's what you want to do. It will lead you to start trusting yourself so you can take chances that will make your life better. My hope is that I can help you tap into your trust and your intuition and find your true voice. I hope I can convince you that grit—a tool that you already have—will help you use your trust and your voice to get everything you want, need, and deserve.

Grit will help you:

Give yourself permission rather than asking or waiting for permission from someone else.

Realize that your passion for what you want, need, and deserve is greater than the fear of trying.

In-power yourself to trust your own voice more than the voices of the past.

Take a step forward into the spotlight on the stage of your own life.

The beloved Disney character, Dumbo, had grit.

In the 1941 movie named for the innocent and misunderstood cartoon elephant, a small, streetwise mouse named Timothy believes that Dumbo's giant ears can act as wings and allow him to fly. Dumbo doesn't believe this, so Timothy gives him a feather and convinces him it is magic and will allow him to fly. Dumbo tries it, and unbelievably, he can fly.

Later, though, Dumbo loses the feather—but he can still fly.

The moral of the story: He never needed that feather. What a surprise—he could fly all along. All he needed was self-confidence (i.e., to in-power himself) and trust. And giant ears.

Same goes for you. You don't need your backup singers to give you permission to fly. All you need is self-confidence and trust. Instead of giant ears, you just need a bit of grit. And your own permission.

Take One Step Forward

Your responses to the prompts below will help you take one step forward toward the spotlight of your life and help you fulfill your personal permission mission.

What is your personal permission mission? The dream or desire you've silenced because you thought you needed approval?

What would you do if you didn't need anyone's permission but your own to go after it? It can be a large, lofty goal (like working your way up to the CEO of a corporation or starting your own side hustle) or multiple smaller goals (like gathering the grit and courage to ask for a raise or to tell your family you'll be reserving Tuesday evenings for "me" time).

Make a list of five goals you believe you could achieve if you would just give yourself permission to try.

Identify three backup singers from your past. Write their names and the most common messages you still hear from them. Think about where those messages come from. What do you get out of playing them on repeat?

Write down any rules that you now realize are imaginary or outdated. Cross them out and replace each with a new rule for yourself.

Journal about one situation where you silenced yourself. Rewrite the scene with what you wish you had said.

Visualize: Create a visible reminder (sticky note, phone wallpaper, lipstick on your mirror) with the phrase: "I only need my permission."

Practice: Begin a daily practice of noticing. Every time you hear an old voice in your head, pause and ask, "Is this true today?"

Take Action: Look at the five goals you wrote down, and circle one. That's your first step. Take it. Small or large, imperfect or polished—just make a move.

Part Two

Your Personal Permission Mission

G **ive yourself permission rather than asking or waiting for permission from someone else.**

R ealize that your passion for what you want, need, and deserve is greater than the fear of trying.

I n-power yourself to trust your own voice more than the voices of the past.

T ake a step forward into the spotlight on the stage of your own life.

Think of your life as a performance on a stage. The spotlight is on you. You're the main act. You're the star of the show. You're bolstered by a chorus of backup singers who harmonize behind you. Their role is to make you sound and look good. They're a supporting cast, each chosen because she can make a specific, important contribution to your performance.

But you have a problem: You're not the one who chose them, or at least not all of them. In reality, those backup singers are the voices and memories of people from your past—both from long ago and as recent as yesterday—who have had an influence on you during your life.

It seems like it would be comforting to have them lined up behind you, ready to catch you if you fall, to cheer you on, and to give you the best advice in every situation.

If only you could count on that.

In fact, those backup singers—the people who raised you, educated you, coached you, and guided you throughout your life—have had a hand in getting you to where you are today. They're partially responsible for your successes, which you achieved by making good decisions, influenced, in large measure, by those important mentors. They also get some credit for your missed opportunities, stalled dreams, and sometimes paralyzing fear of failure, which has led you to avoid taking risks, even when your gut told you to go for it.

You can't blame them for everything, though. You're the one clinging to the lessons you learned from them, starting with your first memories as a toddler. They taught you not to play with matches and to cover your mouth when you cough. They also might have taught you to put others first, ahead of yourself, even when that's not in your best interests. But they also might have convinced you to stick with what you already have and to what you already know—the sure things—instead of stretching and reaching for something bigger and better.

In short, they're running the show. Your show. They're fueling your reluctance to stand under the spotlight and encouraging you to stay back in the chorus with them.

They're stealing your power, and you're allowing it. You're giving them permission.

It's time to in-power yourself with permission, and not theirs. It's time to separate the helpful from the limiting when it comes to blindly following advice that is twenty, thirty, forty years old and no longer applicable to you today. It's time to realize that your decisions belong to you. And while it's wonderful to have the benefit of the wisdom of those who came before you, it's crucial that you use it as a tool, not as a given and not as the only way to get what you want. It's not a demand. It's not a rule that you can't break, no matter what.

It's your show, your life. It's time for you to sing your own song and follow your own rules. To decide who you are, what you want, and how you will get it. Can your backup singers help you with that? Absolutely. Can they limit you if you give them too much power? Yes. Absolutely.

So how can you take your power back? Give yourself the power to use your intuition and experience to determine which of your beliefs are not yours at all. Separate those of family, friends, and mentors who have advised you along your way. Call on your grit to choose which backup singers offered wisdom that you still want to follow after all these years—and which ones you want to silence.

It's time to make new choices, to recast your chorus with voices that sing in harmony with your goals and dreams of today. It's time to break some rules that you never agreed to but still wound up following. And it's time to start the journey on your personal permission mission, one step at a time.

It's time to give yourself permission to break with tradition and in-power yourself to activate your grit. It's time to take a step forward toward your best self, your most abundant life, and your rightful place in the spotlight.

Chapter 7

Whose Life Is This, Anyway?

> Tell me, what is it you plan to do with your one wild and precious life?
>
> **—Mary Oliver**

In a way, our life is a many-act play, and we're the star of the show. We stand at the center of the stage of our lives, and there's a chorus of backup singers behind us. We open our mouths to sing, or to act, or to give a speech. Before we utter a sound, though, we have to muster the courage to belt it out, to show what we've got, to share our wisdom or perspective, and to trust that we've got what it takes, that we've got something worthwhile to perform.

In other words, to show our grit.

During that process, those backup singers, the voices from your past, are doing their thing, too. They're behind you, literally, to back you up. They're there for you, to bolster your confidence, to remind you that you're the star. They know you. They know what's best for you. Or at least they think they do.

And often, we think they do, too. But we're wrong.

The only one who knows what's best for you is you. But you're still relying on the wisdom, judgment, and criticism of others—some long gone—and allowing it to override your gut.

To take the metaphor a step further, imagine anything you're about to do, especially if it's new or outside of your comfort zone. You have to decide whether to belt it out or rein it in. You have to decide if you're going to stand in the spotlight or retreat to the chorus.

Don't worry; those backup singers are going to help you make that decision, right or wrong.

You know who they are. They even have names.

One of them is your dearly departed grandmother, who loved you so much that when you were five, she taught you to say "please" and "thank you" and to wash your hands before dinner. At thirteen, she taught you how to say "no" to a boy who was being fresh with you. At twenty-one, she told you that you were putting on weight and you would never catch a man looking like that. At thirty, she said you'd better hurry up and start having children before your biological clock ran out.

Another is your dad, who taught you never to lie or cheat on a test. Later, he let you know that girls don't need to go to college; their husbands will take care of them so they can raise the children. It was good enough for his mother and for your mother, after all.

Your older sister might have told you that you're beautiful, but you sing off-key. A friend probably said, at some point, that your cooking is delicious, but your housekeeping is subpar. A coworker insisted that he knew better than you about just about everything. A boss fired you or refused to promote you because you just weren't good enough to step up to the next level.

So, just when you're ready to speak up at a staff meeting, say "yes" to wearing a form-fitting bridesmaid's dress, buy your first house, start a business, write a book, choose a spouse, or order a bottle of wine for everyone at the table to share, you freeze—just for a moment, or maybe longer. Instead of harmonizing in the background of your performance—this metaphor for your life—those backup singers are screaming at you in all different keys.

"You're not good enough."

"You don't look good in red."

"You are too emotional for that job."

"You're not sophisticated enough to understand opera."

And you believe it.

Of course you believe it. These notions came mostly from people who loved you and wished you well, right? They came from people you trust (or once did), and they're urging you to reconsider whatever it is you were sure you could do just a minute ago.

And now you're not so sure. You're letting them decide for you.

Who's in charge here? Are you living someone else's life? Are you dreaming someone else's dreams because they dreamed them for you? Are you giving those critics from the past so much space in your psyche that you can't separate who you are and what you want from who they said you are and what they wanted you to be?

I don't know anyone who isn't influenced by the opinions of others, whether you heard those perspectives as a kid or the day before yesterday.

I know I am. So are my friends. And my colleagues, clients, neighbors, and relatives are, too. We all are.

I don't want to say we hear actual voices. It's more like we remember the voices of those mentors from our past. Tucked into our memories are the voices of approval and disapproval that we have carried with us into adulthood and still rely on when it's time to make a decision, take a risk, or otherwise step into the spotlight of our own lives.

Some of them are saying, "Go for it," and just as many are warning you to stop because you won't succeed.

They're not singing in harmony. And even if they were all saying the same thing, do you really want them making your decisions for you? Do you want them living your life for you, so to speak?

One friend, Sofia, shared with her mother her plan to quit a high-paying job on the editorial staff of a national magazine and start her own home-based business as a freelance writer.

Her mother told her, "I wouldn't do that if I were you."

She might have responded by abandoning her plan. Instead, she replied: "I know you wouldn't."

Good for her. But think about what Mom said: "If I were you."

When Sofia told me that story, I pointed out that her mother is not "you." She's herself, with her own limitations, fears, comfort zone, and backup singers.

So, should my thirty-six-year-old friend, who trusts and loves her mother, heed the advice and squash the plan to become self-employed? Or should she consider that her mother never pursued a career that gave her the opportunity to strike out on her own? That her mother is thirty years older, and things were different for women back when she was Sofia's age? That she had a family to help support, so she never would have walked away from a steady paycheck? That she can't imagine herself taking a risk like that, and so she doesn't think Sofia should, either?

Mom is just trying to protect her daughter.

But they're not the same person. Their upbringings were different. Their stage in life is different. Their fears are different. Their situations aren't the same.

Mom is a backup singer who is not in harmony with the experiences, wants, and desires of her adult daughter, at least not this time. In another situation, for another decision, Mom's wisdom might be comforting or encouraging.

When Sofia is wrapping gifts, for example, she can't cut the paper without hearing her mother's voice in her head, asking her why she doesn't measure the paper before cutting it. It's a fond memory of time spent together during the holidays, wrapping presents for family and friends. About half of the time, Sofia cut the paper too short for the gift and had to start over—but they always laughed through it.

To this day, Mom's words remind her to measure, and she does.

Listening to the voices of your past, it seems, is part of being human. Giving them a majority vote in your decisions, however, is not a given.

Consider Walt Disney, who created one of the most successful entertainment empires ever. He was once told by his newspaper editors that he was not creative enough.

Anna Wintour, the inspiration for the movie *The Devil Wears Prada* and *Vogue* editor for the past three decades, was fired from her first job as a junior fashion editor at *Harper's Bazaar.*

A Baltimore TV producer told Oprah Winfrey she was "unfit for television" because she got "emotionally invested in her stories."

You can bet that those celebrated individuals remember all of that negativity. Those naysayers followed them, in the back of their minds, forever. But they chose to never let those backup singers sing louder than their own voices. They in-powered themselves and trusted themselves to dismiss the ones who very clearly were singing off-key.

That's a pivotal moment in achieving your personal permission mission: when we trust ourselves more than we trust the voices of our past, when our passion for our definition of success overrides our fear that those voices might be right and we might be wrong.

That's not always an easy moment to realize.

Those voices from our past, whether from family members, mentors, or even society and culture, helped shape our identity.

Later, we'll unpack some strategies for managing the chorus and getting your backup singers to sing in harmony.

Chapter 8

You Deserve Everything

> The minute you settle for less than you deserve, you get even less than you settled for.
>
> **—Maureen Dowd**

The imaginary rulebook we discussed earlier has a page in it I'd like you to rip out. It's the one that says you don't deserve to have everything you want and need.

You do.

You don't need the permission of your backup singers, your culture, or society to believe in yourself and your worth. The fact is that your worthiness is not given to you. It's not earned. You're born with it. All you have to do is accept it.

In the past few years in my practice as a business coach and consultant, I have met more women than ever who are shattering glass ceilings in their fields and finding greater opportunities for and access to success. So why do I meet so many who are waiting for permission to pursue their dreams?

The answer is that they are waiting for permission that they do not need and should not heed. The only permission they need comes from within. They don't need someone to empower them; they need only to unleash the power of the permission that can come only from themselves.

You'll recall that I call that "in-powering."

Yet so many people—too many people, both women and men—don't own that power. They don't go after what they want and need. They don't follow their dreams.

We come up with all sorts of reasons for forfeiting the success, abundance, and happiness that can come from realizing our goals, and most of them are fear-based. We're afraid we might fail or look foolish. We're risk-averse. We're pretty comfortable where we are, so why rock the boat when we don't know for sure that whatever's next will be any better? We're too polite to object. We'd rather eat glass than speak up.

Let's talk about something that might take you a minute to admit about yourself, and this might sting a bit: You don't believe you *deserve* to have the things you want, the success you crave, the love you yearn for, the life you dream about.

If you did, you would have already given yourself permission to go after them.

So, is that true? You don't deserve it?

I hope you'll let me convince you that you do, in fact, deserve all of that and more. But you won't get it until you believe it too.

If this is resonating with you, you're in good company. Some of the greatest humans in history have suffered from the same affliction: They felt unworthy of success, praise, and awards, even though they had plenty of evidence of their greatness.

One of them was the poet Maya Angelou, one of the most celebrated voices of her generation. For much of her life, Angelou waited for "permission" to pursue her passion for writing and speaking, largely because of society's expectations and her own personal fears. It wasn't until she was in her forties that she stopped waiting and found her own voice.

In her bestselling 1969 autobiography *I Know Why the Caged Bird Sings*, Angelou wrote, "There is no greater agony than bearing an untold story inside you."

While Angelou didn't explicitly use the term "waiting for permission" in her personal reflections, much of her life and work reveals her journey toward breaking free from societal and internal expectations, a clue that she knew the permission she sought had to come from within herself.

In her writings and interviews, Angelou often spoke about overcoming the barriers that those expectations put in front of her. For example, in her autobiography, Angelou wrote about how her childhood trauma led her to silence, and how her eventual decision to speak and share her story was an act of reclaiming her power. In essence, she realized she didn't need anyone's permission but her own to express herself.

Permission, she found, is power.

It might be surprising that people who have the confidence to publish books or act in the movies feel as undeserving or unworthy when they receive praise or awards as the rest of us sometimes do.

The actress Gwyneth Paltrow revealed on a 2021 episode of the podcast *Anna Faris Is Unqualified* that she felt embarrassed when she was nominated, at age twenty-six, for an Academy Award for her role in the movie *Shakespeare in Love*.

She recalled how she felt when she heard the news: "I can't even believe this is happening. I'm not even that good. . . . Well, of course, I'm not going to win."

She did win, and in her acceptance speech, she acknowledged her sister nominee, the iconic Meryl Streep, as "the greatest one who ever was," and added, "I don't feel very deserving of this in your presence."

The nagging notion that we aren't worthy of admiration, wealth, joy, a happy marriage, a great job, a birthday cake on our special day, or a wonderful life is deeply rooted in history and culture, especially for women.

Throughout history, the contributions of women have been undervalued and often ignored or even credited to men. Women have consistently been underrepresented in historical narratives and, in more modern times, in the media.

I can remember watching *The Cosby Show* when I was a kid and realizing even then that the mom, attorney Clair Huxtable, was the only professional woman I had noticed on TV. I wasn't wrong; research has shown that the media, especially in past decades, have depicted women as being dependent on men. That kind of gender inequality can make women question whether they deserve power, or leadership roles, or even success. It can make them wonder if they have permission to step outside of the box society has trapped them in. Movies, TV, social media, and even culture have taught women that their looks and relationships should take priority over their professional achievements.

A group of women business leaders is addressing the lingering lack of realistic portrayals of women in media and entertainment. Shelley Zalis, CEO, Founder, and "Chief Troublemaker" of The Female Quotient, a global community of women in business, partnered with the Association of National Advertisers in 2016 to launch a movement called "SeeHer," whose mission is "to increase the representation and accurate portrayal of all women and girls to drive business growth in the global marketing and media ecosystem, now and for generations to come."

I support that movement because one reason we don't give ourselves permission to stretch beyond the boundaries of the status quo is because we so rarely saw women on TV shows and movies doing it. We did not know we could have it all because we had simply never seen it modeled before.

Another effort to overcome the entertainment industry's tendency to keep women in the background is called the Geena Davis Institute. The actress (from movies such as *Thelma & Louise* and *A League of Their Own*) started the institute to research, educate, and advocate for more inclusive and equitable representation of women and minorities in entertainment. The organization focuses, in part, on more gender-inclusive research in children's media and family films.

Davis's motto: "If they can see it, they can be it."

And if you've seen *Thelma & Louise*, you know those characters were a full-on permission revolution in action.

One more: Oscar winner Nicole Kidman in 2017 pledged to collaborate with a female director at least once every eighteen months. By 2025, she had worked with nineteen of them.

Today, of course, the media portray more professional women on shows, in ads, and in the news than they once did, so girls, at a younger age, are witnessing the reality of what's possible for them as they grow into women.

Some of my favorite movies portray women as strong, outspoken, and capable and feature characters that clearly give themselves permission to go for what they want, need, and deserve.

Among them is the 1980 film *9 to 5*, starring Dolly Parton, Jane Fonda, and Lily Tomlin. As office workers, they face sexist, patronizing, and exploitative treatment from their chauvinistic boss. They give themselves permission to stand up to him and to reclaim their personal power, not to mention make some groundbreaking changes in their workplace.

The film underscores the themes of this book: You don't need permission from others to stand up and make things happen. You only need to in-power yourself.

Still, according to State University of New York law professor Carolyn Cocca, just 26.7 percent of the DC and Marvel characters are female, and only 12 percent of the protagonists in mainstream superhero comics are women, at least in 2017, when she wrote *Superwomen: Gender, Power, and Representation.*

My own theory about why more women don't give themselves permission to move upward and onward is that we are far too loyal to the permissions and cautions we have heard from authority figures we once admired. They may be long gone, but in our minds, they are still singing backup and holding us back.

We can't change how we were raised, and we can't change the statistics of the past. But we can remove ourselves from the status quo by doing one thing: giving ourselves permission to go after what we want, in spite of norms, expectations, and even history.

That requires a change of mindset. You have to believe that you deserve it.

If you've been reluctant to go for it because you felt, even a little bit, that you didn't deserve what you would be going after, consider these first steps:

1. **Engage in self-reflection.** Take a deep dive into figuring out what you need, desire, and value. Consider what your rights are, what your boundaries are. One study revealed that when we engage in regular self-reflection, we tend to better understand our needs and goals, and what we deserve from relationships, work, and life.

2. **Practice self-compassion.** Research has shown that people who treat themselves with kindness, care, and compassion are more likely to understand their own worth and believe they deserve positive treatment from others.

3. **Set boundaries.** Another researcher found that people who set boundaries in relationships and at work are more likely to understand—and demand—what they truly deserve.

4. **Stop comparing.** Social comparison theory suggests that when we evaluate our self-worth based on our perception of others, we sometimes feel we deserve less than we actually do.

5. **Look at the evidence.** If you believe you don't deserve an award, a speaking engagement, a spot on the neighborhood association board, or anything else you want, consider the skills you have used to excel at something you're good at. Chances are, you have

evidence right there to prove you are competent and deserving. Do this whenever you're offered an opportunity that's a little bit outside of your area of expertise. I bet you'll discover that you did something similar before, and you can do this new thing too.

I want to share something with you that I believe in my soul: Worthiness is not something you have to earn. It's not a gold star for good behavior or a trophy for checking all the boxes. It's something you were born with. From your first breath, you were enough. We're all born worthy, but somewhere along the way, we learn from unhappy experiences, cultural norms, and society's expectations that convince us otherwise.

They were wrong.

Your worthiness isn't up for debate. We are worthy. You are worthy. Embrace that truth and enjoy the freedom and power of giving yourself permission to do, say, and receive everything you want for a happy and successful life.

Chapter 9

Your Emotional Closet

> If you want to fly, you have to give up everything that weighs you down.
>
> **—Toni Morrison**

My favorite question to ask my coaching clients when they tell me they absolutely can't do something is, "Who said you can't?"

My second question is, "Why would they say such a horrible thing to you?" They usually laugh. And then I ask, "What do *you* say?"

Those are excellent questions to ask yourself the next time you're convinced that you're not good enough, worthy enough, or simply not enough.

Who told you that? Let me guess, someone from your past almost certainly did.

Next question: Is it true? Even if it had any truth to it way back when you heard it, is it still true today?

And two other all-important questions to answer when any of your backup singers are saying that you can't: First, what was the motive of the person or people who cast you in such a negative light? Second, is their opinion of you sabotaging your success or happiness today?

Whenever you say to yourself—or admit to someone else—that you can't or you shouldn't, chances are good that you learned that limitation from someone from your past who repeated it to you over and over. Eventually, you developed such an emotional attachment to a belief that belonged to someone else that you have made it your own truth.

You might have some unlearning to do. We all do.

To truly achieve your personal permission mission, the first step is to clean out your emotional closet. That's where your backup singers hibernate until you call them out to help you make a decision.

The mistake we tend to make is that we call them *all* out, when really, we only need the ones who have something useful to contribute to our decision-making. You don't need the ones who downplayed your abilities or talents because they were jealous of you. You certainly don't have to listen to the ghosts of the control freaks who wanted you to do what they wanted instead of what might be better for you. And if you could tune out the pessimists—the ones who shot down everyone's hopes and dreams because they never achieved their own—your confidence might not just build . . . it might soar.

You don't need them all. You might have needed each of them at various points in your life, but now, you simply don't. You know who I am talking about.

Just as you carefully select the actual people you spend your time with, it's important to curate your chorus with just the right singers.

Motivational speaker Jim Rohn introduced this notion in his 2001 book *The Jim Rohn Guide to Personal Development*: "You are the average of the five people you spend the most time with." Rohn's premise was that your attitudes, habits, mindset, self-worth, and even income are, at least in part, shaped by the people you're closest to.

You also are, at least in part, shaped by the people who have influenced your beliefs—especially about yourself—over the years, starting when you were very young.

It's just as unhealthy to hang out, in your mind, with backup singers who tear you down as it is to continue relationships with the people in your life who put you down or stress you out. If they're not cheering for you, it's time to turn down their mic.

Basketball great LeBron James has talked about the collective influence of the people who surround him.

"Sometimes, it ain't about what you know, as who you know as well," he has been quoted as saying.

My beloved late Southern aunt was a gem who helped raise me and imparted so much wisdom, usually in the form of humor, that I often wonder if I would be who I am today without her loving guidance. She lived life out loud. She taught me how to act like a lady but still have fun, how to be polite but say "Bless your heart" when appropriate (if you know, you know), and she tried to teach me how to make biscuits (I still can't get it right.).

I miss her.

But I hear from her often, especially when I'm having a hard time deciding if I should take a risk, make a change, or jump into something headfirst. She had a hunger for life. She was willing to try new things. My memory of the things she taught me becomes amplified when I'm toying with the idea of doing something that is a little outside of what

Southern women do. She would bend the rules. One hundred percent of the time.

I live in California now, and many of the lessons I learned from various aunts and uncles and neighbors and coaches continue to resonate with and guide me. But a lot of them are so old-fashioned that if I heeded them, I would have probably never gone to college, let alone have earned a PhD in communications. I wouldn't have entered the workforce as a professor and later as a sales consultant. I would not have dared to open a business, travel the world, or stand on a platform to deliver speeches to hundreds of audience members at a time. I likely would have married young and have a houseful of children by now; instead, the only baby my husband and I have is our precious dog, Biscuit, and that's by choice.

They wouldn't have done those things, so they didn't think I should—or any young woman should—either.

My smart-as-a-whip granny fantasized about becoming a doctor, but the pull of tradition convinced her that wasn't an acceptable path for a lady of that time. She later stunned me when she shared that she always regretted that choice. I could see the agony in her eyes as she shared the details of how she wanted to pursue her dream. She had it all mapped out. It was as if she were standing at a velvet rope, seeing her dream life before her, just out of reach. But she chose tradition, which, no doubt, was the product of both her upbringing and the societal norms of the 1930s. Those norms were among her backup singers, along with her grandparents, parents, and society's expectations. She lived a good life, but also one of unfulfilled dreams because of the decisions she made or that were made for her.

That woman had plenty of grit, but not quite enough to overcome the odds that were unanimously stacked against her.

Still, she's in my head all the time, often one of my most prominent backup singers. If I were to heed her advice and follow in her footsteps, I might also have unfulfilled dreams. So when I have a decision to make, I have to remember that she grew up in a different time.

These are just some of the voices that I discovered when cleaning out my emotional closet. I evaluated each of the people from my past whose praise, criticism, advice, and demands compete for a solo in my chorus of backup singers. I try to appreciate their loving suggestions while at the same time ignoring the ones that tell me to stop when my gut says to go for it. (I can see Granny shaking her finger at me!)

The fact is that not everyone whose words still influence me all these years later taught me lessons that are right for me today. That advice might have been solid for the nine-year-old Cindy who learned it back then. It might have been spot-on for the person doing the advising, given that person's gender, age, and family situation—in many cases, different from mine today.

As I wrote this book, I stumbled onto some fascinating research from the 1980s by Richard C. Schwartz, a systemic family therapist, whose observations of why we behave the way we do coincide, in some ways, with my theory about backup singers.

Schwartz has said his clients often felt their minds had been shaped by their experiences into distinct "parts" that are not necessarily in harmony with each other. He categorized those parts as "subpersonalities."

Those subpersonalities, Schwartz theorized, are like an internal family, and like external families, they don't always agree. He named this the Internal Family Systems, or IFS, which he developed into a form of therapy to help people bring those subpersonalities into harmony with the individual's "core Self."

I compare that to getting your backup singers to sing in harmony toward a common goal that matches the one you truly want to achieve. But if it feels like everyone in your backup chorus is singing a different song, it can clutter your mind so badly that you can't possibly decide which tune you want to hum.

Finding that hum, that harmony, begins with cleaning out your emotional closet.

Doing that can be well, emotional, even painful. Like hanging on to your great-aunt's old collection of Hummel figurines even though you don't especially enjoy them, remaining loyal to the life instructions you received from a departed loved one can feel respectful and a way to preserve a legacy.

Years after we've left our parents' homes and started our own lives, it can still be difficult to separate their opinions from ours, to create our own right and wrong. Attachment Theory, developed by psychoanalyst John Bowlby in the 1960s and '70s, shows that the emotional bonds children form with their parents or caregivers create a framework for decisions throughout life. As we get older, that same sort of attachment can develop with close friends and romantic partners.

Bonds that strong are hard to shake, even when the relationship is over or the role model is out of the picture. Our parents are the first ones who make us feel emotionally secure, and their opinions and instructions are wound tightly with our sense of safety and validation.

So, we continue to let those influential teachers make our decisions for us, as we replay their words of wisdom, caution, praise, and belittlement when, even as adults, we face a difficult choice.

But those aren't the only reasons we might substitute the judgment of others for our own.

Voices from our past, as we discussed earlier, have helped us shape our identities. Doing what our elders did or told us to do ties us to our history and helps us keep them alive in our memories, the same way that listening to a parent's favorite music or following a family recipe for a meal that tastes like home can make you smile.

It's no wonder that we not only welcome but heed the voices of those backup singers when we need assurance that we're doing the right thing. They help us make decisions that feel safe.

There's value in that. Plus, for some, following even outdated advice can feel like a good way to avoid repeating the mistakes and benefit from the experiences of those who came before. Perhaps an older friend or relative lived through a crisis, and now you're in the middle of one yourself. Heeding warnings or mimicking the response of those wise elders could hold some value for your situation.

Upholding the traditions of those you cared for creates a sense of nostalgia, which researchers have linked to emotional well-being and feelings of belonging.

On a practical note, if you base your decisions on instructions from those from your past, your conclusions might come quicker, especially if you're really stuck on finding your own answer. In her book *The 85% Solution*, Linda Galindo, an advocate for personal accountability, suggests that allowing others to make decisions for us gives us someone to blame if our choices lead to failure.

And sometimes, we use those backup singers like crutches to prop us up when we're afraid or reluctant to take a step forward toward our spotlight, to help us justify our decision to stand still instead of moving toward the stage.

Sounds comfy. But living in a comfort zone built by others can be limiting, even stifling.

Whatever your reasons for substituting the advice of others for your own, consider whether this practice is preventing you from stepping into the spotlight of your life. Weeding out the advice from your past that is no longer benefitting you can be helpful and can lead you to begin to trust yourself and believe that you need to fulfill your own personal permission mission. Adjust your mindset to realize that, along with safety and comfort, some of the advice you recall is no longer valid for the grown-up you of today or the person you want to be tomorrow. It only reflects the limitations of the loved one who offered it. Try hushing any voices that tell you that you can't or shouldn't, or that you're not good enough or that they wouldn't if they were you. Then listen for the harmony of a chorus without those negative voices for advice that is positive, relevant, useful, and most importantly, willing to let you have the final say by making a decision that is uniquely right for you.

Once you have identified your backup singers and have sorted through the lessons you learned from them, you can give yourself permission to override them when their messages don't jibe with your current values and goals. In no time, you will start to recognize that your own opinions, judgment, and knowledge are more valuable than the leftover lessons that have led you to follow rules you didn't write and live a life that isn't fully yours.

Your personal permission mission is achieved by getting your backup singers into harmony with what you sincerely want and who you authentically are. It's a challenge designed to *in-power* you to identify which past lessons serve you and which do not, to consider the advice that has shaped you into the adult you are, and to let go of anything that is needlessly holding you back.

These chapters have, so far, included strategies for getting to this point of balance and self-leadership. In addition, consider this mash-up of advice that might apply equally to IFS and backup singers as you clean out your emotional closets and say goodbye to backup singers who no longer serve you:

1. **Pay attention to your internal conflict.** This occurs when some of your backup singers are reminding you that you're not smart enough to pull something off while others are bringing to mind the praise and admiration they had for you because of your resourcefulness and critical thinking skills.

2. **Consider both sides.** If you feel the adults in your life over the years have genuinely rooted for your success, you might find a little bit of truth in all of their advice. It's almost always the case that there's at least 2 percent of truth in every argument. Don't dismiss any of

the advice you recall just because you don't agree with it. Instead, approach that advice with curiosity rather than with bias. Weigh it and then decide what is relevant to your situation today. Try to understand the concerns of those who pushed you to be cautious. Do a negotiation in your head between the "pro" and "con" camps among your backup singers. Look for any common ground between them. You just might start to hear them harmonizing.

3. **Identify the emotions that you associate with each of your backup singers.** When you're limiting yourself because of fear, guilt, a perceived inadequacy, shame, or something else that you feel instead of know, ask yourself: Who made me feel guilty about this, and what was that backup singer's motive? Who made me feel inadequate? Am I really? And do I want this memory to limit my life?

4. **Determine, deep down, what you truly believe about yourself in this situation.** Sure, our beliefs are shaped, in large measure, by those who influenced us along the way. But over time, we have had slews of experiences and met lots of people, including geniuses and probably a few jerks. Despite our lingering attachment to the opinions we heard when we were younger, we have loads of evidence about our own abilities, and about our likes and dislikes. Who are you, really? What do you sincerely want? What do you believe you truly deserve?

5. **Make your decision, and make the decision yours.** If you take the time to listen to your backup singers and to evaluate what they're reminding you of, your decision will be informed. It will be right for you.

Whatever you call your inner voice, remember that it's yours. The voices from the past have their place—and it's up to you to keep them in their place. In the end, you, and nobody else, will deal with the consequences of your decisions.

Chapter 10

Change the Narrative

> When we deny our stories, they define us. When we own our stories, we get to write a brave new ending.
>
> **—Brené Brown**

The backup singers knocking around in your memory can be pretty harsh. Among Josie's is her father, a surgeon, who was the academic star of his family while growing up, telling his ambitious daughter, a straight-A high school student, that she'll never get into medical school—because her grades aren't high enough. Six years later, when she graduates with honors from college, she never applies. Another one is the uncoordinated big sister telling her talented preteen sibling that she makes a fool of herself when she dances with the older kids, even though she always busts those moves with rhythm and style. At her high school prom years later, the shy teenager feels too embarrassed to dance with her date.

Often when someone who knows you well and has earned your trust criticizes you, that feedback is helpful, propelling you to work harder, practice more, or make a change for the better. Sometimes, though, the comments are made out of jealously, fear, insecurity, or even spite.

When you're just a kid, you don't know the difference. So you internalize it as true, and it becomes a part of your identity, and it stays part of your identity. It becomes the narrative you write about yourself, the script you live by.

As an adult, you recall those unflattering assessments whenever you consider taking a risk, trying something new, or otherwise stepping outside of your comfort zone. You believe you can't do it because people you trusted told you that you can't.

Beliefs can change. But when you play that old record over and over again in your head, when you heed the advice again and again against your own better judgment, who is responsible? A long-ago role model from your childhood? Or worse, is it you?

That syndrome, that tendency to drag the hurts of the past into the present—courtesy of the backup singers who are only too happy to remind you—isn't an affliction only of mere mortals.

During her 1999 commencement speech at her alma mater, Academy Award winner Natalie Portman confessed that she fleetingly thought Harvard had admitted her by mistake.

"I felt . . . that I wasn't smart enough to be in this company, and that every time I opened my mouth I would have to prove that I wasn't just a dumb actress," she told the Ivy League audience.

Selena Gomez, an award-winning actress and singer, revealed in a September 2024 piece that appeared in *Page Six* that when she recalls all of the negative things she said about her appearance and talent early in her career, "It makes me sick. . . . It burns me out."

I know a smart, fun woman who, in her early forties, felt that even her friends didn't respect her intelligence, perhaps because she loved to party and have fun. Julissa enrolled in graduate school and finished her master's degree with a 4.0 average. She literally felt like she needed a credential to prove to them that she was smart. Or, perhaps, she had to prove it to herself.

Isn't it time to stop trying to convince your backup singers, dead or alive, of your value? Isn't it time to embrace your own talent, intelligence, beauty, creativity, resourcefulness, and know-how as a given? It does not matter what anybody has ever said to the contrary. Isn't it time to stop playing that record on repeat?

I realize that what I am asking you to do is not an easy thing.

In her book *The Verbally Abusive Relationship*, interpersonal communications specialist Patricia Evans, PhD, explains that going over those harsh words again and again leads to internalizing them; that is, you eventually believe what she calls the verbal and emotional abuse that was piled on you by people who were (or are) trying to control you. That leads to negative self-talk, which reinforces the negative messages. Sounds like backup singers to me.

Your backup singers might have had the best intentions. They might not have intended to hold you back with their criticism and misguided life lessons. But if those lessons are not serving you now, why do you continue to consider them?

Why are you letting people from your past write your future? Is it yours? Or is it theirs?

Negative self-talk indicates low self-esteem, which typically is rooted in early childhood experiences involving critical parents, teachers, siblings, peers, and others who are influential with you when you're young. By internalizing those negative messages, we develop a critical (usually very loud) inner voice that mirrors the disapproval of those people—in other words, your backup singers. That disapproval becomes baked into your identity, and the memory becomes a fact: Your sister doesn't just think you're a bad dancer; you are one. You obviously weren't intelligent enough for law school. You're fun to hang out with, but you're not as smart as your friends. You are, indeed, undeserving.

Lesson for today: No, you're not.

It turns out your harshest backup singer, out of all of the dozens and dozens of voices from your past, is *you.*

What people have said about you is not who you are. But too many of us live it as if it is true. We live our lives based on the impressions of others, or on the basis of what others thought was true, good for us, proper, wrong, or expected.

A theory from way long ago—1902—explains this perfectly.

Sociologist Charles Horton Cooley suggested, basically, that perception is reality. His Looking-Glass Self Theory says our self-image is shaped by our perception of how others see us.

Sit with that. Ponder it. Do you see yourself through the eyes of others or through your own?

Then answer this: Say you're shopping at the mall, and the entrance to your favorite store has two doorways. One says "beautiful," and the other, "average." Which one would you walk through?

Dove, the company that makes hair, skin, and body care products, answered this question in 2015, when it set up those two entrances at shopping centers around the world.

Most of the women approached the doors, paused, looked around (likely seeking permission), and then walked through the "average" door.

In an accompanying survey, 96 percent of women said they would not describe themselves as beautiful.

I wonder who told them they are not beautiful? I wonder which backup singer whispered to them as they saw the two doors?

The interesting thing about the survey is that those who walked through the "beautiful" door said later their choice made them feel "triumphant," while those who chose the "average" door felt saddened.

Dove's point: Characterizing yourself as beautiful is a choice.

So is buying into the negative messages that others bombard you with all your life. And even if you have lived up to this point as if you are "less than" just because someone convinced you of that, it's not too late to make a different choice. The key: Give yourself permission to choose something different. Give yourself permission to hush the backup singers whose advice, criticism, and negativity no longer serve you—if they ever really did. Give yourself permission to rewrite the narrative of your life that you have bought into for so long. Let's be honest, you are the one allowing the backup singers to still call the shots. You convinced yourself that they were and are right.

Give yourself permission to give yourself permission. Take back the pen. Write your own story.

Back to that looking glass. Consider looking for something else when you look in the mirror. Forget about what others see or think about you. What do *you* see? Do you like it?

Earlier, we worked on cleaning out our emotional closets. What did you keep? What did you toss?

Now what do you see?

How about the lies that made you feel that you are not beautiful? And they are lies, even if someone else believed they were true. That does not make them true. It is not true that you're not smart or desirable or lovable or competent—or whatever else you think you're not but wish you were.

How about the notion that you can't do what you want to because some wise elder told you that you couldn't or shouldn't or shared with you that he or she wouldn't?

Overcoming a lifetime's worth of negative beliefs about yourself won't happen overnight. It takes time. It takes grit. It takes resolve. But cognitive behavioral therapists say it's possible. Billionaire founder of IT Cosmetics, Jamie Kern Lima, was able to do just that when she met with obstacles when trying to get her company off the ground. She shared in a *Goss* article, "I really needed to turn down the volume on the negative self-talk and instead turn up the volume on the gut feeling that I had inside me telling me . . . that my brand was going to thrive."

Here's some advice to help you do the same:

Listen to yourself. First, you need to be aware of the negatives you believe about yourself. These are often revealed by your negative self-talk; that is, by how you put yourself down in the silent conversations you have when you're alone. I believe that if you can—and are willing to—identify a problem, you have a good chance of overcoming it.

Remember, you're a backup singer, too. Why are you putting yourself down?

Next, consider whether any of the criticism or negative assessments of your backup singers is even true. Do you have evidence from your life that it is? Or, more likely, that it isn't? Evans says healing begins when you recognize that those negative thoughts you're carrying around are abusive and absolutely untrue.

Then, replace the negative thoughts with positive thoughts, or at least with balanced ones. When you hear a backup singer telling you that you can't or shouldn't do something, don't react, but assess. Challenge it. Whose voice is it? Consider the alternative. Reframe it. Unpack it. Call up another backup singer, one who will cheer you on. Turn "I can't do it" to "I can *so* do it!" Call on your grit.

Consider that maybe you don't want to do it, but that doesn't mean you can't.

Also, listen to the language you use when you talk to yourself or talk to others about yourself. Instead of using the word "failure," for example, say "setback" or "round one." Instead of characterizing yourself as a failure because of a setback, talk about what went wrong with the activity and do better next time rather than blaming yourself for it.

Cut yourself some slack. If your best friend called herself an idiot, what would you say? Probably that she's not, that she's smart, that whatever just happened was a one-time thing.

If you could talk to your nine-year-old self, would you criticize her and tell her she's stupid? Of course not.

Show yourself the same compassion. Instead of criticizing yourself in harmony with any negative backup singers who have invaded your thoughts, how about comforting and encouraging yourself?

Use positive affirmations. I remember a skit on an old *Saturday Night Live* episode showing a man looking in the mirror saying, "I'm good enough, I'm smart enough, and doggone it, people like me!" It is hilarious because, although the affirmations were over-the-top for the early 1990s, a lot of self-care and self-help experts today advocate for adding that kind of daily positivity to your self-talk. It's been shown that affirmations can gradually shift your mindset.

Make room for new voices. Too much negative clutter in your chorus of backup singers can elbow out any positive new voices that might serve you better. Examine why you're clinging to the opinions of legacy loudmouths instead of embracing the positivity that you're getting from people who have known you as an adult and have sung your praises. Perhaps their message is so different from the one you're telling yourself that you're having a hard time believing that praise?

Be grateful. Notice the small wins that occur throughout your day. Did someone at work compliment you on your new haircut? Did you get the thumbs-up for a project you proposed? Did you finish your project early enough to make it to the movie you've been dying to see? Did a new friend invite you for coffee? How do you accept compliments? If someone says she loves your outfit, do you tell her where you bought it and what a great deal you got on it, or do you just say, "Thank you" and smile for the rest of the day? "Thank you," by the way, is a complete sentence. No need to downplay or qualify the compliment.

In fact, embrace the friend who complimented you as a new backup singer. A positive, encouraging one.

Those are the little success stories that can make your day, if you'll let them. Congratulate yourself for them and celebrate them. At the end of the day, write them down and feel thankful for them. Research shows that deliberately and regularly practicing gratitude can shift your focus from negative to positive.

Give yourself permission to focus on the many positives in your life and on everything that's absolutely right and wonderful about you.

And then, live *that.* Make your story one of positivity, self-appreciation, and confidence. Make it one of "I can" instead of "I can't." Take back your story. In-power yourself to write a new one. One where you choose the "beautiful" door for yourself. Permission is how to get there.

Chapter 11

Find Your Voice

> It took me a long time to develop a voice, and now that I have it, I am not going to be silent.
>
> **—Madeleine Albright**

The voices that belong to your backup singers—the ones you play over and over in your mind—might always be a part of your decision-making, and that's OK. There's some wisdom in voices from the past.

Still, you have the power to quiet them when they're so loud that you can't hear your own voice over the memory of theirs.

The next time that happens, consider this: Do you know your own voice? Do you know what you want to say, or ask for, or be known for? Do you know what *you* want?

Our backup singers take over when we do not know those things. It's when we don't seem to have the words to express what we want, need, or believe that we let those voices from long ago—and some from not so long ago—speak for us.

Are you ready to take charge of your decisions, your actions, and your destiny? You can start your journey—your personal permission

mission—by identifying exactly what you want. It might surprise you how different that is from what your parents, grandparents, coaches, teachers, best friends, partners, and enemies have wanted for you at various points in your life. It might surprise you to learn that your backup singers—no matter how much they were just trying to help—are no longer helping you. They might be doing just the opposite.

A great example is the Hollywood icon Elizabeth Taylor, who was married seven times. The first time, she obediently married hotel heir Conrad "Nicky" Hilton, reportedly at the behest of her mother and the executives at MGM studios, who apparently believed the union would be good for Taylor's acting career. The marriage ended after just eight months, with Taylor accusing her husband of being abusive. Likewise, Princess Diana revealed that she felt pressured into marrying Prince Charles—and he said he felt pressured, too—and their partnership famously and very publicly ended after fifteen years and a lot of heartache.

Others, however, were determined to forge their own paths despite the objections of their families, some who expected their growing kids to follow in their parents' footsteps, and some who basically forbade them from going into the family business.

The parents of Fleetwood Mac singer Stevie Nicks wanted her to graduate from college so badly that they cut her off when she dropped out to pursue a music career, so she worked as a maid and a waitress to support herself and her friends until they found fame.

Similarly, author Harper Lee, comedian/actress Rebel Wilson, and even the revered pacifist Mahatma Gandhi all went to law school because their families expected them to follow in the footsteps of their elders.

All of them eventually found their voices and wandered far from the path of what others expected of them and into the destinies they created for themselves.

You can do that, too.

What's stopping you? Researchers say many people feel a deep sense of duty toward their parents, especially if Mom and Dad sacrificed their own dreams for their children. After all, our parents—and often other family members, neighbors, and teachers—were once our primary caregivers and emotional anchors. They're the ones who helped us shape our sense of self-worth and identity.

Lots of reasons keep us beholden to the people in our lives who helped us become who we are today. We feel that we never got the approval we sought from them when we were kids, so we need to make them proud—even after all this time, even if they have passed on—by living up to their standards and expectations.

I know a woman who swears she hates all seafood to the point that she will decline invitations to crab feasts and dinner parties, even if all of her friends are going. Once, I asked Alex if she had ever tasted lobster, and she admitted that she had never tasted any kind of fish or shellfish in her life. It turns out her mother hated seafood, and so Alex decided long ago that she hated it, too, without ever trying a bite of it.

Do you recognize yourself in any of these stories?

I call them stories for a reason: They are the stories we tell ourselves. We can't break out of the family mold because the family wouldn't like it. We can't change careers and follow our passion because we've already committed to doing what's safe. We can't get out of a bad marriage because our religion or our culture tells us it's not acceptable. We know we're not good enough because our Aunt Peggy said so when we were nine.

Maybe it's time to change out the lead singer. Maybe it's time you wrote your own story instead of living out the one your mother or spouse or even your children have boxed you into. Maybe it's time to make your story yours and not the product of obedience or duty or tradition or a sense of safety from hanging on to what you have rather than going after what you want.

Maybe it's time to kick some of those backup singers out of your chorus. They might just be stopping you from stepping into the spotlight of your life.

It's definitely time to give yourself permission to do what you want to do without waiting for someone else to approve your decision. It's certainly time to realize that the person who taught you not to talk to strangers and also said that women shouldn't travel alone might have taught you one thing that is a valuable life lesson and another that is absolutely not true, even if she believed it was at the time.

Now it's time to figure out what you want. Instead of listening to the voices that are telling you what they want for you, find your voice. What does she want? Let her speak. Only then can you determine how to get it.

I love this cryptic exchange between the fictional Alice and the whimsical Cheshire Cat from Lewis Caroll's classic children's story, *Alice in Wonderland.* Alice asks:

"Would you tell me, please, which way I ought to go from here?"

"That depends a good deal on where you want to get to," said the Cat.

"I don't much care where . . ." said Alice.

"Then it doesn't matter which way you go," said the Cat.

". . . so long as I get SOMEWHERE," Alice added as an explanation.

"Oh, you're sure to do that," said the Cat, "if you only walk long enough."

A wise cat, that one. The fact is you can't get to where you're going if you don't know where you want to go. You can't find your voice if you don't know what you want to say. You can't use your voice to get what you want if you don't know what you want.

What is it that you want to say? Exactly what your backup singers are telling you? The same thing your mother said all the time? Or do you want something of your own?

What is that?

It's time to schedule some alone time to figure that out. Like Alice in the timeless fable, you'll never get anywhere if you don't know which direction you're going. And the first step toward figuring that out is to make a plan.

Plans can be for personal missions that are specific and single-minded ("I want to get over my fear of speaking up at meetings") or general and ongoing ("I want a life full of adventure and travel").

You can plan for either one of those and for everything in between. The key: Write it down. If you don't, it's just an idea. If you have something concrete that you can look at every day, you are far more likely to put it into action.

As you read on, you will learn something indisputable about me: I always have a plan. Yes, I am that girl. I always advocate for others to have a plan. I believe a plan is the most effective route to achieving our personal missions, our personal permission missions.

Try this exercise. Try writing:

- A list of what you would like to achieve, big or small. Include the lofty, like "I want to retire when I'm fifty-five" or "I want to start my own business," to the short-term, like "I want to learn how to cook" or "I want to get a dog."
- A summary of why you want those things. Understanding your motivation for what you want will help you justify the reason why you deserve to have them. It will also clarify for you what you really want.
- Bullet points for why you deserve to have what you want.
- Every objection you can think of, especially if you know a backup singer would not approve. Then, refute each objection.
- A small first step for every item you identified in your plan. And do keep it small, at least at first. James Clear, the author of the perennial bestseller *Atomic Habits*, famously defined progress this way: "If you can get 1% better each day for one year, you'll end up 37 times better by the time you're done." He argues that these tiny improvements, almost unnoticeable day-to-day, compound over time to create remarkable results.
- A deadline—or a dare, if that's how it feels—to take that first step for at least one of the items on your wish list.

Planning is how you turn wishes and dreams into reality, one small step at a time. You deserve to have everything you want. You are worthy of happiness and success. Don't leave your future up to anyone who is not you.

Finally, don't be afraid to break some imaginary rules on your way to finding your voice, your passion, or your destiny. Remember, most of those rules benefit the ones who created them—not you.

Once you know what you want, give yourself permission to go for it. Once you do that, you will have the power of permission to bolster your resolve.

Chapter 12

Go Ahead: Break the Rules

> If you obey all the rules, you miss all the fun.
>
> **—Katharine Hepburn**

Cinema superstar Julia Roberts showed us what "going for it" looks like when she won her one and only Academy Award for her leading actress performance in the compelling true legal drama *Erin Brockovich* in 2001. She took her sweet time on stage as she made her acceptance speech.

She had been nominated twice before, in 1990 for her role in *Steel Magnolias* and the following year for *Pretty Woman*, but lost first to Brenda Fricker, who acted in *My Left Foot*, and second to Kathy Bates for her role in *Misery*.

And, as she said on stage that evening, she wasn't going to count on winning another Oscar.

So as the orchestra conductor cued the musicians to start playing the wrap-up tune that would indicate to Roberts that she was out of time, she hushed him.

"Sir, you're doing a great job, but you're so quick with that stick!" she admonished him. "So why don't you sit, because I may never be here again." Later, she added, "Stick-man, I see you."

The music stopped. Roberts finished her speech.

She never did win another Oscar.

Roberts, who did not comment on her remark in post-Oscar interviews, clearly gave herself permission to squeeze every moment of joy out of what might be her only statuette win. She presumably understood the value of her fame and stature in the movie industry and capitalized on it at a moment that was important to her.

An Oscar winner himself, the music conductor, Bill Conti, respected her request. Afterward, journalists and commentators gauged the incident as everything from humorous to crass.

But to me, Roberts wasn't willing to settle. She gave herself permission. What was Conti going to do, turn up the volume? She took what she felt she deserved. She put in the work and finally earned her reward—something beyond the $20 million paycheck she took home for her work on the film. Part of that reward, it seems, was a thorough acceptance speech, even if, at four minutes long, it far exceeded the typical forty-five-second allotment of time.

My friend Jake generally considers himself a rule-follower. He doesn't race through yellow lights when he's driving. He would never cheat on his taxes. He waits his turn in line, even when there's an opportunity to cut. And, as a kid, he always raised his hand when he knew the answer to a teacher's question or had an insight he wanted to share with his classmates.

Then one day, during an especially compelling lesson on American history, he was bursting at the seams to add his perspective to an energetic class discussion about Benjamin Franklin's many inventions. He raised his hand, but the teacher didn't call his name. He waved it around like he was the Prince of Wales greeting an approving crowd. He stood halfway up from his chair and sat back down three or four times, but kept his mouth closed, waiting for permission.

One of his classmates blurted out her opinion. Another one did the same. Two more disagreed with them. Not a single one of them raised a hand or waited for the teacher's permission to talk. Jake did, though, because he always followed the rules.

The rule-breakers essentially had created a new rule and replaced the old one: It's OK to speak without permission if someone else does it first. They assumed implied permission. One by one, the students discovered there would be no consequence to talking without the teacher's consent, and soon, everyone, including my friend, threw the raise-your-hand rule out the window and joined in. It got loud and chaotic. Jake was exhilarated.

Years later, as Jake told me the story, he was animated. He recalled the experience as freeing. He remembered feeling more powerful than he ever had when he was following class rules. He even remembered what he said way back then.

He also recalled the lesson the experience taught him: that sometimes the rules change. When he shouted his answer without permission, he wasn't breaking the raise-your-hand rule because that rule no longer existed. A new one—go ahead and blurt out your comment—had taken its place. There would be no negative consequence for following the implied permission instead of waiting for actual permission. Raising a hand was no longer required. Nobody made an announcement; it was just understood. The nonverbal behavior—the student after student who contributed an opinion without raising a hand first—created a new rule system in that classroom at that moment. Jake never would have spoken out of turn if everyone else hadn't done it first.

He might have felt empowered by the group. He might have considered their rule-breaking as permission to do it himself. But in reality, he had a choice. He in-powered himself. He gave himself permission.

Lots of us give ourselves permission to break the rules every day. We come to a rolling stop instead of a halt at a stop sign. We use a friend's streaming account without paying extra. We jaywalk when it seems safe and others are doing it, too. We secretly peek at a text during a class with a no-phones policy.

We don't think twice about it, as long as others are doing it and there seems to be little or no consequence. We create new rules for ourselves: It's OK to run the stop sign if nobody is there to see you do it. Lots of friends share streaming accounts and get away with it.

To be clear, I'm not condoning breaking the law, even a minor traffic law. I'm just saying we do it all the time because we see others doing it. We give ourselves permission to break a rule—even if we're rule-followers—because the rule isn't enforced and everybody else is breaking it, too.

Yet we find it difficult to break imaginary rules that we don't really have to follow.

Here we can move from observation to science.

Social Learning Theory, popularized by psychologist Albert Bandura in the 1970s, suggests that we learn how to behave by observing the behavior of others. If the others' behavior is rewarded or goes unpunished, we figure, "Why not?"

Social psychologist Robert Cialdini saw a difference between how most people behave (descriptive norms) and how we think we should behave (injunctive norms). When we see someone else violating a rule, the descriptive norm shifts, and we give ourselves permission to break the rule. An example: We're more likely to litter in a place where there's already trash all over the ground because our perception is that it's OK in that situation. We would never consider rushing a football field after a big win unless lots of others were already doing it. Then off we go.

Similarly, sometimes we subconsciously engage in unethical behavior when we see others doing it. At that moment, those rules don't seem so legitimate. This is a slippery slope that can lead to a gradual erosion of ethical standards.

To get real science-y, research in the field of neuroscience has shown that something called "mirror neurons" respond to actions we observe others engaging in. That leads us to imitate that behavior.

In plain English, this all means that if you see a Kardashian wearing a blouse unbuttoned to her belly button and being rewarded for it with compliments and opportunities for modeling and relationships with sports stars, well, we might open a few buttons on our shirts, too—even if our backup singers plead with us to button up.

The funny thing about giving ourselves permission to create new rules in the absence of society's adherence to the old ones is that most of those rules were created by the same society that is ignoring them now.

Another point to ponder is that not everybody is given the same rulebook. Women get one; men get another. The rules change from generation to generation. Maybe your family was conservative and your neighbor's was liberal. Different beliefs. Different imaginary rules.

I can think of a few of society's invisible rules that I've broken, and I've had to silence a background singer or two to do it.

My husband and I are child-free by choice. I've been reminded dozens, maybe hundreds of times over the years that our choice is against the unwritten rule that women are supposed to get married and have children. My husband, on the other hand, is rarely questioned about it.

That's because the imaginary rulebook lays a stigma on child-free women. Not so much for men, though. It's only the women who are made to feel less than.

A child-free-by-choice friend, Madi, told me about an international house guest she and her husband hosted. The man, assuming Madi was unable to have children, pulled her husband aside to ask him, privately, why he didn't divorce her and find a wife who would have his babies. The husband politely explained that he doesn't want kids, either.

So many people in my life sincerely believed I would regret my decision once it was too late to reconsider. But I was clear on my plan. My husband and I were clear on our plan.

I created a new rule: Every woman gets to choose for herself whether she has children. I still have to make a choice, but that choice in my new rule system (and it's catching on) has not already been made for me. And I don't have to explain that choice to anyone.

Same goes for busting stereotypes and norms like the one that says the man of the house should be the breadwinner. I love this story the wildly successful singer Cher told Jane Pauley during a 1996 interview: "My mom said to me, 'You know, sweetheart, one day you should settle down and marry a rich man.' I said, 'Mom, I *am* a rich man.'"

Our backup singers have made a lot of rules for us, and some of them stand as tall today as they did when we were toddlers. "Don't run with scissors" comes to mind.

But when you get to a point where you're fed up with following rules created for you by others in a different time, by people who could not possibly know your circumstances forty years into the future, it's time to toss that rulebook and write your own.

It's like your backup singers have handed you a playlist and you're not allowed to sing anything else, even though you're the one in the spotlight, not them. You're standing center stage in your life, not theirs.

On that stage, I make my own rules. An example: When respect is no longer being served, walk away from the table.

Once I was making small talk at a sales convention with a very successful gentleman who, after I told him I live in San Francisco, rattled off a list of things that must be wrong with me if I would choose such a home. As a polite Southern woman, I am, of course, expected to eat the you-know-what he was serving with a knife and a fork and then dab the corners of my mouth and say, "Thank you."

"When is the last time you visited San Francisco?" I asked him.

He had never been to California, let alone my town. So I replied, "I see. Well, I am not sure how you can assess a place you've never visited. And that's my home you're talking about." Then I excused myself.

The always-be-polite rule just wasn't working for me, and no amount of backup singer finger-pointing could convince me otherwise.

I called on my grit, and it served me way better than any imaginary rule for polite Southern women ever could.

I trusted my own voice—the one that said to ditch "polite" in the face of insults from inconsiderate strangers. I trusted my own voice more than I trusted the many backup singers in my head at that moment. Sorry, backup singers, but what worked for you doesn't always work for me.

In fact, sometimes, you have to construct your own rules, and those rules might be different for you than they are for others.

As we've examined in prior chapters, it's hard to detach ourselves from rules that were prescribed to us as children by people we believed and trusted. Then, as we age, we still let the voices of those trusted adults—now our backup singers—limit us when we want to feel free and powerful.

Most of us do question the rules, though, especially when they don't make sense to us, or when they seem to be written to benefit some people and not others. Often, the rules we question are society's rules or norms, or they're the cultural customs that made sense when we were kids or perhaps when our parents were, but they don't anymore.

At least not to us.

My friend Jake gave himself permission to break a rule even though he's not a universal rule-breaker. But he breaks the imaginary ones.

The next time you're doing something—or more likely, not doing something—because there seems to be a rule for or against it, ask yourself the six As of rule-breaking, and then decide if you really need to follow it. Is the rule . . .

Absolute? Is this a hard-and-fast policy of your employer or another authority who can penalize you for breaking it? For example, if you're told to report for jury duty at 7:30 but you arrive at 7:40 and find an hour-long line of jurors waiting to be checked in, have you broken a rule? And next time, can you sleep ten minutes longer?

Acknowledged? Is the rule enforced or even enforceable? If the dress code says male employees must wear jackets and ties, but most, including the bosses, wear jackets without ties and nobody is reprimanded for dressing too casually, have those tie-less colleagues broken a rule?

Achievable? Is it even possible to adhere to the rule? If you're a professor and the college demands that you submit grades for all sixty of your students within forty-eight hours of the final exam, and you grade day and night for two days and still aren't finished, what can you do? And if, the next morning, there's no email from the higher-ups wondering where your grades are, have you broken a rule?

Applicable? Does the rule even have anything to do with the work or whatever it's part of? Does a rule that requires everyone to write their weekly status reports in black ink mean you shouldn't type them on your laptop? That you should print them out instead of emailing them? What? Why? Seriously? And does anybody actually do that, or does everybody type and email?

Altered? Is the rule so often broken that it seems another rule—an opposite one—has taken its place? For example, if nobody is allowed to check personal emails or text messages at work, but everybody does it right out in the open without consequence, is that even a rule?

Absurd? If the rule is so over-the-top that nobody would ever consider following it, would you follow it? One BuzzFeed user reported a company that forbade women employees from sitting together at lunch or socializing outside of the office to avoid the appearance of cliques. Another required female workers who chose to wear open-toed shoes to the office to polish their toenails. Instead of following those rules, many employees resigned.

Whether you are a rule-follower or a rule-breaker, consider whether society's norms and your backup singers' antiquated beliefs are holding you back from achieving success or fulfilling your dreams. If they are, it might be time for you to create a few invisible rules for yourself to live by, no matter what everyone else is doing.

Chapter 13

When You're Just Fed Up

> I've never seen any life transformation that didn't begin with the person in question finally getting tired of their own bullshit.
>
> **—Elizabeth Gilbert**

Any mission is a journey. Your personal permission mission is a quest for the confidence to give yourself permission to go after anything you want, big or small, long-term or just for today. It begins with a change of mindset, from "I don't deserve this" to "I deserve to have everything I want." It will require you to do some introspection and to understand and admit that most of the limitations you put on yourself in the form of "I can't" and "I shouldn't" revolve around the recollections you have of lessons learned from trusted, respected, or even feared authorities who guided and taught you as you grew from a child into an adult—your backup singers.

Many of those who have achieved their personal permission missions have something important in common, aside from fear, trust, and grit: They had reached their limit when it came to tempering their dreams, foregoing their ambitions, putting their lives on hold, or otherwise harmonizing in the chorus of their lives instead of belting out the solo they were born to sing.

At a certain moment, they were fed up. Have you ever been fed up? Reached a breaking point? Decided that something had to give? (You don't have to answer that; if you're human, the answer is yes, yes, and yes.)

Did you feel guilty for feeling that way?

Why can't we give ourselves permission to simply be fed up, with a lazy teenager, a too-demanding schedule, an insensitive life partner, or with anything or anyone who is making you feel stuck? Let's admit that we have a threshold for tolerance, as all humans do, and give ourselves permission to walk away from or at least change a bad situation when that threshold is crossed. Let's resolve that it's OK to break the imaginary rules or step out of our boxes once it becomes clear that we just *can't* anymore with these antiquated social norms and expectations that were written with invisible ink in a different era and that we never agreed to. Let's take a look at how clear—or unclear—our boundaries are, and answer one question. Why do we have to reach a breaking point before we'll even consider giving ourselves permission to take a long-overdue action?

For inspiration, look no further than today's headlines, where you inevitably will find an update about the daily goings-on in the lives of the Duke and Duchess of Sussex.

It's been widely reported that Prince Harry and Meghan Markle left England and their roles as "senior royals" for a less royally prescribed life in America. In their Netflix documentary, *Harry & Meghan*, and in the prince's book, *Spare*, the couple detailed their frustrations with the British tabloids, tensions within the royal family, and racism.

In their book, *Finding Freedom*, biographers Omid Scobie and Carolyn Durand showed that the couple's breaking point came over the lack of independence they had as part of the royal family. The 368-page biography focuses on the prince's irritation with the roadblocks he perceived were keeping the newlyweds from "operat[ing] as an actual family . . . Harry was drained by the unique circumstances of his family."

Combined with social media criticism, scandalous tabloid headlines, and Meghan's dissatisfaction with her new life after marrying into the royal family in 2018, the prince had had enough. So they left.

"There really was no other option," the prince told the audience at a charity dinner in January 2020. His threshold had been exceeded. He had stretched his boundaries as far as he could. He later admitted he had not made the decision to leave England lightly. But staying, he said, "wasn't possible."

Even a titled prince with privilege struggled to reach his personal permission mission. His impetus, like it is for a lot of us, was frustration. He couldn't work it out with the Queen or his father or his brother—the heirs to the throne—and he was simply fed up.

So he gave himself permission.

Everyone's threshold is different, but our reasons for powering through our breaking points are rooted in psychology and, not surprisingly, fear.

When we're frustrated, of course, we tend to complain. I have one friend who complains to her friends about her husband so much that we all thought they would wind up divorced. It turns out he's a great guy and she loves him to pieces. She just needs to vent sometimes.

For her, venting relieves the frustration. But many people won't vent, even to their trusted friends, because they believe admitting frustration will be perceived as complaining, weakness, or failure. We fear our friends (or whomever we're complaining to) might reject us—or perhaps think negatively about the person who has caused our frustration.

In my friend's case, she didn't want or need to change her situation, except to perhaps find a more persuasive way to convince her man to pick up after himself. But others opt for "toxic positivity," the tendency to hold in their frustrations and press on, even when they're miserable. They pretend to be happy, even when they're struggling, to keep up appearances.

I wonder who told them to do that? Perhaps a backup singer along the way who taught them that they can't be both grateful and frustrated at the same time. Or, that they can't, like my friend, love and respect and want to stay with a partner who is sometimes frustrating to live with.

At work, employees regularly hesitate to admit frustration or dissatisfaction for fear they will lose their jobs, or that someone will label them as a troublemaker, or that there will be some sort of retaliation. In a personal relationship, partners and friends might avoid expressing frustration with each other to avoid hurting the other person's feelings.

When it's time for a change, you know it. Listen to your inner voice. Give yourself permission to walk away or confront the culprit, even if the culprit is you. Have you ever been frustrated by your perceived inability to offer your ideas at a work meeting, even though you know they're valuable? Have you ever reached the point of getting really mad at yourself for choosing to put off a health check or a vacation or all of your social obligations for a whole month because you're always working?

Change is hard. It's scary. We're afraid that what we're leaving might be better than the unknown that comes afterward. We're comfortable with what's familiar. And, believe it or not, our brain likes the habits we have and will resist us when we try to change them.

So will our backup singers. They want you to stay safely ensconced in your marriage, at your long-time job, or in the house that you outgrew after you had your second child. That's what they did, after all. They also probably suffered from chronic stress, resentment, unmet needs, and a lack of growth or even hope for any improvement.

Is that the life you want? Look a year into the future. What will it look like if you keep doing what you're doing, even though you're emotionally done with it? Why aren't you leaving/negotiating/taking action/going to therapy/planning your next move?

Aren't you tired? Aren't you fed up?

Are you waiting for permission? Whose? Are you really ever going to get that permission? Probably not. You don't need it anyway. You have to in-power yourself. Give it to yourself.

Take One Step Forward

Your responses to the prompts below will help you take one step forward toward the spotlight of your life and help you fulfill your personal permission mission.

What are your backup singers telling you that you no longer trust?

Recall a time when you trusted your own voice more than that of your backup singers, perhaps when you decided to break an imaginary rule.

Recall a time when you wish you had.

Ask yourself

- Whose rules are you still following that no longer serve you?
- Make a list of backup singers who are in harmony with your dreams and those who are not. Commit to amplifying the supportive ones.
- What would change in your life if you believed and trusted that your choices are yours to make?

Journal about your personal manifesto: Write five to seven sentences about what you value, what you stand for, and what you refuse to apologize for. Keep it visible as a reminder that your life belongs to you.

Visualize: Write the name of the backup singer that you want to lead your chorus this week. Keep it where you can see it. Give him/her a solo every day and let that help give you the courage to take a step toward fulfilling your own permission mission.

Practice: Saying "no." Start small. Say "no" to something you would usually agree to but don't want to do. Pay close attention to how it feels to say "no."

Take Action: Look at the manifesto that you wrote in your journal and choose one thing that you value and refuse to apologize for, and let it be known. Speak up about it this week. Choose one bold step, however small. Write down what your action step will be and when, commit to it, and follow through.

Part Three

Your Personal Permission Mission

G ive yourself permission rather than asking or waiting for permission from someone else.

R ealize that your passion for what you want, need, and deserve is greater than the fear of trying.

I n-power yourself to trust your own voice more than the voices of the past.

T ake a step forward into the spotlight on the stage of your own life.

Inventor and engineer Charles Kettering, perhaps as famous for his many insightful quotes as for his inventions, once said: "The world hates change, yet it is the only thing that has brought progress."

I couldn't agree more. The reason: Change prompts growth, and growth prompts change. And next to grit and trust, growth is a crucial key to achieving our goals.

Still, change is scary. Even thinking about change can cause stress and, sometimes, panic. It can cause us to abandon our mission and goals. It can derail our most carefully considered plans.

So, it's important to realize that to achieve your personal permission mission, your passion for what you want, need, or deserve must exceed your fear of doing what you must to get it.

First, you must overcome your fear. That's not easy. You can't simply give yourself permission to stop being apprehensive and anticipating the worst. You have to work at that.

If you want to make it as a social media influencer, you have to put your face and personality on display for everyone to see and comment on, even though you know some of those comments will upset you. Do you want to be an influencer more than you dread those negative comments? Or is it the other way around? If you want a raise, the only way to get it is to ask for it, and it's possible the answer will be "no." Do you want the bump in pay more than you fear that your boss will tell you "no"? Which one is more important to you?

Fear is a normal human emotion, whether you're about to make a speech, buy a house, end a significant relationship, or dye your hair purple.

Everyone is at least a little bit scared when they try something new or go after something that could result in a negative consequence.

That fear, of course, is learned. The same backup singers who told you that you can achieve anything you set your mind to also instilled caution in you and urged you to avoid taking chances, so perhaps you never do.

The question is: How badly do you want the thing you want? How great is your passion for having or doing it? How much risk are you willing to take to get it? And does that passion, your permission mission, equal more or less than your fear of potential negative consequences?

What are you willing to give yourself permission to do? Have you tapped into your grit so you can follow through?

The good news is that you can outgrow your fear, especially if you adopt a mindset that says failure is part of growth. It's not so scary to take a chance on yourself when you believe that a negative consequence is simply a roadmap to doing it better next time.

So instead of letting your backup singers convince you that you're not a good singer because your sixteen-year-old self wasn't equipped to sing the national anthem at the ballpark, decide for yourself. Since then, have you acquired the skills to belt it out with confidence as an adult? Instead of letting those voices from the past keep you stuck in a dead-end job because the devil you know is safer than the one you don't, you choose for yourself. Do your research about the company you have your eye on, talk to some of its employees, and put your application in.

Along the way, ask those who support you for their input and help. After you start to make progress, if it looks like those backup singers were right, or you realize this is not what you want, then shut it down. This will be uncomfortable and uncertain once you make the change, so prepare for it. And don't give up too early.

All the while, keep this in mind: Nobody has ever died from hearing "No, you can't have a raise," or "You missed that high note, but the rest sounded great." But plenty of people have learned from that kind of criticism and tried again, harder and with the confidence that a second chance can give you.

Chapter 14

Outgrow Your Fear

> All too often we are taught that "fear" is a bad thing. But sometimes the presence of fear is life's way of telling you that you're on the right track . . . So lean into your purpose, trust that all you need is already within you.
>
> **—Sara Blakely**

Like any mission, your permission mission will present you with some challenges along your way to meaningful change. As we have discussed, fear is the biggest one. A lack of trust in yourself is a close second.

In 1967 during a concert in New York's Central Park, the celebrated songbird Barbra Streisand, already a superstar at age twenty-five, forgot the lyrics to "When the Sun Comes Out," the final song before a mid-show intermission.

"It was my worst nightmare come true," Streisand wrote in her 2023 memoir, *My Name Is Barbra*. "It really threw me. . . . I felt an absolute lack of control . . . and it was terrifying."

Streisand, a self-described perfectionist, didn't perform at a live concert again for twenty-seven years.

While her retreat from live shows—she continued to make albums and to record performances—may seem like the opposite of permission, she actually is an example of someone who gave herself permission to stop doing something she no longer enjoyed.

Still, the fear that kept Streisand from the stage until 1994 is something nearly everyone grapples with—much more privately, of course. Whenever we face a demand or an opportunity that takes us outside of our comfort zone, we are afraid we will fail or be criticized or ruin our reputations. And like Streisand, a lot of us throw in the towel after one bad experience, so we'll never know if we can overcome our fear or if we might have turned out to be great at the thing we flubbed.

Fear is a normal emotion, and it's one that you can overcome. It takes some grit—OK, a lot of it—but along the way, you will strengthen your confidence.

The comedian David Nihill admitted during a TED Talk: "I thought I was going to die the first time I performed stand-up. I was shaking. I was terrified. But I didn't die. And every time after that, I reminded myself: I'm scared, but I didn't die last time—so I probably won't die this time."

He added: "That simple thought gave me permission to keep going."

The fact is that if you're never afraid, you might never grow. Fear is a powerful motivator and teacher. It forces us to confront our limitations and vulnerabilities. It teaches us what makes us uncomfortable, which in turn, highlights our core values and beliefs. It shows us what we need to improve. It helps us become resilient.

The only time we ever grow is at the edge of our comfort zone.

In fact, in my view, fear is a prerequisite for growth. And it moves you closer to achieving your permission mission, which happens at that magic moment when you realize that your mission, whatever that may be, is more important to you than your fear.

It's the moment when you give yourself permission to ask for a date, even though you're terrified that your new crush will say "no." It's the magic that happens when you finally decide to go back to school as an adult, even though you're afraid you will be twice as old as everyone in the class. It's the joy of deciding to make an offer on your first house, even though you've been putting it off for years for fear you might not be able to make the monthly mortgage payments. It's the breaking point when you're fed up with what you're missing more than you're afraid to go after it.

It's when you cross the threshold from being controlled by your fear to taking control of it. It's the permission you give yourself to shake your hesitation, hush the warnings from your backup singers, and decide that you want something so badly you don't care if it's the scariest thing you've ever done.

It's time to start the conversation you need to have with yourself so you can overcome the fears those backup singers have instilled in you. It's time to work through the doubts you feel about your own ability to pull off the successes you dream of achieving.

One of my favorite quotes comes from President Franklin D. Roosevelt, who said during his first inaugural address in 1933: "The only thing we have to fear is fear itself."

Being afraid is a primal emotion. And it is so powerful that most of us try to avoid it. But you have handled fear before. And you survived. But ask yourself, will you be content knowing that you let your fear keep you from experiencing joy, or pride or fulfilment?

My friend Rajna really, truly wants to be decisive and give herself permission to do what she feels is right for her. So she musters up her grit and gets started on her personal permission mission . . . and then stops. Over and over again. She calls upon her grit and courage to get going, but it doesn't take long for her fear to overcome her and her backup singers to convince her that she has bitten off more than she can chew.

Fear is her permanent plus-one, but more often than not, she lets it RSVP for her.

Sound familiar?

It might surprise you to know that another superstar singer, Adele, has openly discussed the extreme anxiety she experiences before her performances. She has even canceled shows because of it. Abraham Lincoln, lauded after the 1863 speech known as the Gettysburg Address as one of the greatest speakers in history, reportedly declined at least one speaking invitation because of his fear of criticism and his speech anxiety.

Sometimes, fear can be a bit irrational, especially if our backup singers have conditioned us to expect the worst or if we continually watch violent media. Communications expert George Gerbner introduced a theory—Mean World Syndrome—in the 1970s that suggested that when we watch too much violent content on TV or in the movies, like crime shows or horror fiction, our perception of how scary the real world is can get distorted.

What are you afraid of? Criticism, backlash, being made fun of, gossip, loss of control, letting go, being hurt? Does it hold you back? Does it keep you from giving yourself permission to step into your own or do the things you secretly would like to do? And be honest, are you just a teensy bit afraid of succeeding? Are you afraid that once you knock it out of the park, everyone will expect you to do that every time?

Don't fret: Fear can be a good thing.

For example, one analysis found that the more fear we experience, the less likely we are to engage in risky behavior. It can make us more cautious and convince us to be especially thoughtful about decisions, especially if they potentially involve danger or uncertainty. Fear also can be useful in helping us figure out how to mitigate a perceived threat, according to the analysis published in PubMed Central.

In terms of human evolution, the research pointed out that fear has been considered a survival skill, something we need to let us know when we're in harm's way. Fear can change the way your body feels: Should you flee or fight? It can bring your thoughts into clearer focus, help you react quickly, and make you more attentive, all positives when you're about to make a big decision.

My sense of fear has been a safety monitor for me as I travel the world making presentations. Once, I was riding the elevator to my hotel room when a sketchy-looking man joined me and pressed the button for the floor above mine. My spidey-sense kicked in immediately, and I said, "Oh, I pushed the wrong floor. Sorry!" Then I selected the floor above his so he would get out of the elevator before I did and would be unable to follow me to my room. I will never know what the outcome would have been if I had not pushed the button for the higher floor, but I trusted that little voice inside. I trusted my gut.

Fear can protect us and hold us back, but in this case, it was probably for the best. But excessive or chronic fear is unhealthy.

While fear sharpens our senses, it also can lead us to overestimate potential threats, which distorts our ability to make clear-headed decisions. It can convince us to avoid risk at all costs, which can be limiting. Chronic fear can mess with our immune systems, elevate our blood pressure, interrupt our sleep, and even promote eating disorders, according to the *American Journal of Managed Care*. At its worst, it can manifest as post-traumatic stress disorder, phobias, and depression.

Evolution doesn't get all the blame for our fear, though. A lot of our fears are learned—passed down from our backup singers who used fear to instill caution or terrify us into changing our behavior: "If you lie, your nose will grow." "Don't crack your knuckles or you'll get arthritis." We also learn fear when we experience trauma or an event so unpleasant that we never want it to happen again. Like Pavlov's dog, we can even associate sounds, like thunder, with something scary that happened at the same time as the loud noise. And some people actually are genetically disposed to fear; it's in their biology.

Overcoming fear isn't as simple as giving yourself permission to get over it. Fear is often deeply ingrained. If our fear is born of trauma, that's not something we can simply shake off. For some, years of therapy are required to take control of their emotions and overcome their fears.

But don't consider yourself fear's victim. If you don't give yourself permission to overcome your fear, you're not a victim; you're a volunteer. How about being a victor?

Research shows that exposure therapy, which can involve exposing ourselves to the things we fear, little by little, can help desensitize us and reduce our negative reaction to them. I admit that I still get butterflies before I walk onto a stage to give a keynote speech to hundreds of people. I think that is a sign that I am human. I also subscribe to positive thinking, like "I'm going to help so many people with this speech" instead of "What if they don't like me?" And I imagine the audience being engaged and smiling in the moments and hours before my speech. Both really help me to keep my nerves in check.

Yet I still get butterflies before going on stage.

One audience member asked me if those ever go away. I admitted that they don't.

But I told the woman, a company leader, that I hope they never do. Those butterflies are giving me information: Do more research; rehearse a little bit longer; be sure to know exactly who is in the audience.

I think of fear as a friend. It's a constant companion. It's a constant motivator.

I also have talked with other speakers about how they feel before they walk onto the stage, and we're all in the same boat, so I know it's not just me.

Perhaps the most impactful thing I do to allay any lingering fears I have before a big presentation is to prepare. I make a plan for exactly what I want to accomplish. I do tons of research. I write a detailed outline. I rehearse in front of a mirror; sometimes I even record my rehearsal to get a visual of my body language and facial expressions. I even plan my outfit so I'll feel physically comfortable and confident that I won't trip over my own shoes.

In a way, I'm grateful for my fear because I believe it keeps me on my toes. But I also have learned how to calm the fear. I arm myself with preparation so I know I won't forget anything or be unable to answer a question or sound like an amateur. But mostly, I know that my fear helps me understand how important doing well and making a good impression are to me.

It helps me determine that being a keynote speaker and delivering a helpful message are far more important to me than avoiding those things because they invoke a little fear. It helps me fulfill my personal permission mission, and it can help you fulfill yours, too.

Chapter 15

Imposter Syndrome: Your Constant Copilot

> The obnoxious roommate living in our heads—that voice of negativity and self-doubt that tells us we can't do it, or shouldn't even try.
>
> **—Arianna Huffington**

Perhaps nothing tempts us to give up too soon more than the ubiquitous feeling known as imposter syndrome. And if you don't think every single person suffers from it at one time or another, consider the superstar actor, director, producer, and script writer, Tom Hanks.

He's done comedy and drama. He has appeared on stage, on TV, and in the movies—nearly one hundred of them. He has won two Academy Awards. He's a bona fide star, one of the most famous stars ever.

Yet in a 2016 interview with NPR, Tom Hanks—from *Forrest Gump*, *Philadelphia*, *Toy Story*, and on and on and on—asked, "When are they going to discover that I am, in fact, a fraud and take everything away from me?"

Hanks has admitted during multiple interviews that he suffers from imposter syndrome—the persistent feeling that you are a fraud, even though you have plenty of evidence that you're competent and able. He's not the only one. The dynamic speaker, bestselling author, and former First Lady Michelle Obama has said her imposter syndrome "never goes away." Author, poet, activist, and performer Maya Angelou is widely quoted as saying, "I have written eleven books, but each time I think, 'Uh oh, they're going to find out now. I've run a game on everybody, and they're going to find me out.'"

I could list a hundred more accomplished, amazing humans who admit that they experience imposter syndrome. If I could talk to each one of them one-on-one, I'd say the same thing to all of them: Good for you!

Imposter syndrome may be self-doubt at its worst. Yet, I think it's a true gift from your backup singers.

If you "suffer" from imposter syndrome, that means you have given yourself permission to stretch far outside of your comfort zone to try something unfamiliar—and you're crushing it! It means you have decided that your desire to go for the next big thing is greater than your fear of messing it up. It means that you have considered the pros and cons, listened to all of the arguments your backup singers have for moving forward or standing still, and you've made the big decision for yourself. You decided to listen to your own voice.

If you're worried that people are going to discover that you don't know what you're doing, that means they have not yet made that discovery.

Chances are very good that they never will because you're probably the only one in the room who thinks you're not good enough, experienced enough, capable enough, smart enough, or just plain *enough* to pull off something that might be a bit next-level for you.

Imposter syndrome is a symptom of one thing only: growth. If you're never at least a little bit nervous about elevating yourself to the next level, you would be the exception. Psychologists Pauline R. Clance and Suzanne A. Imes, who introduced the concept of "imposter phenomenon" in 1978, found that the syndrome is common, especially among high-achieving women. In fact, they learned, approximately 70 percent of people experience it at some point in their lives, some when they're just starting out and others with years or even decades of experience.

Sometimes, I feel imposter syndrome, too. Right before I give a presentation, walk on stage to deliver a speech, or even just step into a new room full of people, that itty-bitty sh*tty committee in my head chimes in with, "Are you sure you belong here?"

It's sneaky. And loud. And kind of a jerk.

So, I take a breath. I look at the evidence. I've written books and blogs on these exact topics that I am speaking on. I've been invited to speak to leaders, professionals, and organizations across the globe. I know this stuff.

But like many women, I sometimes can't believe my good luck. And then I realize that I'm not lucky; I'm prepared. I'm experienced. I'm a pretty good storyteller. I have helped a lot of people. I do have something to offer that could truly benefit my audiences.

I'm in the position I'm in because I've earned it.

I wouldn't be surprised if your story sounds similar to mine. That's because it's completely natural to feel a little bit out of your element when you put yourself in a position to do something that you haven't done before, or that most people would never attempt, or that someone, at some time, has warned you that you would fail if you tried.

It's completely natural to feel unsure of yourself when you're stretching and growing and pushing yourself to do more and to do better.

Experiencing that self-doubt just means you're not quite comfortable with the new thing yet. But the takeaway here is that you've given yourself permission to do the new thing. That's growth.

Imposter syndrome can be your friend. It's your constant copilot. So why not give her a cute nickname? (Mine's Critical Cara.) It's not a bad thing unless you let it become your loudest backup singer.

Why? Feelings of imposter syndrome can be incredibly motivating. They can make you feel like you have to prove yourself—to yourself or to anyone who planted the seeds of self-doubt in you during your lifetime so far. Feeling like a fraud can drive you to work harder and get the skills you need to feel like an old pro. The anxiety of feeling like a fraud can lead you to be even more prepared and to work harder. And it can help you see where you actually do need to improve, which could lead you to take the steps you need to make fewer mistakes and set higher standards for yourself.

It's challenging to find logic when you're experiencing an emotional moment before you step onto a stage or in any other anxiety-provoking role, but it's possible.

The X Files actress Gillian Anderson, for example, said she felt insecure playing the role of Eleanor Roosevelt in the Showtime series *The First Lady*, partly because the actress is five feet three inches tall, and Roosevelt was five foot eleven.

"First of all, I couldn't believe I could do it," Anderson told *InStyle* in a 2025 interview. "I really had to stop my self-doubt from getting in the way."

And she did: "You have to convince yourself that you can do things you might not yet be able to do," she said, in hindsight. "And by doing it, or acting like you can do it, suddenly you can, and you're no longer afraid."

Valerie Young, cofounder of the consulting firm Impostor Syndrome Institute, has said imposter syndrome is nothing to be ashamed of. In fact, she has suggested that if you experience it, tell someone. You'll find that you're not alone.

Here are a few of her other tips that I have found useful, along with some based on my own experiences and those of my coaching clients:

- Just because you feel "stupid" in a situation doesn't mean you are. But you knew that, right?
- Expect that imposter syndrome might show up if you're stepping into a situation that you're not quite comfortable with. Young gives the example of someone who is much younger or older than everyone else at a meeting, or if you're the first woman or person of color to achieve something, or if you fit a category that is usually stereotyped.
- If you're a perfectionist, you are especially susceptible to feelings of imposter syndrome. Try to recognize that mistakes happen, and that you'll probably make one. Forgive yourself in advance.
- Give yourself permission to ask for help or even for reassurance.
- Visualize success. And then reward yourself when you do great.
- Finally, know that every one of us, no matter how experienced or knowledgeable we are, has to fly by the seat of our pants sometimes. And when you do, you'll be reminded that you are resourceful and

> you actually do know what you're doing. If you didn't, you simply wouldn't have gotten this far.

Imposter syndrome should really be called the "Grit Glitch" because that's all it is. A momentary glitch in an otherwise incredibly successful life. It's the moment where your backup singers are reminding you of what happened in your past and of what the people from your past had to say. That was then; this is now. And you are in control now. Realize you're growing and embrace the lessons you're going to learn, good or bad, from what you're about to do. And tell "Critical Cara" to "buckle up buttercup, because we are about to do this!"

Chapter 16

Fail Better

> I definitely think failure is important. If you're not failing, you're really not learning.
>
> **—Reese Witherspoon**

If confronting our fears helps us grow, surviving failure helps us blossom.

I loved the reaction of former *The Young and the Restless* actor Shemar Moore when he announced the winner of the 1999 Daytime Emmy for Outstanding Lead Actress in a Drama Series:

"The streak is over! Susan Lucci!"

The statuette finally went to the *All My Children* star after nineteen nominations and eighteen losses.

Lucci, who portrayed the conniving Erica Kane for forty-one years and was then the highest-paid actor on daytime TV, couldn't have given a more gracious acceptance speech to the audience, which rewarded her with a two-minute standing ovation.

"The fact that you have thought that my work was worthy of notice nineteen times is something I will always treasure," she told her peers, and added, for her fans, "I wasn't meant to get this award before tonight because if I had, I wouldn't have that collection of poems and letters and drawings and balloons and chocolate cakes you made me all this time to make me feel better."

And then, "I'm going back to that studio on Monday, and I'm gonna play Erica Kane for all she's worth!"

If Lucci was bitter about the two-decade snub, she never let on. She routinely made light of her status as an eighteen-time loser, once on *Saturday Night Live* and again in a commercial for an artificial sweetener. After her win, she told the media that she "never really thought I'd get" backstage to talk about a victory. During a cast reunion in 2020, Lucci recalled that after her ninth nomination, she "started to black out; I don't know if it was self-protective. . . . My biggest fear [was] that someday, I might just [mistakenly] think they called my name and go up there."

Lucci had become a sort of poster child for the "try, try again" ethic. She said in a video produced by the American Heart Association: "Every time I didn't win, I would go back and try to grow, to grow as an actress and to get better, to be better, better and better and better and better."

Lucci gave herself permission to keep trying, to keep working her hardest. It's unlikely that she was acting just for the sake of winning awards, but the lack of recognition, especially from peers, critics agree, can be humiliating for a performer.

The same is true of those in any profession. Stephen King has said his debut novel *Carrie*, now a cult classic, was rejected by thirty different publishers before it was finally accepted by Doubleday. HuffPost cofounder and renowned journalist Arianna Huffington said she was rejected by thirty-seven publishers for her second book. She went on to write thirteen more books.

Diana Nyad failed four times to swim between Cuba and Florida. The fifth time was the charm. The fifty-two-hour swim was brutal. Her friends and even her staunchest supporters tried to talk her out of it. But finally, in 2013, the sixty-four-year-old Nyad finally made it. Her mantra became, "Find a way," which is what she titled her 2015 autobiography.

All of these people wanted what they wanted, so they kept trying.

Talk about grit!

That's a secret to achieving your personal permission mission: You have to want it. You have to want it more than you fear getting it, more than you're defeated by rejection, more than your feelings are hurt when others criticize you. If you want something badly enough, you won't give up just because others judge you harshly.

One of my favorite quotes about perseverance comes from Nobel Prize winner Samuel Beckett, author of *Worstward Ho*: "Try again. Fail again. Fail better."

Failure can beat you down and put an end to your dreams or it can fuel you to try, try again. Failure, like so many other lessons in life, is a tool for growth.

Most of us fail on a fairly regular basis. Who hasn't failed a quiz at school or fumbled a job interview at some point? Name one person you know who hasn't given up on a New Year's resolution within the first month of the year. Athletes fail to make the team; actors don't get called back for a second audition; sales reps don't make the sale every time. Marriages end. Companies go out of business. Ideas are shot down.

Those who brush themselves off and try again build resilience. As I do, psychologist Angela Duckworth calls this "grit," which she defines as a blend of passion and persistence. She has suggested that grit is more crucial to success than IQ, social intelligence, good looks, or anything else. For her book, aptly named *Grit: The Power of Passion and Perseverance*, she studied dozens of high achievers, from coaches to editors to CEOs to spelling bee champions.

"Grit is having stamina," Duckworth said in a 2013 TED Talk. "Grit is sticking with your future, day in, day out, not just for the week, not just for the month, but for years, and working really hard to make that future a reality. Grit is living life like it's a marathon, not a sprint."

She added, "We have to be willing to fail, to be wrong, to start over again with lessons learned."

Duckworth also found that simply not giving up can increase your chances of success. Each time you try the same thing again, you bring into the effort everything you learned the time before. Eventually, that collected knowledge from all of your prior failures is what leads to the breakthrough. That breakthrough, that success, would not have been possible if you had quit the first time you failed. Separate research in *Harvard Business Review* similarly found that trying again after failing gives us the opportunity to experiment with different strategies and approaches that don't repeat the mistakes we've already made.

Spencer Silver was a scientist at 3M trying to invent a super-strong adhesive. But one of his "failures" turned into one of my favorite things on the planet—Post-it Notes! He accidentally created a not-so-sticky glue, and years later, Art Fry had the genius idea to use it for bookmarks that wouldn't damage pages.

And just like that, Post-it Notes were born in 1980.

Every one of my books and projects starts on my Post-it wall. I jot down ideas, and when they start to take shape, the real writing begins. Without Spencer's so-called failure, this book (and my previous two books) might never have even happened!

Take a moment and recall a recent failure, big or small. If you shook it off and tried again, and eventually reached your goal, how did you feel? It's been proven that our self-esteem skyrockets when we finally achieve a personal or professional mission after multiple setbacks. The sense of accomplishment after overcoming obstacles is enormous.

In fact, failure counts as one of our most valuable learning experiences. And interestingly, the failures that your backup singers have shared with you over the years might help you learn even more.

Researcher Kristy Towry of Emory University studied how organizations and their people manage their learning. Her finding: Learning from others helps us see the big picture more effectively than learning only from our own experiences. When we examine our own experience, she found, we focus on what is happening now or has just happened. Without prior failures, she noted, "We forget what happened before and don't build that into our decision-making."

That's another great reason to approach your memories of advice and guidance from backup singers with curiosity. Sometimes, it's spot-on.

Of course, trying the same thing over and over again without applying the learning that your prior mistakes graced you with can be futile. You know the saying, most often attributed to Albert Einstein: “Insanity is doing the same thing over and over again and expecting different results.” An article in the *Journal of Personality and Social Psychology* points out that it’s not a good idea to expect persistence to pay off with success every time. Outside factors, like the unpredictable behavior of others, are beyond our control and may affect our chances of success.

And if you’re trying everything you can think of and continue to fail, you’re bound to suffer from stress and anxiety, both killers of motivation.

A number of published studies suggest that women are prone to giving up sooner than men are. Women, the researchers found, tend to internalize failure more than men, and they’re more likely to attribute their failure to their own lack of ability. Women also are socialized to be perfectionists more than men, so they often take it harder when they fail and walk away rather than powering through.

My advice: Fail forward. Shatter the stereotype. Show your grit. Keep trying until you reach your destination.

That’s not easy, but you can in-power yourself to keep going. You can do it if you have permission to keep plugging away—and you already have it. You can give it to yourself.

Chapter 17

Know When to Walk Away

> Some people believe holding on and hanging in there are signs of great strength. However, there are times when it takes much more strength to know when to let go and then do it.
>
> **—Ann Landers**

A proven strategy for successful negotiating is that you have to be willing to walk away from a bad deal. Good salespeople know that being willing to walk gives you leverage. It shows that you're not desperate to get what you're asking for and you're not afraid to start over someplace else if things aren't going your way. It sends the message that you won't accept anything less than what you want, need, and deserve.

Yet it's so hard to do. It's painful to walk away from a relationship that once was wonderful even though it has turned intolerable. It's a big decision to leave a job that you have enjoyed for years when your requests for fair pay or a well-deserved promotion are denied. It's tempting to stay in an uncomfortable situation because it's familiar and safe, even if it makes you miserable.

And, of course, fear stops us from stepping away from our status quo because we can't be sure that whatever else is out there for us will be as good, even if what we already have isn't great. And then, there are the backup singers who remind us that they wouldn't leave a sure thing if they were us.

They're not us, of course, but we too often rely on memories of loved ones who left a good job, ended a marriage, or moved away from a familiar neighborhood and regretted it later. So we stay stuck, sometimes for a little while and sometimes forever.

For *ER* actress Julianna Margulies, the decision to walk away from a $27 million offer to continue on the hit TV show that made her a star shocked even those closest to her.

In interviews, Margulies has said she wanted to act on Broadway and look for other opportunities after playing nurse Carol Hathaway for six years. Everyone had an opinion to share with her, but in the end, she said, she trusted her own instincts, which were pushing her out the door. She found success acting on Broadway and later, of course, starring on *The Good Wife*, which earned her multiple Emmy awards.

For many, the promise of money sometimes is the loudest voice in our backup chorus. If you can silence that seductive songbird, however, you might wind up doing what's right for your life instead of just for your wallet.

For Margulies, walking away from the familiar led her to what she has characterized as more fulfilling pursuits. Sometimes, though, walking away, whether it's from a negotiation with an unyielding car dealer, a volunteer role that makes you feel disrespected, or a commitment to do something that has your gut in a twist, is simply the best thing for you, in the moment, no matter what anyone else says.

Other times, it is a necessity for survival. The great Tina Turner, renowned for her powerful voice and electrifying stage presence, walked away from everything she knew to follow her own permission mission.

Turner's strict mother pushed her to become a maid, despite her ambitions for a career as a singer. At age eighteen, she married Ike Turner when she was a backup singer in his band. For years, while she was raking in money and fame as a dynamic performer with boundless energy, she lived, in a way, as a backup singer in her own life, not permitted by her husband to choose her own music, costumes, or even her friends.

Sixteen years in and the victim of her husband's violent behavior and nonnegotiable control, Turner left a hotel room in Dallas, reportedly in her bare feet and with only thirty-six cents and a Mobil credit card in her pocket. Her journey of recovery and reinvention—and toward becoming the main event on her own stage, both professionally and personally—is well documented. By the time of her death in 2023 at age eighty-three, Turner reportedly was worth more than $250 million.

I can't image how much fear she felt, as a victim, as she escaped and as she started over. But she in-powered herself. Her mission was greater than that fear.

The 1960s screen siren Audrey Hepburn walked away from a successful movie career to focus on raising her children and doing humanitarian work. Florence Nightingale rejected the life of a wealthy socialite to pursue a career in nursing and went on to establish the field as a respected profession. Acclaimed writer Edith Wharton divorced her husband in 1913, at a time when such a move was considered scandalous for a woman. She later won the Pulitzer Prize.

Objections came from every direction from the people giving them advice, both in real time and from the memories of past advice, brought to life in the moment by their backup singers.

The next time you're considering walking away from a circumstance that is making you unhappy or unsafe, consider following in the footsteps of these brave women. And ask yourself this: Who said you can't leave?

You'll count a lot of backup singers when you answer that question.

Psychologists say it's hard for women in particular to leave a bad situation because of social conditioning that emphasizes stability and security. For some, the "sunk cost fallacy" is responsible—the notion that if you leave, you'll lose your investment in a career, marriage, or other commitment that you have spent a lot of time and effort on. I have a friend whose daughter lived a miserable life as an attorney throughout her thirties because she—and her mother, her loudest backup singer—believed if she followed her passion for teaching, her law school tuition would have been a waste of money. Women in abusive relationships often express a feeling of helplessness because they believe they don't have the power to leave and nowhere to go if they do.

One San Francisco woman put a unique spin on the concept of walking away. Before Ann Russell Miller, a wealthy socialite born in 1928, met her husband when she was twenty, she had envisioned a life devoted to prayer, possibly as a nun. But she followed the invisible rules of the time and devoted herself to her children instead; she had ten of them, five girls and five boys.

Her son, Mark Miller, wrote in a series of tweets in 2021 after his ninety-two-year-old mother passed away that "she lived a life of privilege, living in a mansion, taking extravagant vacations, throwing parties, smoking, drinking and driving her fancy cars way too fast." But it turns out that she had a different plan for herself. When she was fifty-six, her husband died, and five years later, she became a nun.

Sister Mary Joseph not only walked away from her fortune and lavish lifestyle, but she left her children and grandchildren as well. She never met some of her twenty-eight grandchildren or any of her dozen-plus great-grandchildren. As a Carmelite nun, she existed mostly in silence and had few visitors.

At her farewell party before she entered the monastery, Miller shared that "she had devoted her first thirty years of her life to herself; the second thirty to her children; and that last third of her life would be dedicated to God."

Miller's story is extraordinary. But the good news is that plenty of women have given themselves permission to walk away from situations that were no good for them (or, in Miller's case, no longer served them), and you can, too.

What do you feel stuck in? A house that's too big for you? A relationship that has become boring? A job that demands so much of your time that you don't have a social life? An addiction?

Examine why you don't pick up and go. Is someone telling you that you can't make it on your own? That nobody else will ever want you? That you're not smart enough or pretty enough or good enough to find the success, fulfilment, and happiness that you feel you're missing?

Like a conductor leading an orchestra, you have the power to fire any backup singer in your chorus who is telling you those things. Decide what you want to do, and then conjure up the singers who harmonize with your goals, dreams, and wishes.

You'll give yourself permission once you're fed up with putting up. You'll give yourself permission once you realize that your fears are grounded in notions about yourself that might not be true. You'll give yourself permission once you start to trust yourself to listen to your own voice and find your way once you're out.

Change your mindset. Instead of "I can't do it on my own," how about looking at a drastic change like ending a relationship or quitting a job as an opportunity to be independent? Psychological research has proven that walking away reinforces autonomy, a key component of well-being. When you feel in control of your own decisions, the research shows, your self-esteem will rise and your stress will lower. You also could feel less burnout, anxiety, and depression if you sever your relationship with a toxic personal or professional situation.

You'll also be happier.

Embrace a growth mindset, and you'll have an easier time selling yourself on the notion that walking away from a bad situation just might be the first step toward a better, more rewarding one.

Whose permission are you waiting for? Which backup singer are you allowing to guide you? Call on your grit and give yourself the permission you need. Walk away.

Chapter 18

Nobody Does This Life Alone

> Don't be afraid to ask for help. Sometimes the hardest thing we ever must do is ask for help. We want to show everyone that we can do it all, that we have it under control. But the reality is that asking for help is not a sign of weakness—it is the greatest sign of strength.

—Kendra Scott

Eshita Kabra-Davies ran into some trouble raising capital to start a business that matches fashionable consumers who have expansive wardrobes with customers who are willing to pay to rent those clothes. Traditional venture capitalists, she told Britain's *The Times*, didn't "get" the apparel-sharing concept. So she turned to the successful women among her acquaintances, and the money poured in.

Since Davies founded her London-based company, By Rotation, in 2019, the site has counted 1 million downloads and has accumulated an online closet full of 120,000 upscale outfits, from casual fashions to formal wear, available for rent.

On her road to success, Davies embraced two key concepts that can help anyone achieve the permission mission: First, she recognized that nobody does this life alone; we all need help along the way. Second, she realized that your chances of getting what you want are exponentially higher if you ask for it than if you just hope for it.

In a later chapter, we will review the importance of selling yourself on the changes you might need to make to complete your own personal permission mission. This chapter focuses on how to sell *others* on helping you achieve all the success you want, need, and deserve. And the key to that "sale" is giving yourself permission to ask for help.

I say all the time that nobody does this life alone. There is no way Davies could have funded her start-up by herself; she needed help. So she asked for it, and she got it.

The simple truth is that if you don't ask for help, you are very unlikely to get it. If you do ask, you at least have a shot.

We so often feel that it's better to wait for someone to offer to help us or give us something we need than to come right out and ask. Think about it, though: If you don't say what you need, how are others going to know you need it? And how are they going to know if they have some way to help you get it?

Like so many of the questions I pose, the answer here is rooted in psychology, society, and culture. We don't want to be a burden to others. We fear the answer will be "no," and rejection is a feeling nobody likes. Maybe if we ask for help, others will think we're weak or incompetent or not strong enough to do it on our own. We don't want to be judged. Maybe we don't want to put ourselves in a position of owing a favor in return for someone's help. Or if you were raised like me, you might believe it's impolite to ask others to do stuff for you. You should just do it yourself.

Where did these notions come from? You guessed it: your backup singers.

Face it, many of us value independence and self-sufficiency. For many, it's a core value. Your backup singers passed that ethos on to you. You very well may pass it along to your own kids.

But independence is not something that stands on its own. We can be independent and also collaborative. We can be self-sufficient and also accept input and contributions from others to help us stay that way. We can be on our own and still appreciate others who help lighten our load. We can be entrepreneurial and also delegate to supporting players. We can be a solo act and still groove to the harmonics of the backup singers in our chorus.

Research shows that most of us underestimate how willing others—even strangers—are to help, so we're reluctant to ask. In fact, a study published by Stanford University suggests that saying "yes" to a request for help makes people feel good and happy and can lead to more meaningful relationships. So, the next time you shy away from asking for help because you don't want to inconvenience anybody, consider that you're doing someone else a favor just by asking.

It's a win-win for both of you, exactly what any sale should be.

That's why random acts of kindness go viral on social media, according to a summary of the Stanford study by researcher Xuan Zhao. And here's the important part: "The majority of help occurs only after a request has been made. . . . People want to help, but they can't help if they don't know someone is suffering or struggling, or what the other person needs."

Asking for help, the summary concludes, "can remove those uncertainties . . . and enable kindness."

Sometimes, kindness shows up loud, proud, and wearing a giant clock.

Flavor Flav became the official sponsor and hype man for the US women's water polo team in May 2024—all because he wanted to help. When team captain Maggie Steffens posted on Instagram about the financial struggles many Olympians face, Flav didn't hesitate. "As a girl dad and supporter of all women's sports—imma personally sponsor you . . . and the whole team," he wrote.

That one act of kindness sparked a five-year sponsorship with USA Water Polo, supporting both the women's and men's teams. But Flav didn't just back them with money—he became the official hype man for the sport. He showed up, rallied the crowd, and used his platform to shine a light on a sport that often flies under the radar.

All because one person chose to show up with kindness, because they were asked.

Give yourself permission to enable that kindness, and to get the help you need in the process.

Comedian and *Girls Trip* actress Tiffany Haddish accepted $300 from fellow comedian Kevin Hart when she found herself homeless and living out of her car before she became famous. According to an interview she did with *Vanity Fair*, Hart told Haddish that she could convince "any man" to let her live with him, but the broke star-in-the-making wasn't about to ask for that kind of help. She did give herself permission to accept help from Hart, in the form of the price of a hotel room, and credits that act of kindness—plus his suggestion that she write a list of goals for herself—as the beginning of the end of her struggles.

Haddish reportedly has a net worth of $6 million today.

If you're feeling shy about asking for help, for a favor, for a loan, or for a hand to hold, think of it as an opportunity to connect with a friend, neighbor, colleague, family member, or even a stranger in a way that might just do you both some good.

And then make a plan. As I'll mention often, everything goes more smoothly when you plan ahead.

In fact, asking for help is very much like making a sale. But even professional sales representatives don't simply blurt out their requests without laying some foundation first. When I coach sales pros as part of my consulting business, I always advise them to make a plan for the sale before they ever approach a potential customer.

I like to plan for everything, even the simple stuff. Let's use an example. Say you want to ask your neighbor to drive your daughter to band practice because you have to work late. It's a simple request, but consider the layers.

First, how do you feel about making the request? Are you reluctant because you feel like you're imposing? In your plan, think that through. Have the two of you traded driving duties before? Did the neighbor seem like you were inconveniencing her? Did you feel like she was inconveniencing you?

Next, examine whether there could be any benefit to your neighbor if she says "yes." For example, does she have to drive her own daughter to practice anyway? Could the trip to the school be an opportunity for the two girls to spend time together and forge or deepen their friendship? Is there a return favor you could offer, like taking over carpool duty next week when you don't have to work late?

Come up with ways to make saying "yes" a win-win for your neighbor and a win for you. Remember that most people feel good about helping others. That's a win in itself.

To overcome your reluctance, conjure up what you know about your neighbor. Is she a friend, or nearly a stranger? Is she friendly and good-natured, or does she act like people are imposing on her? Knowing that might help you choose your words. She might appreciate a "please" and "thank you" or an acknowledgment that you realize how busy she is. You might have observed that she is especially busy on Wednesdays, which is the day of the band practice. Tell her you know that.

Then, find a good time to ask. If she is rushing from the car to the house with two arms full of groceries and apparently can't find her house key, that might not be the right time to ask for a favor, but it would be the perfect time to offer her some help. After she gets settled inside, then ask for her help, and offer more of yours in return.

If she says "no," thank her anyway. Let her know you can ask someone else. Don't make her feel bad. If she says "yes," you'll also thank her. And after band practice, show her how much you appreciate her. Send her a follow-up text. Let her know that you're available to drive the girls next time.

Asking for help and accepting help isn't weakness—it's wisdom. A simple ask doesn't have to be a process, but if it's something you avoid doing because you're afraid of the consequences, use the planning process to ease yourself into it. Planning builds confidence. Confidence translates into trust in yourself and alleviates fear.

It is when your desire outweighs your fear that the ask gets easier. So, give yourself permission. Trust yourself. And remember, nobody does this life alone.

Chapter 19

You'll Never Be the Same

> Your new life is going to cost you your old one. It's going to cost you your comfort zone and your sense of direction . . . All you're going to lose is what was built for a person you no longer are.
>
> **—Brianna Wiest**

When former bodybuilding champion Nikkiey Stott decided, about a decade ago, to make the fitness and nutrition changes necessary to enter into that highly competitive world, she felt healthier, fitter, more productive, and prouder with every success.

But on her way to winning all three of the bikini contests she entered, she also felt something unexpected: grief.

Stott, the cofounder of a fitness community called WarriorBabe, revealed on *The Macro Hour* podcast (which she has hosted since 2023) that not every friend or family member supported her new routine. She was eating healthier, working out at the gym regularly, drinking less alcohol, and honoring the commitment she had made to herself to change her body and her life.

Some friends chided her for not eating enough or for working out too often. Others didn't like it that she stopped making excuses for skipping workouts while her friends did not.

"You're saying 'no' to the things you used to say 'yes' to, and some people won't know how to handle it," she said, noting that in many cases, her old friends had bonded with her over the same habits she was letting go.

So in some cases, she lost those friends—or they lost her.

When you commit to changing a habit, a behavior, or even your attitude, what you're doing is changing your life. When you give yourself permission to stop doing something your friends have enjoyed sharing with you, they might not be on board. The same goes if you decide to add something, like working out, taking classes, or joining a book club. Not everyone you love wants to do those things with you, so you don't see them as often.

You might miss them. Surviving that without sacrificing your mission takes grit. Lots of it.

We know we need to take time to heal after the death of someone close, or a breakup, or even after the loss of a job. But it might come as a surprise that when we deliberately make a major change, one that we gave ourselves full permission to do, as Stott did, we go through a grieving process.

Embrace it.

One of my friends, Claudine, used to nod along at every PTA meeting, always volunteering for mundane tasks. When she became president, the "yes" she used absent-mindedly to respond to every request turned into, "How about we try something different?" She streamlined events, pushed for new fundraisers, and expected follow-through from everyone on the committee. Before long, some of her friends, comfortable with the old, passive Claudine, drifted away, finding her new assertiveness off-putting.

Ouch.

Sometimes, a big change—even one that you're happy with—comes with a downside. You might sort of miss your old self. And in Claudine's case, she misses the friends she doesn't see as much anymore.

Many of my coaching clients have experienced this when they made changes in their lives that they wanted but may not have been popular opinion. It's hard to say goodbye to someone you have known for so long. It is your personal brand. But are you living a personal brand that you've outgrown? If you are on your personal permission mission, chances are that you are going to need to make some changes. You're going to miss the old you sometimes.

So, take some time with it. Think ahead about how you will respond to friends and colleagues who want you to stay where you are, probably because that's where they want to stay. Examine your chorus of backup singers for the ones who are warning you to hide in your box, and do your best to say goodbye to them, too.

On her podcast, Stott pointed out that as she spent more time in the gym working out alongside others who also made fitness their priority, those people became her new friends.

"The more you keep showing up for yourself, you're going to start attracting those people into your life," she said.

Stott also noted that it's possible to be both "proud of who you're becoming and still feel sad about who you're letting go. You can still love every ounce of your progress and still feel a little lost in the process."

Growth almost always comes with growing pains. When you're feeling them, consider that you wouldn't have decided to take action if you weren't ready to grow.

As you become more comfortable with giving yourself permission to be yourself, no matter what anyone from your past or present has to say about it, do what I always do—and by now, you know what that is, of course: Make a plan. It could help you sell others on accepting the positive changes you are making. And it could help you take steps to prepare yourself and others for any disappointing consequences, like a shift that might occur in an important relationship.

As Part 1 of the plan, try to identify any of the people in your life who might object to what you're doing: coworkers who don't want you to climb the corporate ladder faster than they do; best friends who want to continue hanging out with you every day after work; spouses who like to celebrate every special occasion with the kinds of food you no longer want to eat. Even though these people are in your life today, they count as backup singers when they try to influence your decisions.

You know these people well; what is motivating their objections? Are they afraid you'll make them look bad as you make yourself look good? Do they enjoy the way things are and resent you for changing them? Are they jealous that you have the confidence to give yourself permission to try things they're afraid of taking on? And finally, are you willing to press forward anyway, despite their objections? Are you willing to call on your grit and resolve to make the "new you" stick? Are you willing to give yourself permission to walk away from backup singers who would hold you back?

Once you feel you understand their motives, it's time to consider ways to address your upcoming changes with anyone you believe might have hurt feelings over your exciting new direction. What can you do to ease the transition between seeing them every night and going out just once in a while so you have time to go to the gym or work on your new projects? How can you explain your decision in a way that will make your pals want to root for you instead of holding you back? In what way can you continue to include your old friends in your new life?

Part 2 of the plan is all about you. Stott said when she looked in the mirror as her body changed, she sometimes didn't recognize herself—physically and emotionally. Stepping into the unfamiliar can be scary. Achieving your goals can be a shock, especially if success comes quickly.

Do the same exercise here: Make a list of anything you believe you will have to give up on your journey toward fulfilling your personal permission mission. Will you have to spend your time differently? Study harder, read more, talk to different kinds of people, answer tough questions? Will you have to abandon any backup singers who like to remind you that you're too weak to change? Was your comfortable, old brand easier? (Yes, it was, but growth is the point!) How will you prepare yourself for feelings of loss as you outgrow old habits, activities, backup singers, and even friends?

As you let go of the people and things that you won't be taking with you as you move toward success, allow yourself to grieve what you leave behind. Even necessary goodbyes come with emotion. Look into the not-so-distant future. How would you like to see yourself? How would you like others to describe you? Who will you be adding along the way? Celebrate them. Deliberately create a new and improved you that will get you there.

And then sell yourself on it. Give yourself permission to blossom into the best version of you. With permission comes power, and with power comes opportunity—and sometimes grief. But grief is the price of growth. Feel it. Honor it. And keep going.

Take One Step Forward

Your responses to the prompts below will help you take one step forward toward the spotlight of your life and help you fulfill your personal permission mission.

What do you want so much that you're willing to overcome your fear of going for it?

How will you overcome that fear?

What beliefs about yourself no longer belong in your life? What are the reasons you keep believing them?

When you hear the voice of doubt or criticism, whose voice is it really? And does it deserve to stay?

If you believed that you are already enough, how would you act differently today?

Journal about three limiting beliefs you carry with you today. Then write a letter to your younger self, reminding her that she is and always will be enough.

Visualize: Choose which fear is holding you back and visualize yourself moving through it. What does it look like to leave it behind?

Practice: When doubt surfaces, pause and ask: "Whose voice is this?" If it's not your own, thank it for trying to protect you and then gently replace it with: "I am enough."

Take Action: Clean out your emotional closet. When a limiting belief is stalling or stopping you from taking a step toward the life you want, pause, reflect, and remind yourself that your voice is leading you and it knows the way and then take a step toward your future.

Part Four

Your Personal Permission Mission

G ive yourself permission rather than asking or waiting for permission from someone else.

R ealize that your passion for what you want, need, and deserve is greater than the fear of trying.

I n-power yourself to trust your own voice more than the voices of the past.

T ake a step forward into the spotlight on the stage of your own life.

Trust is a state of mind that can make life easier or more complicated. At the forefront of the balancing act is the unfortunate fact that most people trust others more than they trust themselves.

That's because too many of us don't in-power ourselves to do what we believe is right because we're too caught up in what others think. We fail to tap into the power of our own voice, our true inner voice—the one that should be singing louder than any of our backup singers.

If you're going to achieve your personal permission mission—your goals in life, a milestone, a change in your behavior, anything that's important to you—you'll have to take action. Taking action requires risk: sometimes a little and sometimes a whole lot. Taking a risk requires you to trust that you're making a decision that won't harm you.

It all starts with listening to your own voice and then in-powering yourself to do what it's telling you.

Do you trust yourself to make that decision? Do you trust yourself with decisions that will affect your here and now, and in your future? Do you in-power yourself to discard the memory of long-ago criticisms and advice from those who warned you away from risk, no matter how small?

I hope you said "yes." Now, answer this: Are you sure?

Too often, we assign the responsibility for our decisions to others. When we were kids, we did this intuitively; parents presumably would take care of us and make choices that would help us grow, learn, and thrive. As we grew, we started making some of our own choices: what to order at a restaurant, which outfits to buy, how to wear our hair. Sometimes, we made bad choices, like drinking too much soda or hanging out with a neighbor who was always in trouble at school. If they were paying attention, our parents might have intervened and saved us from ourselves. If they weren't, we (hopefully) learned from our mistakes and acted more responsibly the next time.

All of us draw on those lessons we learned as we grow into adults.

Where we take a wrong turn is not outgrowing that dependence on Mom and Dad, on siblings or our friends and their parents, or on others who helped us shape our identities and determine how confident we are in making decisions for ourselves. We did what we were told when we were kids, and as adults, we sometimes remember those lessons—that is, we hear the voices of our backup singers—during times of indecision. And so we still do what we were told when we were kids.

We still trust others more than ourselves, allowing them to influence our decisions. And because we allow that influence to continue, we never learn to fully trust ourselves, to trust our own decisions, to make our own choices, and to take our own chances.

To achieve your personal permission mission, you must trust your own voice more than anyone else's. You must give yourself permission to have the final say, even if what you say is different from what your backup singers say.

That takes grit. And it takes the decision to give yourself permission—to in-power yourself—to sing your own tune. It takes the wisdom and confidence to trust yourself to sing your solo.

Even if you never really declared full independence from the influence of your backup singers, it's not too late.

The fact is that you have sung solos many times before. You did it in real time when you were a kid and faced a new situation when your parents weren't around to tell you what to do. As an adult, you can probably recall a few times when your gut feeling was so strong that you decided to override the directions of the chorus when everyone was singing a different tune. It's likely that you make decisions on your own all the time, but you rely on past advice just as often.

The point is that you have evidence that you can do this on your own. You can separate good advice from bad because, assuming you have figured out what you want, you know good from bad. Pay attention to that evidence; as you collect more of it, you will trust your own ability to live your own life more and more.

Along with it, you will believe more in your own worth and value. For many, especially women, that takes some serious internal selling: You have to convince yourself that the negative remarks you believed when your caregivers said them aren't true today, if they ever were. That becomes easier once you examine the values you want to live by and, frankly, when you get fed up with singing someone else's song, living a life that someone else prescribed for you.

Trust. It's true that we misplace it sometimes in people who don't deserve it. We are human. We make mistakes and we learn from them. But your backup singers are not learning any new lessons. They are frozen in time. Give yourself permission to trust yourself with all of your experiences, more than you trust the wisdom of past voices and the demands of those who surround you now. Give yourself permission to in-power yourself to move forward and to listen to your own voice.

Then, one permission mission after another will be easier for you to achieve.

Chapter 20

Trust Yourself

> There is always one true inner voice. Trust it.
>
> **—Gloria Steinem**

You know you don't have to listen to your backup singers or do what they say, right? You know you're not six anymore, and you won't get in trouble if you decide to eat ice cream for dinner or wear your pajama bottoms to the store, correct?

You also know when something is right for you and when something is wrong for you. You have an inner knowing, an ability to decide for yourself, and you know that. So why don't you give yourself permission to follow your gut?

The answer to that question is wrapped up in how much you trust yourself to do the right thing, make decisions on your own, and succeed if you take a risk.

At some point, most people are reluctant to trust themselves to make the big decisions. So, we rely on the wisdom of others to guide us, to instruct us, to pressure us, and sometimes, to decide for us. We remember the decisions our parents made. We remember the advice of teachers, coaches, and best friends over the years. And we allow them too much influence over the decisions we're making for ourselves, even years later.

Earlier, we explored the reasons why our backup singers still have so much influence over us, even though we're grown. We identified fear as a huge motivator in favor of standing still, not taking chances and doing what we've always done because it feels safe and because that's what we learned we should do.

Now, let's look at the confidence gap—the disparity between what you actually are capable of and what you perceive you are capable of. It's the difference between knowing how to spell every word in the dictionary because you studied for a year and the belief that you're going to come in last place in the spelling bee. It's the difference between competence and confidence.

That confidence gap leads to low self-esteem and a fear of failure. And fear, as you know, is the greatest barrier to achieving your permission mission. After all, your mission has to be greater than your fear of going after it, or you simply will not give yourself permission to go after it.

A lack of confidence can prevent us from trusting ourselves. Fear prevents us from trusting that we're capable of deciding for ourselves. It convinces us that we can't trust our own inner voices and our own gut feelings instead of whatever the loudest voices in our chorus happen to be singing this time.

Look at who else has felt that way:

Kurt Vonnegut, the celebrated novelist who wrote the bestsellers *Cat's Cradle*, *Slaughterhouse Five*, and *Breakfast of Champions,* described his ability as a writer like this: "When I write, I feel like an armless, legless man with a crayon in his mouth." Michelangelo, a sculptor by training who painted the majestic frescoes on the ceiling of the Sistine Chapel, reportedly admitted to his brother, Giovan, in 1509, "I am no painter." Agatha Christie, the bestselling novelist of all time, expressed a lack of confidence in her writing, for which she was celebrated, awarded, and extremely well paid.

As First Lady Eleanor Roosevelt said: "You gain strength, courage and confidence by every experience in which you really stop to look fear in the face."

That, in my opinion, is how you learn to trust yourself. You look fear in the face, you take the risk, and you succeed. That proves that you are competent. If you fail, you take what you learned from that mistake and do better next time. Success by success, you learn that you can do the things that you thought and said you couldn't, probably because a backup singer at some time said that you couldn't. As you collect evidence of your competence, you replace your feelings of incompetence with the knowledge that you are capable. You bolster your confidence.

You learn to trust your instincts and rely less on the voices from the past that remind you of your former failures and urge you to limit yourself in the same way.

You finally feel like you can give yourself permission to take the next step toward center stage, whether that means performing, speaking in public, quitting your job, buying a car on your own, saying "yes" to a marriage proposal, or taking a huge risk.

"The worst enemy to creativity is self-doubt," *The Bell Jar* author Sylvia Plath once said.

Overcoming that doubt is a critical step toward trusting yourself, which is a key pit stop on the way to fulfilling your permission mission. Overcoming your fears and building trust in yourself are crucial to accomplishing your permission mission.

Why are we so often reluctant to trust ourselves with our own future? Why do we trust other voices more than our own?

A theory called confirmation bias is relevant here: We're looking for evidence that confirms what we already believe, which might be that we can't or shouldn't. That's the opposite of overconfidence, which can lead us to overestimate our abilities. Both of these biases can distort our self-perception, erode our self-trust, and truly mess with our decision-making.

Similarly, when we struggle with the concept that we are worthy and deserving of everything we want and need, that can lead us to mistrust our own judgment.

Sometimes, our emotions override our logic when it comes to decision-making. We might make a decision based on how we feel in the moment instead of considering the consequences of the decision. This clouds our judgment and our trust. And unhappy consequences of emotional decisions might supply us with evidence that we should not trust ourselves to make the best decisions in the future.

And here's something to think about the next time a backup singer is reminding you that you're no good at something: Our memories are very unreliable, to the point that they're often distorted. So, your backup singer—who is really just a memory—might not have accurate information for you to consider when you're deciding between playing it safe and going after your dreams.

My best advice aligns with an insight from the legendary painter Vincent van Gogh: "If you hear a voice within you say, 'You cannot paint,' then by all means paint, and that voice will be silenced."

He could be talking about your backup singers. Silence them by proving them wrong. Boost your trust in yourself by proving them wrong again and again until you have enough evidence to trust yourself more than you trust them. Only then will you in-power yourself to reach your goals.

In other words, challenge the learned wisdom from those backup singers and go for it! Try it. Be curious about how you might do if you give yourself permission to do it.

Easier said than done. Still, if your gut is telling you that something is right for you, why ask someone else's permission to do it, take it, buy it, or go for it?

Nobel Prize–winning psychologist Daniel Kahneman theorized that we think in two ways: by intuition and by reasoning.

Intuition is what you're feeling in your gut. You know something is right or wrong without really thinking hard about it. Intuition, if we trust it, can help us make quick, almost unconscious decisions based on past experiences that have been consistently positive or negative.

Reasoning, on the other hand, is based more on logic and analysis. When you reason something out rather than basing your decision on intuition, you'll slow down a bit and perhaps act more carefully.

Intuition, Kahneman noted, is most reliable in decisions dealing with our areas of expertise. Our brains store up our experiences and training and expertise and can tap that for a quick decision. A doctor, for example, can often diagnose a patient without running any tests because she has seen so many similar cases before. A police officer might know a suspect is lying without ever administering a lie detector test because he has read the facial expressions and body language of so many dishonest criminals during his career.

And while I'm using "gut" and "intuition" as synonyms, neuroscience has shown that our brains are actually in charge of storing and processing the patterns and experiences of our past and drawing on them when it's time to decide on something.

All the more reason to trust your intuition. She knows her stuff. Think of your intuition as a trigger for permission. When you follow your instincts, you're giving yourself permission to trust yourself.

I'm not saying you should ignore every backup singer every time she starts to sing. Instead, I'm suggesting that you listen to your intuition and use your reasoning so you can dispute the lyrics that do not serve you.

To achieve your personal permission mission, work on trusting your intuition, reasoning, experience, and evidence of your abilities, and consider the music from the chorus as a suggestion, not a demand.

You don't have to do what's right for even your most wonderful, most-trusted mentors from your past. You only have to do what's right for *you* in order to achieve your personal permission mission.

Chapter 21

The Salesperson in the Mirror

> If you think you can, you can. If you think you can't, you're right.
>
> —**Mary Kay Ash**

If my late grandmother were reading this book, she would give me "the look."

Permission to put yourself first? To ignore the wisdom of your elders? To utter, "I deserve it" within earshot of the neighbors? She would tell me to close up that emotional closet and leave things as they are.

I love you, Granny, but nope.

I have chosen to break with some family traditions, and I've had to quiet down quite a few screeching, off-key backup singers to get to where I am today, with a doctorate in communications, a happy marriage, and a lifetime of well-earned moments involving meaningful work, outrageous fun, abundance, and happiness.

Granny would give me another look right now and tell me I'm bragging. (I was *very* familiar with those looks!)

I'm going to ignore that advice I learned long ago because this isn't bragging. This is gratitude. And it's the result of three things: (1) I gave myself permission to do it; (2) my desire to define and design my own life was greater than my fear of failing to get it or of losing what I was leaving behind; and (3) I trusted myself enough to believe I could succeed. I sold myself on believing I could succeed.

This was an internal sales conversation for me. And it's one that you should be having with yourself.

For many of us, we have to sell ourselves on the fact that our own voices don't have the same weight as a backup singer. Ours should be louder. Ours should be the loudest voice of anyone in the chorus.

Have you ever had a conversation with yourself while looking in the mirror? There's a salesperson in that mirror.

I'm betting you've got a backup singer or two who has taught you what your place is—second place, most likely—and what's proper, culturally acceptable, respectable, respectful, and flattering. So, a part of you might be pushing back on the notion that you deserve to have what you want and need, or that it's OK to give yourself permission to shake up the status quo.

If someone were selling this notion in a store, would you buy it? Would you buy a bottle of Permission Potion that promised you a happier, more successful life? Inside that bottle would be the permission you need to stand up and say, take, or go after everything you want and need. You would never again have to wait for anyone else to give you permission. You would already have it in that little bottle.

Would you buy that? If you could buy a bottle of confidence, if you could simply buy a dose of permission whenever you needed one, instead of mustering up the grit and courage to give it to yourself (for free), would you buy it?

To embrace the core concept of the permission mission—that you don't need permission from anyone but yourself to do and have the things you want in this life—you'll need to have a serious sales conversation with yourself.

You are going to have to embark on a sales campaign for a single customer: you.

I've spent much of my career in sales—selling, consulting, coaching sales professionals, and writing books about my unique, five-step consultative sales process. So, I can say with confidence that selling yourself on changing your mindset, your beliefs, and your behavior to achieve your personal permission mission just might be the hardest sale you'll ever make.

I say "you'll ever make" because, whether you realize it or not, you have sold your ideas to others many, many times. In fact, you do it every day. Every time you ask for a favor, coax a child to eat something green, convince your partner to go out for Italian instead of hamburgers, or ask a coworker to switch shifts with you at work, you're trying to make a sale. You have to sell the other person on saying "yes" to what you're asking for. This is the crux of my first book, *Every Job Is a Sales Job*, which I wrote to help non-salespeople achieve greater success in their careers and life.

Here, too, I'll make the point that you need to look at the salesperson in the mirror. That salesperson is you.

Selling to others requires some skill, which professional sales reps acquire through training and trial and error. In my view, every sale should be a win-win: a win for the seller and a win for the buyer. I don't believe in high-pressure, manipulative tactics or dishonesty in sales. So, be assured that the process I'm taking you through in this chapter will not require you to do anything icky or shifty. It will gently help you buy into the notion that you deserve everything you want and need, even if you have to step way outside of your comfort zone to get it.

You'll follow a long line of women and men who sold themselves on stepping out of line to achieve greatness.

Let's look at one-time investment banker Candace Nelson, whose Beverly Hills store, Sprinkles, helped start what would become a nationwide cupcake craze in 2005. But, she told the trade publication *Nation's Restaurant News*, very few friends and investors believed in the project. "Everybody said, 'Nobody eats carbs,'" she recalled. "So all signs pointed to we weren't going to be around very long."

They're still around. The bakery, which Nelson and her husband sold in 2014, has locations in six states and Washington, DC, as well as thirty "cupcake ATMs," or vending machines. Nelson went on to own a chain of pizza restaurants—Pizzana—serve as a guest shark on *Shark Tank*, appear on a number of cooking shows, and write two bestselling baking books.

There is no way Nelson would have pursued her business against the advice of so many people if she hadn't first sold herself on taking a huge chance on herself. Her resulting success was not an accident.

Your mission might not be quite as lofty—or risky—as a superstar cupcake baker's. Still, even if what you want is to muster up the courage to drastically change your hairstyle, or to fall in love, or to run for city council, or to leave your childhood behind and move to a big city, the process is the same. You have to convince yourself that it will be OK. You have to sell yourself on the fact that you're smart enough and skilled enough to make it outside of the comfort and safety of your status quo.

Most importantly, perhaps, you will have to sell yourself on the fact that you deserve it, that you deserve success and happiness. What follows is a place to start.

This is my five-step formula that I teach sales professionals, and you can apply these same steps when it's time to sell yourself on in-powering yourself to take a chance, or, frankly, to sell anyone on anything.

Step 1: Plan. Every sale starts with a thoughtful plan, something I touch on multiple times in this book. In fact, everything in life goes smoother when you plan before you act.

If your goal is to sell yourself on the fact that you deserve everything you want and need, engage in the classic exercise of making a pros and cons list. Write down every reason you can think of why you deserve to go after the things you want, and any reasons you believe you don't. Be thorough; your goal here is not to decide *whether* you deserve to be happy and successful (you do), but to convince yourself that you *are* deserving. Go heavy on the pros.

Step 2: Look for opportunities. As you consider your value, scour your memory, your journals, your social media, and your old calendars to see how much you do for everyone else on a regular basis. Consider the many selfless acts, the sacrifices, the times you put everyone first except for yourself. Remember when you felt unappreciated, underpaid, unrecognized. Do an accounting of how much social capital you earned but never cashed in on, or how much money your family and volunteer responsibilities might earn you if you performed those same activities in the workplace. Gather physical evidence of how much you do that makes you a worthy person. Chances are good that your value will reveal itself as undeniable.

Step 3: Listen to establish trust. No sale happens without trust—in this case, trust in yourself. Let your backup singers have their say. Along with the heaps of criticism that you remember whenever you're evaluating your options—because critics usually are louder than fans—you will recall many kind words, encouraging conversations, sincere congratulations, loving guidance, and hopeful best wishes. But just because a voice is loud doesn't mean it's right. Volume isn't the same as value. Continue to listen until the positive voices outweigh the negatives, and you'll realize that so many of the influential people in your life (the backup singers who interrupt you before you take a risk) have been rooting for you all along, even if they might have also at times criticized you or cautioned you. Take all of that into account, but when it comes to selling yourself on moving forward, you need to trust your own voice more than anyone else's.

Step 4: Ask for what you want. In this case, it's permission. Can you give yourself permission to feel worthy? Can you give yourself permission to accept rather than give, at least sometimes? Will you allow yourself to believe you're deserving of fulfilling your dreams and living a happier life? Can you in-power yourself to change your mindset to an attitude that allows you to receive, take, and collect instead of give, give, give?

Step 5: Follow up with gratitude. The amazing thing about counting your blessings is that they multiply when you do it. When you keep track of the things in your life that make you thankful, more of those things appear. So many books about the law of attraction are full of examples of people who act as if they already have what they want, and then it appears. Give thanks every single day that you are a worthy, deserving human. Express your gratitude for every moment that makes you feel worthy and for every person who treats you as deserving. When you achieve a goal or get something you have wanted, allow gratitude to overwhelm you as you realize you deserved it. The more gratitude you feel and express, the more you will have to feel grateful for.

Selling yourself on shifting your mindset from undeserving to absolutely worthy might pay off gradually instead of immediately. But trust me, it will be worth the wait.

Chapter 22

Hey, Beautiful

> You have been criticizing yourself for years, and it hasn't worked. Try approving of yourself and see what happens.
>
> —**Louise Hay**

How difficult it must be to live life as a celebrity. Despite the lavish lifestyles and the acclaim and attention they get from their besotted fans, movie stars, athletes, politicians, and others can barely get a break from the critics who constantly point out how imperfect they are.

We're all imperfect, of course, and thankfully, we don't have the tabloids splashing evidence of that all over their front covers for all the world to weigh in on. Thank goodness we can post on social media without our momentary lapse in judgment or unintended insensitivity going viral.

Still, we all have our critics, people who are eager to gossip about our perceived flaws behind our backs or use our vulnerabilities against us for their own gain. And every time they do, we have moments when we feel that all we are is the mistake we just made, or some immature behavior we exhibited when we were younger, or our most recent failure.

Our backup singers can make us feel that way, too, when we conjure up memories of what a role model or caretaker once criticized about our abilities, intelligence, appearance, or personality. Who hasn't, on occasion, doubted herself when she's faced with a big opportunity because she remembers that her great-aunt Sally told her fifteen years ago she would never be any good at that exact thing?

That is one of those times when we have to give ourselves permission to ignore those voices from the past—even the very recent past—and accept that we're good enough, smart enough, talented enough, and just plain *enough* to figure it out and make it a success.

We have to give ourselves permission to accept ourselves as we are, no matter what anybody else thinks about us, and channel that acceptance into success.

Celebrities do this all the time, and you can, too. They do it in public, and constantly. It takes grit and humility.

And although we deal with critics on a more personal level, our hurt feelings are just as important and our road to acceptance is just as rocky. Still, we can learn from superstars like two-time Olympian Aly Raisman, who was bullied from a young age because of her muscular body. Raisman told *People* in 2017 that the seventh-grade boys at her school called her arms "disgusting" when she wore a tank top, so she stopped wearing tank tops. Now, years later, "I almost force myself to wear tank tops because you have to appreciate your body, and now people compliment my arms all the time," she said. "You can't let someone dictate the way you feel about yourself. It just makes me mad that I was so insecure about it for so long because my arms made me one of the best gymnasts in the world."

Much of the criticism of celebrities, especially women, is about their appearance and, specifically, their weight. But not all of it. Donyale Luna, the first Black supermodel to appear on the cover of *Vogue*, endured criticism over her mixed race. She rejected the labels—and racial slurs—and worked hard to be recognized for her talent rather than her heritage. The 1920s blues singer Gladys Bentley learned early on that she had to embrace self-acceptance when others labeled her as socially "maladjusted" because she dressed in male clothing instead of slinky dresses like other female performers. Simone de Beauvoir, author of *The Second Sex*, a foundational text of modern feminism published in 1949, at one time denied she was a feminist because it was such an unpopular notion back then. Eventually, she accepted her identity.

Grammy winner Billie Eilish, responding to an interviewer's question about whether she feels her beauty ever overshadows her music, said: "This question made me tear up a little. . . . I've never really felt very beautiful or seen myself in that way, so I definitely never struggled with the idea that it would overshadow anything, since I didn't even really see it myself. I've had to really convince myself that I am beautiful. Being a woman is hard."

I wonder who told her she isn't beautiful? And I wonder why she believed it instead of smiling into a mirror and seeing what the rest of us see when we look at her? This brings to mind the Dove experiment with the "beautiful" and "average" doorways that we talked about earlier.

I have a friend, Christina, who has been on a diet since she was thirteen, when her father told her that her thighs were "huge" and an uncle said she was "getting fat." She was five feet five inches tall and 110 pounds. Whether they were teasing or not didn't matter: She spent the next four decades trying not to be fat. She told me that recently, as she flipped through an old photo album, she came across a stunning photo of her sixteen-year-old self wearing a silky prom gown with a halter top. "That stupid girl thought she was fat," she said. I thought, "The stunning woman she grew up to be still does."

I encouraged Christina to accept her beauty and her body. I would encourage her and anyone else to give herself permission to accept herself as she is, whether she weighs 110 pounds or 310, whether she is sixteen or fifty-six or eighty-six. Like Aly Raisman, we're more than just what others think of how we look. We're capable, experienced, intelligent, and creative. The vessel we carry that around in does not define us.

It's clear that the words of my friend's father and uncle live prominently in her memory as very loud backup singers. She believed them then; why wouldn't she when they were the adults tasked with nurturing her as she grew into an adult? Her problem is that she still believes them now.

The Feminine Mystique author Betty Friedan came to terms with the fact that many people simply didn't like her, like the critics who portrayed her as aggressive, abrasive, demanding, and selfish. She did little to soften her image, opting instead to accept it, even when it alienated others. In her biography, *Betty Friedan and the Making of The Feminine Mystique,* author Daniel Horowitz noted that she didn't try to change or seek to be liked. Instead, she focused her energy on being effective, and she was: Her 1963 book sold more than three million copies by the time she died in 2006 and resonated with generations of women.

Psychologists agree that an enduring impact of criticism, especially when it came from your parents and you can't let it go, is lower self-esteem.

If your parents' love seemed conditional on your appearance or accomplishments, it can lead to perfectionism, which is impossible to achieve, and can eat away at self-worth. If they were always comparing you to your thinner/more beautiful/smarter/more athletic siblings or classmates, those feelings escalate into a belief that you don't, and maybe can't, measure up.

So is it possible to shake that off? To ignore it? To silence those backup singers who keep reminding you of those negative lessons you learned as a kid? The experts say yes, but it takes some work.

The late Aaron Beck, cited by *American Psychologist* as "one of the five most influential psychotherapists of all time," suggested in his book *Cognitive Therapy of Depression* that we should question the validity of those claims. In my friend Christina's case, she recalled that she had once made childish fun of her uncle because he snorted when he laughed. All these years later, she realized that he was calling her "fat" to get even with her. Makes me wonder who the grown-up was in that conversation.

Beck suggested that an analysis of the incident that led to your negative beliefs might reveal that it was based on someone's opinion, not on facts, and that the criticism might not have been fair, and definitely might not be relevant anymore, if it ever was.

Some of the advice from prior chapters about our backup singers is relevant here. For example, how about practicing some self-compassion? What would you tell your best friend if she admitted that she feels unworthy because of how she looks or because of a long-ago mistake that she made? Would you encourage her to accept herself as she is? Do the same for yourself.

And then, rewrite that narrative. Instead of focusing on the negative message, create a positive one for yourself, based on everything that's good about you, like your strength, your accomplishments, and your resilience.

Chances are that you and I have never met each other (yet). Still, I can say with utmost confidence that you are so beautiful. You're just right, just how you are.

Can you give yourself permission to believe that? Can you make a positive voice louder than a negative one from your past? Can you work on giving yourself permission to accept yourself as you are and to leverage that acceptance into taking a step toward the life you really want?

Chapter 23

First in Line

> Love yourself first and everything else falls into line. You really have to love yourself to get anything done in this world.
>
> **—Lucille Ball**

If you've read *Little Women* or caught any of the movie or TV versions, you probably remember Beth March—the sweet middle sister who made sacrifices for her family and friends. She was the kind of person who always put others first.

Beth was so selfless and compassionate that when a neighbor's child fell ill, she stepped in to help, despite the obvious risks to her own health. In fact, Beth ended up catching scarlet fever and never fully recovered. She died from the lingering effects of the disease around age seventeen.

Similarly, her sister, Jo, like all four of the March daughters, was raised to be kind and caring. She, too, often sacrificed her personal desires and dreams in order to help others. But Jo had an independent streak as well, with ambitions to become a writer.

The novel takes Jo to a place Beth never saw: the front of the line, center stage in her own life, a space where there is plenty of room both for family obligations and her passion for writing. She sells her short stories to local magazines, which allows her to help support her family. She writes a novel that gets published. She teaches classes at a school for boys that she helped her husband open.

In short, Jo found a way to put herself first while still living according to the societal and family rules prescribed for girls and women from religious households in the Civil War era.

Even in modern times, that can be hard to accomplish. Often, we have to choose one or the other: our own dreams or the dreams someone else has for us. When that someone else is a parent or other respected authority figure, the choice can seem that it's made for us, not by us.

Can I suggest that it's possible to make another choice? To give yourself permission to put your own wants and needs ahead of someone who you feel is holding you back, especially if that someone is putting his or her own wants and needs ahead of yours?

In fact, there's plenty of evidence that it's entirely possible.

In the book (and movie) *Eat Pray Love*, Elizabeth Gilbert's journey is not about travel and exploration; it's about permission. After her divorce, she realized that she had spent years trying to please everyone around her and had completely lost sight of what actually made her happy. So she hit pause. She gave herself permission to put *herself* first for the first time in her life.

In the year that she traveled through Italy, India, and Indonesia, she rediscovered her passions. Her memoir is filled with those soul-nudging moments that remind us that it's okay to take a break, to say "no" to the "shoulds" and say "yes" to our own needs.

In a Q&A session in Dallas, Gilbert shared that "in Mandarin Chinese, they have two words for selfish. One means doing that which is beneficial to you and the other means hoarding, greedy, and cruel. We, in English, have pushed those two words together."

Let that sink in for a moment. What she is saying is that self-care isn't selfish. It's survival. And sometimes, it's the first step to becoming who you were meant to be.

The point at which she took control and began her journey was the moment she embraced her personal permission mission. Even though she was unclear on where this journey would lead, that moment was the turning point when she knew that what she wanted and needed was more important than her fear of doing what she had to do in order to get it.

Three questions for you:

1. Whose needs are you putting ahead of your own?
2. Why are you doing that?
3. Is it preventing you from reaching your own goals or getting something that you want or need?

I don't disagree that there are times in our lives when we need to devote ourselves to others—our children, our partners, our parents—because they truly need us. But consider if, like Jo March, you might be able to do both: carve out time for yourself while still tending to the obligations you perceive you have to family, work, and even friends. Or, like Gilbert, are you tired of complying with rules that you didn't make or agree to, ones that are draining your energy?

If you're feeling fed up, it's time to give yourself permission to change your situation, to figure out how to do what you want and what those who depend on you need—at the same time. Or to resolve to get out of an unfulfilling situation, even if the people around you don't understand your motives. Or to speak your truth even if others don't want what you're saying or doing to be true.

It might be time for you to step out of the role that you have been playing. The version of you that bends and shapes into whatever others need so you can fill whatever expectations others have of you in any given situation.

We know those roles can be changed because so many others have done it: Edward VIII, who was the king of the United Kingdom for less than a year before he abdicated the throne in 1936 to marry American Wallis Simpson, who was divorced and considered unacceptable as a partner for a British monarch.

At some point, we all have to do something we don't want to, especially if we have a job or family. That doesn't mean you should not make yourself a priority and do the things you *do* want to do. It's important to engage in activities that are meaningful to you personally and to devote yourself to the pursuit of your dreams. It's important to strike a healthy balance among work, family, and other competing obligations.

I love the point that the *Barbie* movie character Gloria, played by America Ferrera, made during the film's pivotal monologue. Gloria, a working mom with a love for Barbie dolls, talked about a system that is rigged against women: "I'm just so tired of watching myself and every single other woman tie herself into knots so that people will like us," she said, noting that women are expected to be and do what others want.

"It's literally impossible to be a woman," she said. "You are so beautiful, and so smart, and it kills me that you don't think you're good enough. Like, we have to always be extraordinary, but somehow we're always doing it wrong."

It's common for women to prioritize others, largely because we have been socialized as caregivers and nurturers, roles that invoke selflessness. Some women feel responsibility for others in relationships, family, or work, often to their own detriment. In fact, in some cultures, women are praised for being "martyrs," and for some, that could be a comfort. In others, society seems to link a woman's worth to her ability to care for others. Women who buck those norms often report feeling guilty about it. And those who engage in self-care can be considered indulgent and even selfish. Then there's fear: of judgment and of disappointing others.

That's a lot. And while men might be more apt to make themselves a priority, they face some obstacles as well—different ones.

If women are socialized as caregivers, most men grow up learning that their role is to provide for and protect their families. Traditional masculine norms emphasize qualities like strength, independence, and stoicism, with a focus on meeting the needs of their families. These ideals can make it difficult for some men to prioritize their own needs, as they may be judged as weak or as failing to fulfill their roles.

Luckily, society is nudging toward a greater acceptance of self-care as essential rather than an indulgence. A side benefit, some studies show, is that when women practice self-care—whether you define it as indulging in a facial, writing in a journal, or planning your next career move—they can better care for others.

It worked for Jo March. It might work for you, too, no matter what your backup singers tell you when you're carving out time to take care of yourself.

Chapter 24

Experience Emotion

> The best and most beautiful things in the world cannot be seen or even touched. They must be felt with the heart.

—Helen Keller

A good friend of mine volunteered to host a graduate student from Pakistan during his year attending a university where she teaches. The student spent a lot of time with my friend and her family. They invited him and his international classmates over for Thanksgiving dinner and stuffed them all with turkey and pie. They took him snow tubing in the mountains, where everyone screamed and wiped out and got up to do it again and again. They introduced him to the mayor of their city at a backyard cookout they threw in their new friend's honor. They had a blast taking him sightseeing and witnessing his awed reaction to seeing America's iconic monuments for the first time.

During his nine-month visit, however, they never saw him smile.

My friend asked him if he wasn't having fun. He assured her that he was. "Then why don't you smile, even when we take pictures?" she asked. He explained it was "the way" in his culture. Men don't reveal their feelings by smiling, laughing, crying—any of it. They're expected to practice restraint and remain composed.

The whole time he was in America, which he repeatedly said he enjoyed, he never once gave himself permission to smile along with his happy hosts.

I know someone who never smiles, too. She is the niece of another friend. Her face is so unmovable that I sometimes wonder if it's made out of glass. My friend has jokingly asked her if she is afraid that if she smiles, it will crack.

You'll rarely see a posed photograph of the classic Hollywood actress Greta Garbo, most famous in the 1920s and '30s, with a smile on her face. She was often questioned about her stoic expression, and she said she would rather express herself through her acting roles. In fact, the famously private actress, often described as lonely and reclusive, was known for her ability to convey her emotions through nuanced facial expressions other than smiles.

Whatever the reason, any of these people could be sending a message—and unintentionally creating a personal brand—that leads others to believe they are unapproachable, distant, cold, super serious, or just plain unhappy. In the case of my friend's niece, others feel she never enjoys herself and, perhaps, doesn't enjoy their company, which is hurtful. In the case of Garbo, who often complained of an unhappy childhood, it's possible she actually was unhappy most of the time.

It is, of course, hard to give yourself permission to smile when you don't feel you have anything to smile about. That takes grit, for sure. But there's lots of evidence that smiling is good for you: It can enhance your mood, reduce your stress, and even boost your immune system. A bonus:

You know the expression, "When you're smiling, the whole world smiles with you"—from an upbeat 1930s song popularized by jazz great Louis Armstrong? It turns out that's true: Smiling is contagious.

Smiling at someone can significantly boost that other person's mood. It can release endorphins in both you and those who witness your smile, making both of you feel better. It's an icebreaker; when you smile, others will perceive you as approachable. Plus, they'll probably smile back, which starts that happy cycle over again.

Granting yourself permission to feel joy could be an even greater health and mood booster. Dr. Tiffany Moon, an anesthesiologist and former cast member of *The Real Housewives of Dallas*, has said that joy isn't simply a fleeting emotion; it's a vital component of a fulfilling life. In her bestselling book, *Joy Prescriptions: How I Learned to Stop Chasing Perfection and Embrace Connection*, Moon made this claim, which she said changed her life: "Joy isn't a luxury. It's a necessity."

Not smiling seems like part of a bigger issue for some people who are overly guarded when it comes to revealing their emotions. Just like the niece who seems not to want anyone to know when she's happy or amused, some people don't want others to know when they're upset, sad, angry, or annoyed.

We tend to assume people's emotions without knowing the entirety of the situation. For instance, "resting b**** face" is a pretty common term these days. But cultural reasons like the graduate student had, or personality traits and disorders, or even neurological factors can influence whether someone ever shows emotion. So, we should always approach the lack of expression in others with curiosity instead of judgment.

But if you're withholding your own feelings because you feel you shouldn't show them, you might want to ask yourself: Who told you to hide how you feel?

The Pakistani student explained that in his country, showing emotion, especially for men, can be interpreted as a sign of vulnerability. His lack of expression, he said, is deliberate.

Is yours?

At their core, though, joy, smiles, happiness—they're more about choice than circumstance, at least for most of us. That means it's possible for you to feel and share your emotions if you choose to. Can you choose to? Can you give yourself permission to feel all the feels and wear them on your face for all to see?

As much as I enjoy going to the theater for plays and musicals, one of my best memories from attending a live show is from the time I saw a comedy as part of an event I attended with a fairly large group of women, including some I didn't know very well. One of those women watched the whole thing with a huge grin on her face—ear to ear, as they say—mouth slightly open, eyes bright. It gave me so much pleasure to see how much she was enjoying herself, and it rubbed off on me, making me feel a bit more confident in expressing the pure joy I was also experiencing during the performance.

Perhaps someone from your past told you one time too many to "wipe that smirk off your face." Or if you cried because you were upset or sad, did someone call you a crybaby? When you admitted you were afraid—of a monster hiding under your bed or of the reaction your teacher might have if you didn't know the answer to a question in class—maybe others labeled you as a fraidy-cat. Did anyone ever tell you to pipe down when your laughter over something you found hilarious could be heard all over the house?

Years later, are you still hiding your smile because of that memory? Do you hold back your tears so nobody will think you're not mature enough to handle stress or sadness? Do you keep it to yourself when something scares the bejeebers out of you? Do you still laugh under your breath so your unadulterated joy won't bother anyone?

You can thank your backup singers for that. Something else you can do is give yourself permission to embrace your emotions, from overjoyed to grief-stricken, and allow others to join in the fun or to comfort you through your sadness.

I've said many times that nobody does this life alone. If you withhold your smiles, laughter, tears, anger, and fears from those closest to you, how can they be there for you? And frankly, I doubt they would want you to keep them in the dark.

Friends, neighbors, family, and colleagues generally are willing and even eager to offer support when you need it. Have a little faith in the people you have chosen to surround yourself with.

Anyone who isn't a narcissist, sociopath, or psychopath has the ability to empathize with others. A theory called the Empathy-Altruism Hypothesis suggests that empathy is what drives people to offer help when they sense that someone is lonely, for example. And studies show that sharing our emotions is a social behavior that most people relate to because they, like all of us, also have emotions and share them. That sharing, whether we realize it at the time or not, often is our way to seek support, understanding, or even validation.

In other words, people want to know when you need support, and they want to support you. Plus, they want you to support them when they're in need.

My take: It's OK to smile when you're happy. Or to cry when you're sad. Some studies even say crying at work, once taboo, is even becoming OK in the workplace—depending on the company's culture, of course.

Golden State Warriors head coach Steve Kerr gave himself permission to show raw, honest emotion during a pregame interview in May 2022. He opened with, "Any basketball questions don't matter," and used his time to speak about the heartbreaking mass shooting at Robb Elementary School in Uvalde, Texas, where nineteen children and two teachers lost their lives.

Gun violence is deeply personal to Kerr—his father, Malcolm H. Kerr, was shot and killed in 1984 by extremists while serving as president of the American University of Beirut.

While fighting back tears, Kerr slammed his hands on the table in frustration and shared, "I'm so tired of getting up here and offering condolences to the devastated families that are out there. I'm so tired. Excuse me. I'm sorry. I'm tired of moments of silence. Enough."

One piece of unsettling news, however, is a reported decline in empathy levels among college students, who may have become desensitized to the emotional aspect of face-to-face interactions as they have gotten more engrossed in digital communication.

So, if someone ignores your display of emotion, realize it's not you; it's the culture. And if someone teases or criticizes you for it, take a cue from actress Meg Ryan's character, Karen Emma Walden, in the 1996 movie, *Courage Under Fire*. She is the captain of a medevac helicopter, which is shot down during the Gulf War. Stranded with her all-male unit, tensions run high. Walden starts to cry, just a little.

"Oh great," a staff sergeant on her team says. "The captain's crying."

Walden retorts: "It's just tension, asshole. It doesn't mean s***."

Like he didn't feel like crying, too? Of course he did. He just didn't have the courage to do it in front of her. Unlike the captain, he didn't give himself permission to express his authentic emotions instead of hiding them.

That is because we're conditioned differently as we're raised. Don Barden, PhD, shares in his book *Here Come the Girls* that women are typically "encouraged to develop and express emotional intelligence and nurturing behaviors, while men are socialized to suppress emotions and prioritize assertiveness." It's not that men don't feel emotion, but they are taught to suppress their emotions and even prioritize assertiveness. A 2015 documentary called *The Mask You Live In* examines the societal pressures on men to hide their emotions, keep friendships at the surface level, and even resort to violence to resolve conflicts. So it is clear that those gender stereotypes are, for men, as valid as the pressure to put others before ourselves is for women.

Next time you're working your hardest to bottle up your emotions so nobody will know your true feelings, ask yourself why. If your reason revolves around the echo of an adult telling a child-sized you to "pipe down" or "suck it up," give yourself permission to ignore it.

You're not a child anymore. You are an adult, and you are now free to express your emotions in the way you feel is appropriate for you, right now, in the situation you're in. Give yourself permission to embrace your feelings unapologetically.

Take One Step Forward

Your responses to the prompts below will help you take one step forward toward the spotlight of your life and help you fulfill your personal permission mission.

Who do you trust more than yourself? Why?

Do you believe you can trust yourself to make your own decisions?

Describe at least one situation in which you made a decision that was contrary to what you believe a parent or another former caregiver would have advised you to make.

How did it feel to own your decision?

Journal about what you wish you had the courage to do, say, feel, or express. If there were no boundaries, no rules, no repercussions—let it all out.

Visualize one of the things you wrote down coming true. Pick one and focus on it for the week.

Practice listening to your own voice about making decisions for yourself this week. You know the answers; listen intently.

Take Action: Make a decision for yourself by listening to your inner voice. No matter how big or small. And celebrate your decision.

Part Five

Your Personal Permission Mission

Give yourself permission rather than asking or waiting for permission from someone else.

Realize that your passion for what you want, need, and deserve is greater than the fear of trying.

In-power yourself to trust your own voice more than the voices of the past.

Take a step forward into the spotlight on the stage of your own life.

At this point in our journey, it's time for you to take a step forward toward achieving your own personal permission mission. Are you ready?

Look back at the list you made at the end of Part 1, when I asked you to consider a few actions you would like to take but have been reluctant to because somebody, at some time in your life, convinced you that you shouldn't or couldn't. It's time to muster up all of the grit in your being and take one step forward—a giant step or a baby step. It's up to you.

What does one step toward the spotlight of center stage look like for you? Where does the plan, as you work toward your personal permission mission, say you should begin? A tiny bit closer to achieving your personal permission mission is still closer.

If you have in-powered yourself to find a new relationship, for example, a small step forward might be to sign up for a dating app or to ask your closest friends if they know someone you might like.

You don't have to go on a date yet. Just start looking.

If you feel like you can now trust your own voice more than the voices of your backup singers, you might set your sights on indulging a passion for something you never "allowed" yourself to do because you know your parents or grandparents wouldn't approve. For example, if you would like to start joining local fundraisers for a cause you support, a first step might be to log onto your neighborhood's Facebook page and find a buddy.

No need to rush to the next event. Just find out about it.

What have you discovered in this book so far that will help you take that first step? Have you realized that your passion for doing or having something is greater than your fear of going after it? Are you fed up with the status quo? Are you tired of following the imaginary rules?

Are you ready to succeed, achieve, and excel?

Have you identified what is holding you back from stepping into the spotlight of your own life?

In these final chapters, we'll take a look at some of the challenges that you might be facing: unfulfilled wishes that are completely within your reach but that you have not grabbed because you feel you don't deserve to have them come true. Or more likely, you don't believe you could possibly make them come true.

Has your mindset nudged toward optimism by now? Even a little bit? That's something.

We'll rally around the inspiration we felt when reading the stories of people who overcame their imposter syndrome, fear, and lack of trust in their own intuition to then overcome those same things ourselves. We'll confront the backup singers who are preventing us from taking that first step.

The topics we'll cover in Part 5 might resonate with you: a reluctance to say "no," a desire to take a stand, the tendency to settle for less than you want or deserve, a nagging feeling that speaking up or "stirring the pot" will inconvenience others—even if staying silent leaves you dissatisfied. Consider the evidence, research, and examples of women who have overcome their fears, doubts, and lack of confidence to go after and achieve their goals, both big and small.

Taking one step forward brings you one step closer to success. Taking one step forward will get you moving in the right direction. That baby step will create momentum for the next step and then the next, until the spotlight is shining on the tips of your toes and all you have to do is say "yes" to the flood of light that could and should and will wash over you.

Taking one step forward means you're no longer standing still. Why stand still if you don't really like where you're standing?

You need only one thing to get started on the path to having everything you want, need, and deserve, and that's permission. And you only need permission from one person to get that started, and that's you.

Chapter 25

Permission to Own Your Worth

> There's no prerequisites to worthiness. You're born worthy, and I think that's a message a lot of women need to hear.
>
> **—Viola Davis**

Selling yourself on stepping into the spotlight of your life isn't the only sales job you'll need to embrace as you come to believe you are a worthy person who deserves to have everything you want and need.

You also will have to sell that fact to those who are in a position to help you fulfill those needs or deliver what you want.

You know how. You have been selling your entire life. And you have sold yourself already on the bad news, so why not sell yourself on the good? And if you need some help, refer back to the five-step sales process from Chapter 21 that professional salespeople follow as they negotiate a sale. The pros know that the key to any sale is taking the bold step of asking for what you want. Otherwise, if you don't ask, how would anyone know what you want?

As you muster the courage to make the ask, you'll very likely have to ignore any backup singers who have convinced you in the past that it's not polite to ask or that you should settle for what you're offered.

I'm from the South, so "polite" is my middle name. But that doesn't mean I will settle for less than I deserve. I give myself permission to ask for what I want. For everything I want.

You shouldn't settle, either.

Viola Davis (*How to Get Away with Murder, Fences, The Help*) gave herself permission not to settle. She is an incredible actress who has won an Oscar, an Emmy, and two Tony Awards, and despite all those accolades, she was still getting paid less than her white counterparts.

Let that sink in.

In interviews, Davis has been very honest in sharing that her awards bring equality. While others were celebrated *and* compensated, she was expected to just smile and be grateful.

But she didn't stay silent. She claimed her worth and said: "You're a black Meryl Streep . . . we love you. There is no one like you," she said, "Okay, then if there's no one like me, you think I'm that, you pay me what I'm worth."

She drew a line in the sand, and her declaration was a call to action—especially for women and people of color—to not settle. It was a reminder that praise without the paycheck isn't real progress.

When others don't recognize our value, it's up to us to hold our ground.

Tennis great Billie Jean King took an unprecedented action to collect respect for herself and other women athletes when she challenged Bobby Riggs, a former number one player, to a televised match—and won. Riggs, fifty-five, had bragged that he could defeat even the best women's player—then the twenty-nine-year-old King. He also said things like "Women belong in the bedroom and kitchen, in that order" and "I want to prove that women are lousy, they stink, and they don't belong on the same court as a man."

To his credit, he very publicly ate his humble pie after King beat him during the tennis match. From the suffragettes who fought tirelessly for women's right to vote to the stars who championed the #MeToo movement, history is full of women and men whose rights, accomplishments, and hard work were overlooked, ignored, demeaned, and questioned until they stood up and demanded their due.

You don't have to be a celebrity to follow their lead.

Engineer Robert Kearns is a great example of an everyday working man who took on the automotive giants who stole his invention—an intermittent windshield wiper. Kearns spent nearly thirty years in legal battles against Ford and Chrysler, despite great personal sacrifices. The conflict ended in 1995 with an $18.7 million court award.

When you are offered less than you deserve, in terms of money, recognition, respect, attention, influence, or anything else that is important to you, do you settle or do you let everyone know what you want, need, or deserve? Do you ask for what you want, or perhaps, like Davis, expect it?

Why do we sometimes settle for less than we deserve in relationships, the workplace, or even society? Sometimes it's because we don't give ourselves permission to advocate for ourselves. But often, it's because of those darn backup singers—well-meaning moms, grandmothers, and others who taught us to be nonconfrontational and even self-sacrificing.

So many of us never learned how to negotiate, sell our point of view, assert ourselves, or even recognize our own worth.

If you're not comfortable doing any of that, you're in good company. Research on social conditioning has shown us that women are far less likely than men—7 percent compared with 57 percent—to negotiate salaries, often because we fear others will think we're difficult, aggressive, greedy, or ungrateful. Worse, a 2020 report in *Harvard Business Review* revealed that women who negotiate for higher pay are less likely than men who do the same to land the job.

Stats like that can make a fear of backlash seem reasonable. And we know that permission doesn't happen until our mission outweighs that fear.

Still, value and worth are not concepts reserved for the workplace. A common concern among women who achieve—or aim to—is the fear that others will judge them for stepping outside of the family or cultural status quo.

Every Sunday, my friend Annamarie's family has dinner at her mom's house. And every Sunday, Annamarie cooks. She works full time and late hours as a server in a fancy restaurant, but somehow she always manages to put together a feast of family favorites. I have been invited a few times, and it is like a holiday every week.

The rest of her family shows up every week, empty-handed and hungry. No one offers to help. No one offers to set the table. They eat and retire to the living room while Annamarie cleans up. But no one ever says thank you. Not once.

One Sunday, while clearing plates, she overheard her brother say, "She just loves doing all this stuff. Keeps her busy." That night, something snapped. Annamarie told everyone that she is no longer making Sunday suppers. She said, "If I'm not valued, I'm not volunteering." They laughed, thinking it was a joke.

But the next week, Annamarie did not cook. In fact, she did not even attend the family dinner. Her family called, apologized, and expressed their gratitude. Sometimes, it takes your absence for others to recognize your presence.

In the late 1980s, sociologist Arlene Kaplan Daniels coined the term "invisible work," which is described as the work that women typically do in the home to keep things running smoothly. Daniels shared how this type of work is often undervalued. And this "invisible work" can lead to burnout and diminished self-worth.

This notion is explored in filmmaker Pamela Tanner Boll's 2008 documentary, *Who Does She Think She Is?* The film explores the struggles of women artists balancing their creative work with family responsibilities and society's rulebook. It brings life to the battle many women face when exploring and asserting our identities and creativity. It means overcoming resistance and dealing with feelings of doubt. It means limiting our sense of worth to how others define us and to whether they give us permission to shine brighter than we did before.

Backup singers can instill a feeling that conforming to others' expectations is all the success we need, that we're valuable only if we do what they want us to do.

Fear keeps us stuck in bad relationships: the fear of being alone, the fear that others will judge you if you divorce or stay single, the fear that you won't find a better partner if you leave the one you have, even if that partner is lousy.

For now, consider a few action steps that can help you when it's time for you to ask for, demand, or even expect something more than you're offered, when it's time for you to in-power yourself to take your first step forward toward center stage.

First, do the introspection needed to recognize your own worth. Knowing your value and believing it will help you find the confidence you need to ask for what you're worth.

Second, ask for help. As you know, my mantra is, "Nobody does this life alone." Look for allies, like mentors and professional networks. Find someone to help you prepare for the moment you will ask for a raise or a first date or a day off or a favor from a neighbor.

Next, screen out the backup singers who are telling you not to make waves. Remember that as well-meaning as family and friends might be when they tell you to settle, they're not the ones in your low-paying job or unsatisfying relationship. They're not the ones who feel undervalued or unhappy. They might not even understand your true value and worth themselves. Or theirs. Do what you need to do to get your chorus singing in harmony.

And, as I've said in nearly every chapter, make a plan. Anticipate every possible answer and formulate a comeback for it.

Most important, your worth is not determined by others. Give yourself permission to respect your own value and true worth.

Once you believe in yourself, others will, too.

Chapter 26

Permission to Act, Not Ask

> I am no longer accepting the things I cannot change. I am changing the things I cannot accept.
>
> **—Angela Davis**

A trailblazer like Grace Brewster Murray Hopper didn't spend much time during her eighty-five years on Earth asking people for permission.

Hopper earned a PhD from Yale in 1934, taught at Vassar, earned the rank of rear admiral in the Navy, and helped invent a computer language called COBOL, the first to use word commands rather than symbols. She was an innovator and a problem-solver with the confidence to get right to it without waiting for anyone's blessing.

In fact, she is widely quoted as saying, "It is better to ask for forgiveness than permission."

While Hopper didn't create the phrase or the notion, she popularized it and lived by it.

Hopper defied written-in-stone norms, like the ones that 1930s society embraced about women staying in the background in fields like the military, technology, and academia. She was someone who envisioned her own success and set out on a mission to achieve it, again and again.

She is joined by other brave women throughout history who made bold moves without waiting for someone else to green-light their good ideas or empower them to be fearless or audacious or even heroic. Among them: astronaut Sally Ride, who defied gender expectations to become the first woman in space; Amelia Earhart, who overcame resistance from naysayers as she attempted to fly around the world; and Shirley Chisholm, the first Black woman elected to the US Congress and the first woman to run for president in 1972, despite opposition from her own Democratic Party and even from civil rights leaders and feminists. She lost in the primary but paved a path for future generations.

Not only did they not ask for permission, they also bucked the opposition by giving it to themselves.

These were powerful women whom nobody empowered. They in-powered themselves. Like Hopper, they believed "the best thing to do is to do it." And boy, did they—and without asking for forgiveness afterward, either.

So why is it that we stop ourselves from doing what we want because we think we don't have permission or authority? Why do we feel like we need permission to do something we know we can do or we truly want to at least try to do?

As with most things, our parents taught us that we need it. They conditioned us to seek approval instead of granting it to ourselves and to rely on the wisdom of our elders instead of on our own. That makes sense for a little kid, for sure. But that conditioning followed us into adulthood, so we continue to look outward for permission and validation.

I have a friend who won't eat more than two cookies at a time, even her favorites. Her father had a rule: "You can have as many as you want, but never more than two." Anyone in the five-sibling household would be punished for sneaking a third. She hasn't lived with her father for a couple of decades now, and she still never indulges.

If she's waiting for her long-deceased father to empower her to eat whatever she wants, she'll be waiting forever. The only true empowerment, in my opinion, is self-empowerment. It's in-powerment.

It comes from within. Just like permission.

Others have noted that relying on others to make decisions for you—to give you permission—is a way to protect yourself from failure. If someone else says it's not OK, that must mean it's too risky. If others say to go for it, taking action feels safer.

And then there are those cultural norms that seem to be in the front row of our chorus of backup singers whenever the opportunity to make a bold move arises. They sing in your ear: "Respect authority." "Conform to the norm." "Do what's expected."

Those norms, though, can seem like a natural enemy of permission. They include protocols that apply to everyone in general and don't take into consideration the unique needs and talents of individuals. Policies and procedures—of society, families, workplaces, and even relationships—can stop someone from giving herself permission as a way to avoid confrontation or punishment. And the biggest natural enemy of permission: fear. We're afraid of losing a job or a relationship if we do what we want instead of compromising. We fear that others will perceive us negatively if we step out of line without raising our hands. We're afraid we won't fit in if we give ourselves permission to show our superpower, to sing our solo.

Social media doesn't help. It has made us constantly seek the approval of others—and to expect immediate feedback. That's just permission in a digital format, and without it, too often, we're hesitant to act.

In a way, when you rely too much on your backup singers as you make a decision, you're asking them for permission to do it.

The trailblazers in the previous examples very likely did discuss their options with trusted advisers, and they almost absolutely remembered relatives and authorities from their past who constantly told them to sit still and quit fidgeting. Certainly, Earhart's loved ones feared for her safety—and they were right to; she was never seen again once her plane disappeared in 1937. But she climbed into that cockpit anyway.

That doesn't mean she made the wrong decision. It was her decision. It was she who gave herself permission to take the risk that might have fulfilled her mission to become the first woman pilot to fly around the world.

Chances are good that she already had a pretty solid decision in the works for herself before anyone ever tried to talk her out of it.

You've experienced this before, too. You have reached a point when you knew you were going to do something, no matter what anybody else said. That is the second when you are in complete control of your decision, even though you know you're not in control of the outcome of that decision. The moment when you let your voice lead the chorus of backup singers.

That is the moment when you accomplish your personal permission mission.

I know you can accomplish this because you have done this very thing many, many times already. We all have.

You did it nonstop when you were a five-year-old. You've done it often when something is really, truly important to you. You do it every time you take a chance—even a minor one—and ask for something or do something even though you know it might have negative consequences.

You have in-powered yourself before, and you can—and will—again.

Those were golden moments when you realized that your mission was greater than your fear. They were those "aha" moments when it struck you that your backup singers—past and present—are advisors, not dictators. They were breakthrough moments when your opinion, your voice, was more important to you than anyone else's. They were the moments when you stepped into the spotlight where you have always belonged but thought someone else had to invite you to claim it.

Those were your moments in the spotlight, right where you belong. You already know you can get there.

So do it again. And don't you dare ask for forgiveness once you do.

Chapter 27

Permission to Define Yourself

> Find out who you are and do it on purpose.
>
> **—Dolly Parton**

Your backup singers likely have had an outsized impact on who you are today. You might not realize, though, that those same influencers have contributed more than their fair share to how *others* think of you.

Wait. Did you think you controlled that narrative? That you could decide how you want others to perceive you and describe you, and then they would?

You could, for sure. But do you already?

If you have never deliberately created a personal brand, or if you don't think you need one, or if you've never heard of one, that doesn't mean you don't have one. You have one, whether you realize it or not. It's been created by the people you interact with. Your personal brand is what *others* think and say about you, based on how you behave and what you say.

I learned how important it is to create a defined personal brand and live according to that brand every day as a way to ensure that others would think of me in the way I would like them to.

Not long before I was scheduled to defend my dissertation and graduate with a PhD in communications, a trusted professor pulled me aside and gave me what would become one of the best pieces of advice I have ever gotten. He said, "Girls who look like you aren't supposed to be smart."

I was too stunned to ask him what in the world he meant. Was he talking about my blonde hair and feminine wardrobe? Either way, in that moment, something clicked. I knew that I had to take control of the way I was presenting myself. It was my responsibility to make sure that others would have the same impression of me that I had of myself.

Personal branding wasn't something I had thought much about until then. Now, I know that by neglecting to very deliberately create a personal brand, I was leaving it up to others to create one for me.

In my book, *Sell Yourself: How to Create, Live, and Sell a Powerful Personal Brand*, I define "brand" as "the impression you make on others."

In a way, your personal brand—conscious or not—becomes a voice that reminds others what they have observed about you. If you're always messy in the break room at work, for example, that might be the main thing you're known for, even if you're the most talented person out of all of your coworkers and you thought *that* was your personal brand. Your brand is what people say about you when you're not in the room, even if they say something different to your face.

So, it's critical to give yourself permission to take control of the impression you make on others. Give yourself permission to take the time to figure out exactly what you would like that impression to be.

And then live that.

Speak, behave, dress, and otherwise present yourself on-brand. You can't be on-brand if you don't know what your brand is.

For example, you might want people to think of you as a polished professional, but the minute you show up late to an 8 a.m. Zoom call with yesterday's mascara smudged under your eyes and a background that reveals you're still in your bed, your brand is "sleepy," or "sloppy," or "woke up two minutes ago."

It only takes one time to create a lasting impression.

If you haven't created a thoughtful and authentic personal brand that you can live, day in and day out, you're allowing others to assume what your brand is. You're allowing others to define you.

A solid personal brand is one you can live every day. It's one you can call up as a guide whenever it's time to make a decision or take an action. It's one that will keep you consistent. It's one that will remind you to show others what you want them to see.

And it's one that might be contrary to what your backup chorus has been singing in your ears ever since you were a kid.

That's OK, maybe even good. Creating a personal brand is a chance for you to separate what others have believed about you from who you really are and what you aspire to become. It's a chance to claim what is uniquely you and break free from any traits you have adopted from others and carried around with you just because they are familiar. It's an exercise in defining not only the person you are but the one you know you can—and want to—become. It's one thing to say, "I want this." It's quite another to say, "I *am* this."

You have the final say. You can decide to follow the rules those backup singers believed in and taught you, or you can give yourself permission to override their outdated advice and forge your own path. No matter how loud those voices get sometimes, it's still possible—and in my opinion, crucial—to define *yourself*, with as much or as little influence as you see fit from the people you knew as a child and from the people you know now.

Your personal brand can and should become the first chapter in the rulebook you write for yourself.

A powerful personal brand is one that others will buy into because it's what they see all day, every day, when they see you.

They will "buy" you as a polished professional, or as a cool musician, or as clever and fun because that's what you're selling every time you walk out of your house.

Give yourself permission to create a powerful personal brand, to live it every day, and to sell yourself according to that brand.

Think of someone who has made a strong and lasting impression on you. Those are people who have unshakable personal brands.

One of those people for me is Dolly Parton.

When I think of her, I think of big hair and a bigger voice, lots of makeup, a sweet smile, and a great sense of humor. She always looks the same; she always acts the same. Her personality and her performance style are consistent.

That's her brand. She never deviates. She has been honest about how she fashioned her look after the "town tramp" and is often quoted saying she sleeps in full makeup, just in case her house catches on fire and rescue workers have to get her outside. She doesn't want them—or any fans who might be on the street watching—to see her looking any different from when she's on stage.

She created her brand. She lives her brand—perhaps in the extreme. She knows what she wants others to think about her, so she conducts herself in a way that will get her what she wants.

It's no accident. It's a strategy. She is selling it to us every day. And we all buy into it because she sells it so consistently that we could never imagine her looking or acting in any other way. I'm not saying you should wear your makeup to bed, of course. But once you leave your house or turn on your camera for a Zoom or a social media vlog, look the way you want people to remember you looking. Speak to them in the way you would like them to describe to others. Say things that they can repeat without representing you as off-brand.

Live up to your brand. The way you present yourself to the world is what the world will believe about you.

To create your powerful personal brand:

Know what you are selling. Do you want others to view you as an emotionally intelligent professional? Does the Instagram account where you post memes talking about other people and their shortcomings sell you as an emotionally intelligent professional? Even if you post the memes in jest, are you selling something else?

Make a choice. We're all multifaceted people, and our brands can incorporate all sorts of qualities and capabilities: professional, athletic, charitable, creative. But if those facets contradict each other—like polished professional versus sexy social media show-off, the people who interact with you will choose for themselves which one is really you.

Choose a brand you can live. Your brand can be aspirational; that is, you can create a brand that will help you present yourself as someone who is ready for the next big thing. But it should be authentic and not so out of character that there's no way you can live up to it. For example, if you're introverted, branding yourself as a performer or public speaker might be a hard sell.

Define what success means to you. What is your goal? What do you have to do to achieve that goal? How do you have to dress or interact with others? Do you have to change habits or stop behaviors that might be holding you back? Are you willing to hush any backup singers who once told you that you couldn't or shouldn't go for this goal?

If you were to overhear your colleagues or neighbors talking about you, what would you like them to say? Once you have that answer, you'll know exactly how to brand yourself.

Chapter 28

Permission to Evolve

> The whole point of being alive is to evolve into the complete person you were intended to be . . . when you stop long enough to hear the whisper you might have drowned out.

—Oprah Winfrey

If you could be only one thing for your entire life, what would you be?

Most of us can't answer that question because all of us are vastly multifaceted. I'm a daughter, a sister, a friend, a wife, a dog mom. I'm a former singer, dancer, and college professor. I've traveled much of the world. I love boats and cheeses. I am a business owner. You're reading my third published book. I've lived in Florida, Georgia, Washington, DC, California, and even Germany.

Like most of you, I have, and hope to continue to, crammed as many lives into this one lifetime as I possibly can. How could I choose one thing?

While it's critically important for each of us to create, live, and sell an authentic and powerful personal brand, it's no less vital to our success and happiness to constantly update, add onto, subtract from, and refine that brand.

Look at the famous 1920s fashion model Lee Miller, often called the muse of her good friend, Pablo Picasso, or remembered as the romantic and creative partner of visual artist Man Ray. In her own right, she was a widely sought-after photographer's model for *Vanity Fair*, *Vogue*, and *The New Yorker*.

But her circumstances drastically changed in 1928 when one of those photographers licensed some of her images to Kotex, which used one of them in an ad for menstrual pads. After that, she was typecast as the "Kotex girl," and her modeling career shriveled up.

Miller didn't choose to end her modeling career, but she pivoted without blinking. She traded her place in front of the camera for one behind it. She studied photography and reinvented herself as a surrealist, shooting everything from fashion to portraits of famous people.

Of this rendition of her former fashion-model self, she said: "I'd rather take a photograph than be one."

Then, another pivot. Miller found her next passion: war photography. She became the first female photojournalist to follow the US Army to the front lines during World War II. She photographed Nazi concentration camps while working as a war correspondent for *Vogue*.

So many lives during one seventy-year lifetime. Miller's very full life ended in 1977.

Very few people stay the same year in and year out. During some parts of our lives, we're focused on one career, and then we switch to something that suits us better as we grow and age, often more than once. We're devoted to our families, our children, our homes, and our neighborhoods, and then loved ones pass away or grow up, or we outgrow them and move on.

For each stage of this multifaceted life, we rebrand as our interests and responsibilities change.

Just like so many others. Miley Cyrus, who played the spunky-but-wholesome schoolgirl Miley Stewart by day/pop singer Hannah Montana by night for the Disney Channel, ditched that kind and playful image once the show ended. Her brand took a 180-degree turn as the real-life pop star took on a new persona as edgy and provocative. And then, she transitioned into a more mature persona.

Vera Wang, once a competitive figure skater and editor at *Vogue*, made a pivot at age forty—launching her first bridal collection and building a global fashion empire that redefined elegance and reinvention. Dwayne "The Rock" Johnson, once a WWE star, stepped outside of the ring and built a blockbuster career in Hollywood—becoming a top-paid actor. Rihanna, the chart-topping pop and R&B singer, stepped back from music to launch Fenty Beauty and then Savage X Fenty, building it into a billion-dollar brand.

Are you working on a second act, or a third, or even thinking about it?

Are you waiting for someone to give you permission to step out of your comfort zone? Are you waiting for your backup singers to all sing in harmony before you'll take a chance on yourself?

Good news: Your wait is over. You don't need permission from anyone but yourself.

Sure, it's scary to make a change, especially a big one. But remember, you achieve your personal permission mission only when your drive and desire to reach your goal exceeds your fear. Your first step to overcoming that is to figure out why—or if—it's time for you to update your brand.

Here are some questions you can answer to help you determine if you're in need of a brand refresh:

1. Have you ever deliberately created a personal brand for yourself? As we discussed earlier, everyone has a brand, even those who never created one on purpose. Your brand, as you'll recall, is the impression you make on others. So, if you would like to make an impression as a dynamic speaker but you have never looked for an opportunity to step onto a stage, nobody will believe you're a dynamic speaker. You would need to deliberately create an authentic brand that positions you as a dynamic speaker, then live that brand every day by accepting lots of speaking gigs and giving a dynamic performance. Only then will others "buy" you as a dynamic speaker. Until then, they will assume your brand is something else.

2. Is your brand still working? For Lady Gaga, for example, her penchant for extravagant costumes and sometimes provocative behavior subsided as she evolved as a musician and actor. She replaced her meat dress and excessive face makeup with a more natural and simpler look, which she has described as more authentic. The pop star herself has even suggested that her wild fashion choices often overshadowed her music. And in a 2017 article in Brit + Co, the performer admitted she was hiding behind her outrageous persona.

"I don't think the world was ready to see who I really am, because I wasn't ready to be myself," she noted of her old brand. Of the new one: "I'm saying, 'This is me, with nothing.'"

In fact, she told the interviewer the changes are permanent. "I can't . . . become Lady Gaga again," she said.

That brand, it seems, is finished.

3. Have you outgrown your original brand? If you created the perfect personal brand for yourself when you were in high school, college, or at your first-ever job, chances are good that you have grown past it. You no longer need a brand that will position you to get a great summer internship or to start your career. You need one that will showcase your experiences, skills, expertise, and evolving interests. Your life looks different now than it did when you were twenty. Your brand should, too.

That doesn't mean you have to start from scratch. By all means, keep the parts of an old brand that are still working for you. But update, tweak, add, subtract, and recreate the parts of it that you must in order to get to the next level.

4. Are you ready for the next level? Maybe you're happy where you are, and that's great. Give yourself permission to bloom where you're planted for as long as that works for you. But if your situation has changed, like Lee Miller's did, or if you're bored and want a change, take a look at the impression you're making on the people who can help you stretch. Maybe you're in the mood for something different.

Spice Girl Victoria Beckham rebranded from a girl-power pop star to a global fashion icon, launching her own label for clothes, shoes, accessories, and beauty products in 2008. Drew Barrymore, as famous for her off-screen antics with drugs and drinking as for her roles in *ET* and *Charlie's Angels*, has settled into a new brand as a talk show host whom the media describe as "warm" and "motherly." And in one of the most dramatic switches I've witnessed, which I love, is *Baywatch* beauty and former *Playboy* centerfold Pamela Anderson rebranded "from bombshell to barefaced" when she acquired a part ownership in the skincare company Sonsie. She has been posing make-up free to promote the products.

5. Did your brand blow up when you went off-brand? Some of the most remarkable rebranding stories started with a mistake. A great example: Prim perfectionist Martha Stewart, the first self-made female billionaire in the US, made her fortune by building a media empire based on lifestyle and homemaking. Then, she went to jail.

When she had finished serving her time in 2005 for charges related to insider trading, she rebranded—in her sixties—from what some characterized as unlikeable and untouchable to relatable, human, and fun. She posed for the cover of *Sports Illustrated*'s swimsuit edition in 2023 wearing a one-piece with a plunging neckline. She struck up and publicized a friendship with rapper Snoop Dogg; they even hosted a well-received reality TV series from 2016 to 2020 showing the odd couple cohosting dinner parties. Stewart does fun cameos on commercials and talk shows. She has made such an impression that *The New Yorker* ran a headline posing the question on everyone's mind, is she a "comedy genius?"

All of these celebs made major changes to their brands, grew into them, and succeeded in their second acts, at least in part, because of those new brands. Did they ask for permission to change the way others see them? Only from themselves.

Chapter 29

Permission to Run Your Own Race

> Stop comparing yourself to the person walking ahead of you or behind you. Walk your walk.
>
> **—Michelle Obama**

Demi Lovato grew up in the spotlight—a Disney star and global pop icon all before she was old enough to vote. But behind the scenes, the pressures of fame and comparison to others in the industry pushed her into a spiral of self-doubt and inadequacy, with body image issues and perfectionism that drove her to eating disorders and addiction.

In 2018, after a near-fatal overdose, Lovato let go of the pressure to be perfect and began using her voice to speak truth. Today, she's more than a survivor—she's an advocate for mental health, recovery, and self-worth.

Like Lovato, *Beverly Hills, 90210* star Tori Spelling faced years of self-doubt and constant comparisons to her castmates, making her feel like she didn't measure up.

In her early twenties, hoping to feel better about herself, Tori had cosmetic surgery. She later admitted it was a mistake, one driven by insecurity.

The results weren't what she hoped for, and she dealt with pain and health issues for years.

And instead of easing the pressure, the media attention got even worse. It wore her down emotionally and mentally.

Trying to keep up appearances led to financial stress, personal struggles, and a lot of self-doubt. Tori now says she wishes she hadn't made those choices—and more than anything, she wants her daughters to know they never have to change themselves to feel worthy.

Sometimes, those comparisons inspire people to greatness. Elvis Presley, for example, reportedly tried to match or surpass the styles of other rock 'n' roll stars like Chuck Berry and Little Richard, eventually settling into his own unique brand as a performer but always picking up ideas from his fellow greats. Troubled singer Britney Spears, who posed nude while pregnant for the 2006 cover of *Harper's Bazaar* (à la Demi Moore, who struck the same pose for *Vanity Fair* in 1991), has talked about her envy of multiple female celebrities. In the book *Madonnastyle* by Carol Clerk, for example, Spears revealed, "I have been a huge fan of Madonna since I was a little girl. She's the person that I've really looked up to. I would really, really like to be a legend like Madonna."

The great Mark Twain considered these kinds of comparisons as hero worship. "Our heroes are men who do things which we recognize, with regret, and sometimes with a secret shame, that we cannot do," he once said. "We find not much in ourselves to admire; we are always privately wanting to be like somebody else. If everybody was satisfied with himself, there would be no heroes."

It's helpful to draw inspiration where you can, from those you admire and those whose reputations and success motivated you when you were growing up—including your backup singers. But it's important to be yourself, to create your own personal brand, and to live your life authentically, even if you, like all of us, are a compilation of the people you've known and the experiences you've had.

Living an authentic life means trusting yourself enough to *be* yourself, not to be just like someone else.

Often, that someone else is displaying the best parts of her life on social media. I know I'm not the first one to tell you that the people you encounter on socials have as many troubles as you do; they just don't show it in their Instagram stories. They might seem better off than you, but "seem" is the operative word here. They show you what they want you to believe, and that's not the whole picture. It's a highlight reel.

Nobody is perfect. So once you realize that you're not perfect (because that's impossible), don't get sucked into the myth that the people with flawless skin, toned bodies, expensive clothes, gorgeous partners, and constant adventure and fun in their lives are better than you. It's likely that they're just trying to outdo the posters *they* follow who seem to have it even better than they do.

Comparing yourself and your life to the curated posts of those you follow is downright dangerous.

One example is Nina Langton, a Connecticut high school student who attempted suicide at age sixteen and went to rehab after she developed an eating disorder and body image insecurity. "I was spending a lot of time stalking models on Instagram," she admitted to *TIME* for a 2017 article about the dangers of cell phone use by teenagers, "and I worried a lot about how I looked." Later, her mother realized she should have limited the girl's smartphone use.

Even back then, the US Department of Health and Human Services had discovered that depression and suicide attempts had risen among adolescents. Researchers then could not link that upswing specifically to social media use, but today, they can.

In 2024, US Surgeon General Vivek H. Murthy wrote in a *New York Times* commentary: "The mental health crisis among young people is an emergency—and social media has emerged as an important contributor." The nation's top doc wrote that kids who spend more than three hours a day scrolling on socials are at double the risk of anxiety and depression, and that nearly half of adolescents say social media "makes them feel worse about their bodies." Murthy called for a warning label on social media platforms.

Likewise, research from Harvard correlated heavy social media use with greater body dissatisfaction because the idyllic images so many people post of their supposed perfect lives and appearance can lead to negative self-comparisons.

If this resonates with you, take it to heart. That goes double if you're a parent.

You might remember the old saying, "keeping up with the Joneses." Theories abound about its origins, but the notion that we want to look as good as others, own as much as others, and present ourselves as equal with others—often no matter what the cost—is as relevant now as ever. Some call this "lifestyle inflation" or "lifestyle creep." It can make you go broke.

More than 60 percent of respondents ages eighteen to twenty-seven—Generation Z—who answered a 2024 LendingTree survey said they feel pressure to spend in order to keep up with their peers. Many of those young adults will borrow money to spend on lifestyles that they can neither afford nor sustain. A study from the University of California, Berkeley showed that many of the people who lost their homes during the housing bubble of the mid-2000s had spent beyond their means in an effort to keep up with their neighbors by purchasing homes that symbolized success.

The classic explanation comes from the Social Comparison Theory, popularized in 1954 by psychologist Leon Festinger, who suggested that we determine our personal value by comparing ourselves to others. Festinger identified two kinds of social comparison. Upward comparison is when we compare ourselves to people we believe are better off than we are. That can make us feel inadequate. Downward comparison, by contrast, has us comparing ourselves to those we believe are worse off, which can be a big relief and build up our self-esteem.

Examine why it's so important to you to have or be what someone else has or is. Are you jealous?

Don't worry; you're not the only one. But instead of letting envy or jealousy drive you to keep up with the Joneses, think about it as an opportunity to motivate yourself to figure out what you truly want—not because someone else has it, but because it's important to you—and then to grant yourself permission to do *that*.

Can you give yourself permission to realize that most of the time, other people only show you the best and brightest parts of themselves? Can you give yourself permission to stop comparing yourself to others?

Can you give yourself permission to run your own race and let others run theirs?

The author of the fabulous bestselling book *The Let Them Theory*, podcaster extraordinaire Mel Robbins, has this advice about making comparisons: "If you struggle with comparing yourself to other people, the best way to stop doing that is to work on your own happiness and your own success. Here's why: The happiest and most successful people are way too busy doing what makes themselves happy and successful to worry about comparing themselves to other people. Working on yourself and making yourself a better and happier and more successful person, that is the only way that I know of to truly stop comparing yourself to other people."

I love that. Here's my take on what might help you let others do their thing while you do yours:

- Stop beating yourself up for not having the life or the things that others have. You don't really know what's going on inside their homes, their relationships, or even their minds. Run your own race. Be clear about what you want.
- Hush any backup singers who might be pushing you to be more like someone else—someone besides yourself. Realize that this is just left over from childhood, when a parent or teacher, probably, at one time or another, asked you, "Why can't you be more like so-and-so?"
- Consider whether you really want or need what someone else has. Does your colleague really have a better wardrobe? Does your neighbor truly have a nicer spouse? Is the house next door any more

respectable than the one you have decorated with love and in which you have shared your life with your family?

My best advice:

- Turn your dang phone off. The more you scroll, the worse you're going to feel. Avoiding social media has been proven to reduce upward social comparison and improve self-esteem.
- Focus on your own goals and how to achieve them rather than envying someone else's success or possessions. Success is a personal achievement, based on your own life plan. Nobody but you can make you successful.
- Stop using comparisons to validate yourself. Will you really be a better person or a greater success if you buy the same fancy car that your boss has? Tally your own successes, and drive the car you picked out for yourself, even if it was years ago.
- Finally, practice gratitude. When you are genuinely thankful for what you have, when you can appreciate the people, things, and successes that you have in your life, your envy will disappear.

Give yourself permission to count your blessings. And then, run your own race, not somebody else's.

Chapter 30

Permission to Kick the Sorry Habit

> It takes years as a woman to unlearn what you have been taught to be sorry for. It takes years to find your voice and seize your real estate.

—Amy Poehler

Whenever I hang out with my friend, Andrea, she seems to say "I'm sorry" about everything.

"I'm sorry I'm asking so many questions." "I apologize, I don't understand what you mean." "I'm sorry I picked a windy day for our hike." "I'm so sorry the restaurant is closed." "Can we postpone our lunch? Sorry, I don't mean to be any trouble."

I literally don't know if I should forgive her or ask her to quit apologizing! She didn't do anything wrong except apologize to me.

You certainly know someone like this: a friend or colleague who constantly says "I'm sorry," even when she has said or done absolutely nothing to apologize for. Maybe you have apologized to a stranger who knocked into you when you passed each other on the sidewalk or to a colleague who interrupted you midsentence while you were making a point in a meeting. (Excuse you for speaking while female!)

Girls creator and star Lena Dunham admitted in a 2016 LinkedIn article that she does it: "I say 'sorry' all day, which doesn't make sense considering I'm not a warlord, a drunk driver, or a pizza delivery guy speeding down 6th Avenue on a fixed-gear bike scaring the s*** out of pedestrians. I am a woman who is sometimes right, sometimes wrong, but somehow always sorry."

Same with Andrea, who doesn't need to apologize for the weather. Surely, she had nothing to do with the wind, but she apologized for it anyway.

Andrea and Dunham are far from the only ones who do this, especially among women. Women are more likely than men to apologize, even when they know they're not at fault. They're also more likely than men to believe they *are* at fault, which leads to more unnecessary apologies, according to research published by the National Institutes of Health. In a study, the authors found that women reported apologizing more often than men, and they also reported committing more "offenses." "Men apologize less frequently than women because they have a higher threshold for what constitutes offensive behavior," the authors wrote.

That's not all bad for women, though. Other research found that people who apologize a lot are perceived as being warm and even moral. But we also sometimes look at them as less assertive, less powerful, and even less competent. Those every-other-sentence apologies are viewed as insincere, which they are because they're almost like a habit rather than a show of genuine remorse, which is much more likely to be received positively.

So why do so many people feel the need to apologize so dang often? Communications experts and psychologists suppose that women are conditioned by society and our childhood caretakers to be polite and agreeable, even deferential. Women generally are socialized to want everyone to get along, so we apologize to keep the peace. Men, on the other hand, often are encouraged, as they grow up, to be more assertive and less concerned about maintaining harmony, so they say "I'm sorry" less often.

Karina Schumann, an associate professor of psychology at the University of Pittsburgh, wrote the study in 2010 when she was a doctoral student. She explained: "Men aren't actively resisting apologizing because they think it will make them appear weak or because they don't want to take responsibility for their actions. It seems to be that when they think they've done something wrong, they do apologize just as frequently as when women think they've done something wrong. It's just that they think they've done fewer things wrong."

That's not to say you shouldn't apologize when you know you have done something wrong.

In May of 2020, Ellen DeGeneres made a very public apology on her daytime talk show to address accusations of her running a toxic workplace.

"I learned that things happen here that never should have happened," DeGeneres said, "I am so sorry to the people who were affected." She went on to say, "I take responsibility for what happens at my show."

Her reputation as the "be kind" lady may never quite be the same, and there is some debate on whether her apology was sincere, but she did take responsibility.

When I do something wrong, I acknowledge my role in it; I apologize directly to the person I've hurt, I learn from the incident, and I try to do better next time.

Acknowledging your role in any exchange that went sideways can go a long way toward repairing the relationship you might have damaged. And it can help you forgive yourself when you feel you need to, and then give yourself permission to move on from it.

Nobody is suggesting that you should apologize when you're not guilty of anything. So before you do, consider: Did you do something wrong, like hurt someone's feelings or cross a boundary? Or are you just apologizing to try to ease or avoid tension or a confrontation? Which backup singer is telling you to apologize all the time?

Give yourself permission to stop.

Is there another way to be polite or defuse tension besides saying you're sorry? How about replacing "Sorry I'm late" with "Thanks for your patience"? Or "Sorry, I have a question" with "I'd like to ask a question"? Try it!

You might not even realize that you're constantly apologizing for things you have no control over or didn't do. Start noticing how often you say "sorry." Track it in a journal. Write down why you said it. Being more aware of your language—and of how people react to it—could lead you to break what really is a bad habit.

Examine the beliefs that can lead you to apologize for everything under the sun. For example, do you believe you're responsible for how others feel? Do you think it's your job to keep the peace in every situation? Do you feel that apologizing—or taking responsibility—for every little thing that goes wrong or could go wrong will make others like you more?

Anticipate what might go wrong or how someone might react if you don't say "sorry" every time you speak. You might not have to think very long to realize the answer is likely "nothing."

Practice removing "sorry" from your vocabulary, except when you really have something to apologize for. Choose your words carefully. Make your apologies sincere; otherwise, they will seem far less heartfelt.

Notice how you feel when someone else constantly says "sorry" to you. Annoying, isn't it?

If this is a struggle for you, make an effort to not say "sorry" at all for one full week. This is a challenge that Dunham accepted from her father to try to cure the actress of her sorry habit after she apologized to him "10 times in 10 minutes" and her producer threatened to "lovingly murder [her]" if she said "sorry" again. In her LinkedIn column, Dunham recalled that she first noticed what she calls her "apology addiction" when she apologized "profusely" to a classmate who invited everyone in the class except for Dunham to her birthday party. "Sorry for my tears. Sorry you had to be mean. Sorry I'm not the kind of person you'd want to attend a Sunday afternoon romp at the YMCA. Sorry," she wrote.

She might have been sorry, but not for anything she did. She likely was simply feeling sorry for herself because the classmate left her out.

Give yourself permission to stop apologizing when you have nothing to be sorry about. Give yourself permission to ignore the backup singers who remind you whenever you're feeling vulnerable, a lack of confidence, or threatened that it's better to say "I'm sorry" than to confront the situation or the feelings you're having in that moment.

Saying "sorry" all the time is actually tarnishing your reputation and your personal brand, leading others to wonder if you have done something to be sorry for and expressing a belief that you're somehow wrong all the time. You're not.

Give yourself permission to kick the sorry habit and claim the power that your unnecessary apologies are stealing from you.

Chapter 31

Permission to Forgive

> Forgiving isn't something you do for someone else. It's something you do for yourself. It's saying, "You don't get to trap me in the past. I am worthy of a future."
>
> **—Jodi Picoult**

Forgiveness, like permission, is something that works best if you give it to yourself.

You can forgive others for wrongs you perceive they committed against you. But your forgiveness does not automatically absolve them in their own minds. Before that can happen, they have to forgive themselves.

The same is true for you.

If your goal is to be free of guilt and self-blame, and you're waiting for someone else to liberate you, you'll be waiting forever. That's because even if you hear what seems like magic words—"I forgive you"—you might realize that the other person has just released herself from her pent-up anger and resentment, but you continue to carry your guilt and shame. And you will until you say those same words, "I forgive you," to yourself, and truly mean them.

You might feel better knowing the other person doesn't hold a grudge or blame you for whatever it is that happened between you. You might appreciate the other person's effort to absolve you of whatever harm both of you feel you have caused. But research shows that the weight of your guilt, shame, self-condemnation, or whatever emotions you have about what you did will linger.

Psychological research makes a distinction between external forgiveness (when someone else forgives us) and internal self-forgiveness (when we forgive ourselves). Each kind of forgiveness serves a different psychological function. A 2014 report in *Social and Personality Psychology Compass* found that when we hurt someone, we do as much damage to ourselves—specifically to our self-image—as we do to the other person. So even if someone forgives us, our brains and emotions often hold onto any bad feelings about ourselves that started when we committed the offense.

Being forgiven actually can go a long way to resolving some of our guilt over something we *did*. But it doesn't alleviate our shame, which is something we *feel*, according to the *Handbook of Forgiveness*. It's the difference between believing you did something bad (guilt) and believing you are bad (shame). Shame is a very personal feeling that nobody else can feel for us or cure us of, even by saying, "I forgive you." Shame is something our backup singers are well versed in (they seem to help us remember what we did wrong more than what we did right), and it can mess with your self-concept if you let it.

A final point is that sometimes we don't really believe that another person has forgiven us or has accepted our apology, even if she said she does. Or perhaps we believe that a simple "I'm sorry" just isn't penance enough compared to what we did to be sorry for. In that case, the only way to lift the emotional weight is to give yourself permission to move on.

Still, there's no harm in apologizing when you feel you're in the wrong; it's part of taking responsibility. A sincere apology can go a long way toward rebuilding trust and repairing rifts in relationships. While self-forgiveness is the ultimate cure to the emotional turmoil that comes when we perceive we have done something wrong, saying "I'm sorry" and meaning it could help you as much as it does the other person. Plus, a heartfelt apology can disarm another person who might be feeling angry or resentful toward you.

But what about those times when forgiveness just isn't on the table? Maybe the other person isn't ready to forgive. Or maybe they can't—because they've passed away or are no longer mentally present. Are you supposed to carry that burden forever?

Research says "no," luckily. Self-forgiveness does not depend on external forgiveness. But it does require you to acknowledge any harm you might have caused, to feel genuine remorse for doing the harmful thing, and to accept responsibility for what you did. If you practice self-compassion in the process, you can do all of this without wallowing in shame.

Psychologist Everett Worthington, who spent his career studying forgiveness and wrote several books on the topic, noted that when others won't or can't forgive you, self-forgiveness can still help you heal yourself emotionally, especially if you have done everything you can to repair any damage you've done.

So, like permission, effective forgiveness seems to be a solo exercise. Giving yourself permission to forgive yourself, even when the other person doesn't forgive you, is a positive push toward achieving your permission mission.

That doesn't mean you shouldn't forgive others when you feel they've hurt you.

Like a sincere apology, forgiving others can ease your stress, anxiety, and depression and even improve your self-esteem. That's because holding onto anger or resentment toward others can throw your body's stress hormones, like cortisol and adrenaline, into overdrive, which can raise blood pressure and make your heart rate soar. Worthington's research found that forgiveness helps calm you down.

Others have studied the impact that forgiveness can have on repairing relationships that might have been torn by whatever someone else did to upset you: If you are quick to forgive, chances are better that you will have long-lasting personal and professional relationships than if you continually cast blame and nurse your resentment.

For those who cannot or will not give themselves permission to self-forgive, the consequences can be lifelong.

The actress Jane Fonda, for instance, felt guilty for years after refusing, at age twelve, to see her mother on a visit home while she was being treated at a mental hospital. Her mother died by suicide shortly after, and Fonda blamed herself. She didn't understand at the time that her mother suffered from bipolar disorder.

"I went through life with a lot of guilt, the way kids do," she said, in a conversation about healing through self-forgiveness. "I thought it's all about me. It's all my fault."

Years later, Fonda was able to review her mother's medical records and came to terms with the role her mental illness played in the death.

"Everything fell into place," she said. "I wanted to take her in my arms and tell her how sorry I was. Also, I was able to forgive myself. It had nothing to do with me."

Fonda also talked about forgiving her mother instead of blaming her. It turns out that assigning blame to others when you know or are pretty sure you're the culprit is a poor substitute for self-forgiveness.

Psychologist Bernard Golden, founder of Anger Management Education in Chicago, wrote in *Psychology Today* that blaming others might make you feel better in the moment, but over time, especially if you make it a habit, can lead to feelings of powerlessness. It can make you feel like you're a victim.

In the 2018 article, Golden gave the example of a husband who struck his wife after she told him, while he was drunk, that she wanted a divorce. "If she didn't say that I wouldn't have hit her," the husband said in his defense.

Golden gave multiple examples of the aggressor who blamed the victim. And in each case, he said, the tendency to blame others most likely was learned from their parents.

Parents are likely among your loudest backup singers. But if they spent more time blaming each other—or even you—when things went wrong, or if they let you off the hook every time you owned up to a mistake, you might've grown up without learning how to truly take responsibility, apologize, or even learn from your bad behavior so you can do better next time. With that kind of background, your permission

mission journey might be slightly uphill when it comes to self-forgiveness. How can you forgive yourself, after all, when you're never at fault? Forgiveness is personal, whether you are giving it to another person or yourself. And it starts with giving yourself permission.

Give yourself permission to forgive yourself. Give yourself permission to accept responsibility for any harm you might have caused another person, without blaming the victim. Give yourself permission to say "I'm sorry" and mean it.

Once you do, you can get on with the business of achieving your personal permission mission.

Chapter 32

Permission to Say "No"

> "No" is a complete sentence. It's given me this tremendous sense of power.
>
> **—Anne Lamott**

It's hard to say "no" when someone asks nicely. Or when you really do owe the person a favor. Or when it's a request from a boss or close friend. Or when you're trying to solidify your brand as a hard worker.

But it's harder to deal with the potential consequences of a "no"-free vocabulary: emotional burnout, personal sacrifice, lack of boundaries, overcommitment, no time to take care of yourself.

There are perks, of course, especially for people pleasers and those, like me, who are "helpaholics"—a word I actually trademarked. People love friends, neighbors, and family who are always available, always happy to help. Your reliable "yes" might make life easier for someone who frequently needs favors, so you chaperone more than your fair share or often spend evenings planning for the fundraiser. You're the go-to friend, and even if you never seem to have any time for yourself, you enjoy living a personal brand that others would describe as "helpful," "friendly," "accommodating," "a lifesaver."

The upside of "yes" is powerful, as we'll see in the next chapter. But an overall reluctance to say "no" to any request is just about guaranteed to affect your quality of life and even your mental health.

Take Zoe, a full-time working mom who volunteers as a PTA leader, a Scout troop leader, and for several other community causes. She says "yes" to every request for help or leadership. She wants to make a difference for her kids, build connection, and be an active part of the community.

She does it all—attending school meetings, organizing fundraisers, planning troop activities—eagerly and on time. She honors her commitments. Other parents, teachers, and neighbors absolutely appreciate her dedication. Her friends joke that she's "the Energizer bunny" of the neighborhood.

What they don't know is that Zoe barely has time to sleep, eat properly, exercise, or even catch a moment for herself. That is, they didn't know it until a few weeks before the school year ended, when Zoe started missing meetings, canceling events, and snapping at her family and fellow volunteers. When a fellow PTA member asked if something was wrong, Zoe broke down and described everything she was juggling—and what she was giving up to keep up with it all.

"I never say 'no,'" Zoe admitted. "Everyone depends on me. I don't want to disappoint anyone. I don't even have time for myself anymore."

The PTA member gently suggested she step back from some responsibilities and focus on her own well-being. Zoe took the advice, and she quietly withdrew from many volunteer roles and missed several school events. Word spread that the once unstoppable volunteer was burning out.

It turns out that saying "no" is sometimes the only way to protect ourselves—from ourselves. But for many, especially those who care deeply, saying "no" feels impossible.

Like Zoe, we might want to say "yes" to everything. When opportunities and requests come flooding in, we want to seize them. We want to grow, connect, and contribute. Saying "yes" can open doors and build relationships.

How many community projects, family holiday gatherings, and work social events have you been in charge of? Are you feeling fulfilled by them? Or are you feeling drained? Pay close attention to what you are really getting from these obligations.

Once we wake up to the fact that doing everything for everyone leaves little time to take care of ourselves, burnout has already set in, as it did for Zoe. She dropped out of most of her commitments, but a better route might have been to establish firm boundaries, set priorities, and embrace her core values so she could use them to help her decide which events and opportunities to embrace and which to let go.

Technology entrepreneur Ben Horowitz, author of the 2014 book *The Hard Thing About Hard Things*, coined the term "ruthless prioritization" and says it's tough making decisions about where to put your focus. But it's harder to decide what to let go.

Too many of us don't let go, and wind up in the same boat as Zoe: overcommitted, unhappy, and unfulfilled.

Priorities help us set boundaries. Have you drawn yours when it comes to family, friends, coworkers, and others who routinely ask you to do things for them?

To set firm boundaries, consider what your limits are. If you regularly sacrifice what's important to you or what you would rather do to pitch in for someone else, how's that working for you? If it makes you angry, uncomfortable, resentful, or exhausted, it's time to redraw that map. Then, muster up your grit and communicate your new boundaries when others impose on you. "I don't have a moment to spare lately." "That's not something I feel comfortable doing." And be consistent. If someone is pressuring you to say "yes" when you've already said "no," say "no" again. And again and again until the person hears you. "No" really is a complete sentence.

And what if you're being loud and clear, and others do not respect your "no"?

Hold firm. Remember that "no" means "no" and you have every right to say it. Give yourself permission to make "no" a fact, not a request. It doesn't mean, "Maybe." It doesn't mean, "Try to convince me." It doesn't mean, "I'm not sure."

It could mean, "Not now," and if it does, make that clear. Be as clear as you can about your intentions when you say "no."

To make it easier to give yourself permission to respect your own boundaries, consider:

Making a plan, of course! Determine what your priorities are, in general, for the month, for the week, for today. As you schedule your time, keep your priorities top of mind.

Keeping a calendar. Having a handy list of what you have already said "yes" to—and consulting it before you say "yes" to anything else—will give you perspective about what's actually possible for you to do in the amount of time that you have. Your schedule should include work and family responsibilities as well as volunteer, social, travel, and extracurriculars like classes you may be taking or practices and meetings for sports teams and committees you might enjoy being part of.

Block out some personal time on your calendar, and treat it just like any other nonnegotiable commitment: a lunch hour, a daily walk, time at the gym, meditation, therapy or personal coaching, and—very important—sleep. Schedule it.

That way, you can check your calendar before saying "yes" to anything else and know if you realistically can fit it in without sacrificing something else. If the new thing is more important than something already on your schedule, trade it, don't add it. Squeezing someone or something in is the on-ramp to overcommitment.

Redefining "no" from a negative to a positive. In *The Assertiveness Workbook: How to Express Your Ideas and Stand Up for Yourself at Work and in Relationships*, Randy J. Paterson suggests reframing "no" from something to feel guilty about to a word that helps you maintain healthy boundaries and honor your priorities. Think of saying "no" not as a rejection of the person asking for help but as a commitment to your own health, happiness, safety, and welfare.

Protecting yourself. We've all seen the heartbreaking stories—women who let a stranger with a sob story into their home, or family members who say "yes" to financially supporting a capable-but-unemployed adult child, and even folks who donate money they can't afford just because they don't want to seem impolite or seem uncaring. Don't let your "yes" put you in danger or allow someone to take advantage of you.

Feeling the power of "no." If you accept that you have twenty-four hours in a day and they're already spoken for, it might be easier to decline an invitation or a request—without guilt. Giving yourself permission to say "no" to things that you don't want to do or don't have time to do, and feeling OK about that decision, comes with a sense of power—over your own schedule and your time. Because time is finite, why spend it on activities that don't bring you joy or move you toward your goals just because you're afraid to say "no"?

Being nice about it. A "no" doesn't have to be or feel rude, either to you or to the person you're turning down. You don't really need to explain your "no" to anyone; if you don't want to say "yes," then you don't want to and you don't have to. But how about sugarcoating it just a bit, with something like, "I would love to, but not this time. I can't make it work," or "That sounds like a terrific project. I know you'll be able to find someone else to help you."

And what if your boundaries are breached? Giving in will pull you back into your comfort zone, but it won't solve the problem that led you to "no" in the first place. Instead, you can hold firm and realize that allowing someone to nudge or push you into a "yes" is the same as giving your power away. You're giving *them* the power of permission—power that rightfully belongs to *you*.

Someone else is not going to give you permission to say "no." And, even if they did, you don't need their permission. The only permission you need, you already have. Your own.

And let me reiterate and be crystal clear here: "No" is a complete sentence.

In fact, "no" is a gift you give yourself. It helps you reclaim your time, your energy, and your priorities—so you can focus on what truly matters to *you*, not just what others are pressuring you to do.

Chapter 33

Permission to Say "Yes"

> Say yes, and you'll figure it out afterward.
>
> **—Tina Fey**

Shonda Rhimes, the creator of *Grey's Anatomy*, *Scandal*, and *How to Get Away with Murder*, did an experiment a few years ago: "I would say 'yes' to all the things that scared me. Anything that made me nervous, took me out of my comfort zone, I forced myself to say 'yes' to."

She accepted public speaking gigs, even though she had a deep fear of public speaking. She accepted social invitations that she ordinarily would have turned down because of her social anxiety.

Then, she said in a 2016 TED Talk, "A crazy thing happened. The very act of doing the thing that scared me undid the fear, made it not scary. My fear of public speaking, my social anxiety, poof, gone."

But the most impactful "yes" she uttered in place of what usually would have been "I don't have time right now" was in response to an invitation by one of her three young daughters to play, just as she was about to walk out the door to attend an event.

"I don't like to play," Rhimes, who wrote a book, *Year of Yes*, about her experience, admitted. But she "made a vow" to say "yes" whenever one of the girls asked her to play. "I said 'yes' to less work and more play, and somehow, I still run my world."

She added: "The more I play, the happier I am and the happier my kids are. The more I play, the better I work."

And then: "It's amazing the power of one word. 'Yes' changed my life. 'Yes' changed me."

Yes, indeed. "Yes" is a powerful word. And giving yourself permission to say it, even in the face of fear or uncertainty, is a powerful act.

What are you saying "no" to that's holding you back? Is it your backup singers? Some imaginary rulebook? Can you envision what your world would look like if you said "yes" instead?

Often, we decline invitations and opportunities because of fear, just as Rhimes did. Have you turned down the opportunity to give a presentation even though you know the topic like the back of your hand? To take a relationship to the next level, even though it's going really well? To apply for a promotion because it's possible you won't get it? To travel with a friend to a country you've never been to because you're afraid?

Did you look back with regret? Can you imagine how your life might be better or at least different if you had said "yes" to any of those opportunities?

I heard about a woman who, without knowing about Rhimes, did a similar experiment. She and her husband had moved away from the home they shared for thirty-plus years to a state with warmer weather and more golf courses once they retired. Within a year, her husband passed away, and after a couple of months, she gave herself permission to start making a new life for herself. She decided to say "yes" to every invitation for a full year.

By the end of that year, she had joined a pickleball team, seen a dozen plays, eaten dinner at the homes of nearly all of her neighbors, gone on two dates, and joined a quilting club. When friends and family asked if they could visit—she lives near a beach—she said "yes." When they invited her to visit them, she said "yes."

The result: Her life is full of new friends and her schedule is packed with fun activities, many that she had never considered trying before.

"Yes" gave her the power to move on. Permission—her own—gave her the power to get to the "yes."

It turns out that saying "yes" pushes us to face our fears and embrace opportunities for growth. It leads us to become more comfortable with uncertainty. It forces us to hush any background singers who are cautioning us to stay where things are familiar and comfortable. It bolsters our natural grit.

Neither Rhimes nor the widow said "yes" mindlessly; they obviously turned down invitations that might bring them harm or cross their boundaries. But otherwise, they welcomed every chance to step outside of their comfort zones in a way that led them to unexpected opportunities and personal growth.

Research points to other benefits associated with saying "yes." For example, Wharton School professor Adam Grant, in his 2013 book *Give and Take: Why Helping Others Drives Our Success*, suggests that when we're generous with our time (that is, when we say "yes" to others who ask for help or favors), it's good for our relationships and reputations.

Psychologists have found that agreeing to help others and accepting invitations can win you some new friends and strengthen the social relationships you already have. According to research published in *Psychological Bulletin*, opening yourself up to more regular socializing can foster a sense of well-being. A study called "Altruism, Happiness and Health: It's Good to be Good" suggested that saying "yes" to requests for help can make you happier and healthier, and even help you live longer. Another report found that when we agree to new experiences, we gain resilience, confidence, and even new skills, which boosts our confidence.

Combined, that adds up to a fresh perspective and enhanced creativity, and it can even help you feel more satisfied with your life.

A positive response also can indicate to others that you're open to new ideas and adventures, especially if you're accepting new challenges. It can be part of a personal brand that shows others you are positive and agreeable. "Yes" can be a tool for learning new things. Plus, as Rhimes pointed out, it can invite more fun into your life.

In another TED Talk, Richard Branson, who founded the Virgin Group—Virgin Records, Virgin Atlantic, Virgin Galactic—has credited his success, in part, to his willingness to say "yes" to opportunities even when he was uncertain he could handle them.

"If somebody offers you an amazing opportunity, but you're not sure you can do it, say 'yes,' then learn how to do it later," he said.

Of course, as we learned in the last chapter, too much "yes" can cause burnout, overload your to-do list, rob you of personal time, and even promote resentment if you're agreeing to do things you really don't want to do. So, creating boundaries is important. For example, you could say "yes" to opportunities for fun and educational experiences but "no" to invitations to participate in time-consuming activities that seem more like work than fun and to requests to lend money to or run errands for others.

Your "yes" should be for offers that come with the possibility of learning, growth, and smiles, even if they push you outside of your comfort zone and toward the spotlight of your life.

Saying "yes" is one more way to give yourself permission to try new things and meet new people. It's a way to give yourself permission to take chances and have unexpected experiences.

So say "yes" to giving yourself permission. Then, give yourself permission to say "yes."

Chapter 34

Permission to Show Up for Yourself

> How you show up for yourself will speak volumes when it's time to show up for others. You cannot fill the cup of your neighbor or loved ones when you're depleted. Take care of you. Take care of them. In that order.
>
> **—Alex Elle**

It's probably safe to say that Oprah Winfrey is one of the busiest women in the world. She once said she worked one-hundred-hour weeks when she was a news reporter in Baltimore early in her career. Yet, she swears she takes every single Sunday off from work to do absolutely nothing.

"I always give myself Sundays as a spiritual base of renewal—a day when I do absolutely nothing," she wrote on her website. "I sit in my jammies or take a walk, and I allow myself time to BE—capital B-E—with myself. When I don't, I absolutely become stressed, irritable, anxiety-prone, and not the person I want to be in the world."

We may sometimes believe we're doing absolutely nothing, but that, in itself, is an important act. It means we're taking care of ourselves. We're resting and relaxing. We're recovering from a busy day or week. We're regenerating our energy for the next thing.

We have to stop thinking that resting is not a productive use of our time. Rest is a verb. It is *doing* something. But we have to sell ourselves on the idea.

Rest. That's not nothing, in my book.

As novelist Anne Lamott (*Bird by Bird*, *Traveling Mercies*) is often quoted as saying, "Almost everything will work again if you unplug it for a few minutes, including you."

That's easier said than done, isn't it? When is the last time you spent even a couple of hours away from a screen, like your phone, laptop, or tablet? We're glued to them, in part, because we don't want to miss an important message from work or our family.

Consider this: We've all got an internal radar that lets us know when we really need to step it up a notch, and we always do it on cue, right? But do we have an internal alarm system that lets us know when it's time to hit pause?

And even when your exhaustion and your aching body do tell you to stop for a minute and tend to your physical, emotional, spiritual, and mental health needs, how often do you say to yourself, "Later"?

You'll get to *you* once you finish your project, meet your deadline, take care of your children, cook dinner, run to the dry cleaner, or do this one little thing (and then another and then another).

A meaningful break is actually a great investment in your personal brand; getting overwhelmed can change your behavior in a way that you might regret later. There's a huge return on investment when you rest. Any good employee/parent/friend who works hard and then relaxes and refreshes will be better equipped to work faster, help more, feel better, and handle challenges once the break is over.

And by break, I don't mean a quick cup of coffee. I mean all day Sunday off. Or a summer vacation with no work. Or a long weekend hiking or attending concerts or strolling through a museum or getting a facial and a pedicure. If Oprah can do it, so can you.

Think of it this way: You wouldn't drive a car without regular maintenance and tune-ups, would you? The same is true for people: We can't drive ourselves day after day without recharging our batteries every now and then.

If you already give yourself permission to rest on a regular basis, good for you. If you don't, dig into the reasons why. Did a backup singer, like a successful, ambitious parent, model the all-work-and-no-play behavior you have adopted into your own life? Are you afraid of the pile of emails you'll face if you turn your back on your inbox for a few days? Are you so busy with your children that you can't imagine how you would spend any downtime you allow yourself to take?

Let's look at a different consequence: the one that inevitably will catch up with you if you keep running at full speed for long enough.

First, preliminary results from a new study by a group of university researchers found that overworking can change the structure of your brain, and not for the better. A research team from multiple universities said regularly working long hours can mess with your ability to regulate your emotions, remember things, and solve problems. The researchers defined "long working hours" as fifty-two or more hours a week.

Besides that, doctors and researchers have long reported that long working hours can put you at risk for cardiovascular disease and other health problems, and it can cause issues for your mental health as well.

Add to that the huge possibility that you will simply burn out. Another study, from recruitment firm Reed, found that 85 percent of workers have experienced symptoms of work-related burnout. And a third, published by the University of Utah Health, said burnout can lead to depression, anxiety, exhaustion, and withdrawal.

All of that adds up to a less productive, less efficient you.

So if you're still afraid of the negative consequences of taking a vacation, think instead about the negative impact of not taking one.

Working too many hours is just one part of a bigger problem, however, and taking a vacation is just one part of a more involved solution. Research shows that women, especially those with full-time jobs outside of the home, do not make time for self-care. When you're juggling your paid job with your job at home, whether that's running a household or taking care of children or aging parents, or both, you're engaging in what psychologists call the "double burden." You have a shift at work and then a second shift at home. Your obligations are twice what they are for many others.

And being the caring caregiver that you are, you most likely prioritize the care you give to others over the care you really need to give yourself.

In a survey from the nonprofit foundation Transamerica Institute, 55 percent of caregivers admitted they put their own health second to the health of those they care for. The paradox of that, according to Hofstra University professor of cardiology Dr. Jennifer Mieres, is that you could be setting yourself up to burn out or get sick, which could leave you unable to care for anyone else.

And you could become a victim of "compassion fatigue," a phenomenon trauma researcher and psychologist Charles Figley characterized in the 1990's as "the cost of caring." When you repeatedly expose yourself to the suffering and trauma of others, you can experience emotional, mental, and physical exhaustion, which can actually diminish your capacity for empathy. It's almost as if the suffering and trauma are yours, so you experience the same symptoms of those you're caring for.

The cure: Take a break. Get enough sleep. Take care of yourself.

It's the same concept as putting on your own oxygen mask first during an airplane emergency and then helping the person sitting next to you. If you can't breathe, you won't be able to help anyone do anything.

The actress and athleisure entrepreneur Kate Hudson summed it up this way: "When we take care of ourselves first, we are in a much stronger place to take care of those we love."

Showing up for yourself—and doing it first instead of putting your needs and hopes at the end of a long line behind what everyone else wants—isn't just about your health. It's also about your success. And it's also about what you believe you deserve.

Remember this: Burnout is not a badge of honor.

When is the last time you gave yourself permission to say "no" or "not now" to a request for your time when you had already planned something for yourself? Did you ever get back to the thing you wanted to do?

I love this quote from the Sam Levenson book, *In One Era and Out the Other*: "Remember, if you ever need a helping hand, you'll find one at the end of your arm. As you grow older, you will discover that you have two hands: one for helping yourself, the other for helping others."

And I once again want to point out that nobody does this life alone. *Ask* for that help from others. And when it's your turn, offer it.

Here are four ways to give yourself permission to show up for yourself:

1. Recall the advice you remember your backup singers offering you as a child, and evaluate whether it's in your best interest, even if the person who gave it meant it to be. A mom whose full-time job was to raise her children and run her household—but did not also work outside of the home—certainly would have had a different perspective than you do, if you're someone with the "double burden." And during that era, it might have been considered selfish or even negligent to schedule in time for career, rest, hobbies, and any sanity-saving activities that recharge your batteries today.

2. Reclaim your time. Add your personal needs and goals to your daily to-do list. If your daily jog is important to you, schedule it, and consider it as much a priority as your child's school play or your work deadline. Unless someone else's need is an actual emergency, make yours a priority during the time you have it scheduled. Likewise, schedule some downtime every day, when you can read, rest, or even . . . take a nap. Doesn't that sound divine? Even twenty minutes can refresh you for the remainder of your day.

3. Treat yourself as kindly as you treat others. Bo Bennett, the author of multiple books on critical thinking, said it well: "Never expect people to treat you any better than you treat yourself." Give yourself permission to be your own best friend.

4. Look for moments to show up for yourself. Keep track of the ones you accepted and the ones you missed. Seeing a list of what you are *not* doing to show up for yourself can help you understand how important it is to do it.

If you don't show up for yourself, perhaps someone else will step in. Perhaps not. Look at the evidence so far. How's that working for you? What are you waiting for?

Give yourself permission to show up for you. Treat yourself as well as you treat those around you. You're worth it.

Chapter 35

Permission to Sell (Negotiate)

> If you feel like you're not worthy enough to ask for what you want, you just need the courage to show up and ask. So even if your voice shakes, your palms sweat, or your breath quickens, ask . . . You've already deserved it for a long time.
>
> **—Alexandra Carter**

Earlier, we talked about the power of saying "no." But what do you usually do when someone says "no" to you? Or offers you less than you want or are worth?

You could say "OK" and get on with your day. That's called "settling."

Or instead, you could negotiate an arrangement that gets you a "yes," or at least gets you closer to it.

That's called "selling."

You just said, "Ick," didn't you? Did you have an unhappy experience with a pushy salesperson at some point and have forever viewed sales with suspicion? Has that bad seed become a backup singer who is telling you right now to skip this chapter?

Stay with me for a minute.

I've spent most of my career in the sales field, and I'll share with you three things that I know for sure: First, the icky, slimy caricature of the used car salesperson simply does not apply to most people who have found success as sales professionals. Second, sales is a two-way street. On one side is the person who is selling, and on the other is the person who will potentially buy something. Done correctly, the buyer wants or needs something, and the seller has a product or service that will fill that need. The seller also wants or needs something: to sell that product or service. If the two can negotiate terms that benefit both of them, like an acceptable price and delivery date, the sale is made. It's a win-win.

Third, and you might want to sit down if you're not already: You, and everyone you know, has engaged in this sales process, both as a buyer and as a seller, many, many times. In fact, you buy and sell every day. And you are really good at it.

I don't mean that you, the buyer, pull out your credit card and make an actual purchase every day (although there's nothing wrong with a little retail therapy now and then). And I don't mean that you, the seller, cold-call strangers and convince them to buy insurance, roof gutters, or a weight-loss supplement.

Instead, I mean that you, the team member, really want to leave work early on Thursday so you can go to an appointment, and you can only do that if your coworker agrees to cover for you while you're gone. You're the seller. The coworker, on the other hand, is a good friend and is available during that hour, and she can say "yes" or "no" to your request. She is the buyer. If she says "yes," she fulfills her desire to be kind, helpful, and a good friend, all hallmarks of her personal brand.

Win-win.

But it's not always so simple. Maybe she's willing to cover for you, but she wants something in return. She needs to leave early next Thursday so she has time to get dinner ready for a family get-together at her house. So she asks for a trade. She'll cover for you if you cover for her next time. She's negotiating.

You're available next Thursday, so you agree. The sale is made. Another win-win.

Let's back up. What if the coworker says "no"? She would like to help you, but she needs to rush out on Thursday to get her teenager to drama practice, and if she covers your clients that afternoon, she won't be able to finish her paperwork in time to scoot out the door right at quitting time. What now? You can shrug your shoulders and try someone else. Or you can keep selling.

What if you skipped your lunch hour on Thursday and helped her get the paperwork done? You had planned to do your own paperwork at that time anyway, and you actually already had planned to make that offer as a way to return the favor if she agreed to cover for you.

This arrangement works for both of you. You get what you want; your friend gets what she wants. That's a good sale.

Every time you ask someone for help, or for a favor, or to agree with you about something, you're selling. Every time you agree to give the help, do the favor, or agree with the other person, you're buying.

All day long, every single day.

We read about negotiations every day among celebrities who want bigger salaries and world leaders who want peace or trade agreements. A good example is the cast of the TV comedy *Friends,* which banded together to sell their network on paying each of them $1 million per episode in their final two seasons on the air.

They didn't know it, but they followed my five-step sales process, the one that I outlined earlier and the one that I encourage you to use in your daily transactions. It reaped a win-win agreement for the cast and the studio:

Step 1. Plan. According to a 2025 article in *Parade*, which cited *The Wall Street Journal*, *The New York Times*, and others for the details, each member of the *Friends* cast earned $22,500 per episode in season 1. But in season 2, they were paid different amounts, from $20,000 to $40,000 per episode, depending on their characters' popularity. Before season 3, David Schwimmer, who played Ross and reportedly earned the most, suggested to the others that they collectively bargain for their next raise. At that time, Warner Bros. had offered the least-popular player $75,000 per episode, while the others would earn more. As a team, they accepted $75,000 for each. According to the late Matthew Perry's memoir, *Friends, Lovers, and the Big Terrible Thing*, the team was betting on strength in numbers.

Step 2. Look for opportunities. Each season after that, the group substantially upped its collective per-episode rate every single year, until season 9, when each actor's salary was $1 million per episode. Matt LeBlanc, who played the hapless Joey on the show, said the six players took advantage of the opportunity to leverage their growing star power.

Step 3. Listen to establish trust. All told, even the staggering per-episode amount added up to approximately just 16.6 percent of what the production house Warner Bros. earned from the show, which ran ten seasons and is available on reruns and streaming. Warner Bros. made $4.8 billion from *Friends* as of 2024, according to *Forbes*. The show averaged twenty-five million viewers each week and was TV's top-rated comedy for six consecutive years during its decade-long run.

Any sale goes smoother when the seller (the cast) understands the position of the buyer (Warner Bros.). It's much easier to create a deal that benefits both parties when those parties listen to each other and learn what the other wants. In this case, Warner Bros. wanted the full cast to stay on, and the actors wanted to be paid what they believed they were worth.

Step 4. Ask for what you want. This is easier for superstar sitcom actors who know the studio is eager to keep them on a hit show than it is for us mere mortals, but the process is just as effective for everyone. Lisa Kudrow, who played the ditsy Phoebe, said the actors—especially if they're as closely associated with their on-screen characters as the *Friends* ensemble was with theirs—were thinking about their job security when they asked for $1 million per episode.

"I don't think it's out of line to ask that, you know, 'Make me a partner in this endeavor in some way,'" Kudrow said.

The pay raise made Kudrow and costars Courteney Cox and Jennifer Aniston the highest-paid women on TV ever, as of 2002.

Step 5. Follow up with gratitude. In his 2022 memoir, Perry, who played Chandler and died in October 2023, expressed his gratitude for Schwimmer's willingness to forgo the highest salary in the ensemble in season 3 in order to give the full group the opportunity to collectively bargain for even more in future years.

"David had certainly been in a position to go for the most money, and he didn't," he wrote. "I would like to think that I would have made the same move, but as a greedy 25-year-old, I'm not sure I would have. But his decision served to make us take care of each other through what turned out to be a myriad of stressful network negotiations, and it gave us a tremendous amount of power."

LeBlanc, likewise, has applauded Schwimmer for his generosity.

Your situation, of course, is far more down-to-earth than that of those celebrities. But this consultative sales process can work for you just as well when you ask for a raise, a promotion, a date, or a side salad instead of fries when you order dinner.

All of those are potential sales. You rely on someone else to fill a need that you have, whether it's for $1 million per episode or to borrow your dad's car. You plan how to ask; you look for just the right moment to ask for it; you figure out how your dad might benefit from saying "yes"; you ask for exactly what you want; and then you say, "Thank you," whether the answer is "yes" or "no." Gratitude for a "no" is your first step toward getting a "yes" next time.

Shift your mindset so you can spot a sale-in-the-making whenever you hope to get anyone to do anything for you. And then, apply my tried-and-true five-step sales process.

Still feeling the "ick"? Give yourself permission to sell your friends, family, coworkers, neighbors, and others on helping you when you need help. You'll learn two things: First, they'll help you if they can. And second, every one of them has sold *you* on helping *them* with something at some point.

Selling is a fact of life. Sales is not only a business skill; it's a life skill. You sell every day, so you might as well sell like a pro.

Chapter 36

Permission to Explain Nothing

> Don't explain. Don't ever feel less than. When you feel the need to apologize or explain who you are, it means the voice in your head is telling you the wrong story.
>
> — **Shonda Rhimes**

My husband and I love children, but before we were even married, we knew that having our own was not part of our plan. That's our story. Simple as that.

I'm giving myself permission not to explain further.

That's not always so easy. Friends, family, colleagues, and even complete strangers have tried to press me into explaining my decision. The key word here is "my." It's my decision, and I get to decide when and with whom I want to share it. I do not owe anyone an explanation. And neither do you.

And I'll tell you that over the years, I have developed the grit to stick to that.

My child-free friends tell me the same thing. One of them had two elderly aunts who never had children. She never asked them why, even though she was curious. She asked her mother-in-law, who had known both women for sixty years before they passed away, and she didn't even know. She had never asked.

That was a bygone time. Today, everybody feels entitled to know everyone else's business. Thanks, social media.

But some things are simply private. Like the reason why I decided not to go to a reunion. I just didn't want to. I don't know that I had a reason others might deem as good enough. But my feeling at the time was that I didn't want to go. That was good enough for me.

I didn't explain it to anyone. I simply said, "I've decided not to go." This chapter is about giving yourself permission not to explain anything to anyone unless you feel like explaining. It's about giving yourself permission to keep your private stuff private. It's about your personal permission to respect your own privacy and insist that others respect it, too.

As curious as I might be about someone like the sultry-voiced Marlene Dietrich, a mid-twentieth-century Hollywood star who stirred controversy by wearing men's suits, ties, and tuxedos, I respect her decision to keep her reasons to herself. One time, French police stopped her in Paris for wearing men's clothing, which apparently was illegal for women in 1933. Her androgynous style made her something of a fashion icon, but it sparked outrage, accusations of indecency, and even questions about her morality.

She never explained.

A 2017 article in *The Guardian* described the German-born actress's look as a "carefully curated image [that] was a political stance as well as a fashion statement." It claimed that "the bold sexual taunt behind her haute couture gender-switching was designed to be both titillating and subversive."

Although Dietrich's bisexuality was an open secret, it was not something she talked about publicly.

Toni Morrison, who wrote eleven novels, including the Pulitzer Prize–winning *Beloved*, is another influential woman who cut others off when they pressured her to explain herself. An example: In a 1998 interview, Australian journalist Jana Wendt asked Morrison to explain when she would "incorporate white lives . . . in a substantial way" into her books. The author snapped back: "You can't understand how powerfully racist that question is, can you? 'Cause you could never ask a white author, 'When are you going to write about Black people?'"

Explaining yourself is the cousin of asking for permission. When you justify a nosy question with an answer, you're basically trying to justify your decision or action.

So let them demand, but explain only if you want to. Give yourself permission to keep your explanations to yourself. Give yourself permission to honor your own personal boundaries.

Often, people believe they have a right to know your business if you're doing something that flies in the face of social norms. They're not comfortable when someone steps outside of what's ordinary; they might even consider it wrong or unacceptable. Some, especially narcissists, may even feel entitled to the information.

Others simply might hope to understand you better or even to deepen your friendship or connection by asking you to share personal information. They might want to consider your viewpoint if it challenges their own, possibly to decide if they should change their own position on the matter.

And sometimes, it's just curiosity, which can feel intrusive to the one on the receiving end of the request for an explanation. If you're the one doing the asking, consider whether demanding an explanation from someone is insensitive or intrusive.

It's possible to deflect intrusive questions. Some strategies for warding off the Nosy Nellies:

Answer the question generally rather than specifically. For example, if someone is asking you to explain your personal decision not to have children, answer by telling the many reasons any woman might have for making that choice.

Add humor. If a nosy colleague wants to know what your salary is, say it's not nearly enough to pay for the lavish lifestyle you aspire to. That keeps the conversation friendly but lets the intruder know you're not going to give up the information.

Explain why the information is private without explaining your personal situation. Example: If someone asks how many clients you have, you can explain that the information is proprietary.

Change the subject. Like politicians so often do, say you find the question interesting, but you want to discuss a more pressing, perhaps more related issue instead.

Put off giving an answer. Say you want to think about your answer before discussing it. That way, you have time to decide if you want to respond. And the intruder might forget to get back to you.

Give a nonanswer. In response to a "why" question, like "Why aren't you married yet?" respond, "I'm just not." Then, let the silence speak for itself.

Come right out and announce your boundaries. "I'm not going to answer that" or "That's personal" will let the intruder know to stop asking.

Turn it around. Instead of answering the question, ask the intruder one. If the question is, "Why don't you have children?" your answer could be, "Why did you decide to become a parent?" or "How old is your daughter now?"

Be blunt. If the intruder presses on despite your gracious attempts to deflect the interrogation, and if you're willing to ruffle her feathers a bit, come right out and tell her it's none of her business.

An intrusive question can feel like an accusation or a judgment. Chances are good that any major life decision you have made came after lengthy consideration, an examination of the pros and cons, discussions with those in your inner circle, and a healthy back-and-forth with the backup singers who routinely insert themselves into your decision-making in the form of memories of their advice and judgment from the past.

You don't owe an explanation to anyone else. Give yourself permission to keep your private life private.

Chapter 37

Permission to Shatter the Mold

> We must reject not only the stereotypes that others hold of us, but also the stereotypes that we hold of ourselves.
>
> **—Shirley Chisholm**

If you have ever felt relieved, after watching an old movie, that you're not expected to squeeze into a frilly dress with a laced-up corset every morning, you can thank Coco Chanel. One of the twentieth century's most influential fashion designers, Chanel put women in everything from roomy little black dresses without waistbands to wide-leg pants, which represented a gaping departure from the constraining, fitted styles that were popular at the turn of the century. Her simple, elegant designs bordered on androgynous, which defied fashion norms at the time.

CNN Style quoted her as saying, "Nothing is more beautiful than freedom of the body," and called her work "a form of female emancipation."

Today, Chanel, who died in 1971 at age eighty-seven, might be called a "disruptor," a term for visionaries who introduce a product or service so unlike the status quo that it changes the way business is done in that industry. She is joined in history by countless other women who have shattered cultural and societal norms with their innovative ideas and brave actions.

One who preceded her was Nellie Bly, an aspiring journalist who, in the late 1800s, wasn't satisfied with being assigned to the women's pages of the local newspaper, as was routine at that time for female reporters, considered too delicate for news about crime and politics. So she cooked up a scheme to prove she had the reporting chops to compete in the male-dominated news field: She pretended she was insane and got herself committed to the Women's Lunatic Asylum on Blackwell's Island. For ten days, she suffered alongside the patients, who bathed in icy water, ate rotten food, and were physically abused by staff.

The New York World published her multiple-part exposé, "Ten Days in a Mad-House"—later compiled into a book—in 1887. She was promoted to investigative journalist, and she forever changed the role of women in journalism.

Similarly, engineer Mary Jackson—you might remember her from the movie *Hidden Figures*, based on a true story—broke the mold for women of color. The movie showed her working alongside mathematicians—all Black women—at NASA, helping to launch America's space program.

Jackson, who worked as a "computer" for NASA in the 1950s, wanted to be an engineer, but the rules said Black women were not allowed to enroll in the night classes she needed to take in order to get the promotion. So she petitioned the court to allow her to learn alongside the white students, and she won.

Her bold move—to give herself permission to push and fight until she was allowed to attend a segregated school—allowed Jackson to become NASA's first Black female aerospace engineer.

Here is how far up the ladder of success women have had to climb: In 467 BC, playwright Aeschylus included a line in the play *Seven Against Thebes*, a phrase that has lived forever after, in various forms: "Let the woman stay at home and hold their peace." In a 1723 compilation of proverbs titled *Gnomologia: Adagies and Proverbs,* the intellectual/physician/preacher Thomas Fuller included this as a saying he considered "witty" and "wise": "A woman is to be from her house three times: when she is christened, married and buried." More modern renditions of it include, "A woman's place is in the home."

Yet centuries earlier, Cleopatra VII, the Egyptian queen born in 69 BC, waged a war on Rome and lives on in history books as the prototype of the femme fatale. In the fifteenth century, the one-time peasant girl Joan of Arc led the French army to victory during the Hundred Years' War, and Queen Elizabeth I, born in 1533, ruled England alone after rejecting marriage proposals that would have required her to share her power. Catherine the Great, who lived in the eighteenth century, overthrew her own husband to become the Empress of Russia.

More recently, Brian Chesky, cofounder and CEO of Airbnb, helped transform the hospitality industry by creating a model that lets people rent out their homes and spare rooms to travelers who don't want to pay high hotel prices. Drew Houston revolutionized the way we store computer files when he cofounded Dropbox. Travis Kalanick replaced hailing a taxi with sharing a ride as the cofounder of Uber.

Disruptors, all of them.

So if you ever recall long-ago advice from a background singer who told you that you don't belong in a certain industry or aren't suited for something you aspire to, approach it with a healthy dose of skepticism. History has amassed plenty of evidence to the contrary. So have the stories of many modern disruptors, like the pioneering hip-hop duo Salt-N-Pepa. The group made a name for themselves by rapping boldly about taboo topics such as sex, relationships, feminism, and social issues. They were the first female rap act to be certified platinum for their single "Push It."

"People say for women, [we were] a turning point in hip-hop and opened some doors for a lot of ladies," said Cheryl "Salt" James. "So that's just a good feeling to know that we were able to do that." And they were the first female rap group to win a Grammy in 1995 for "None of Your Business."

Consider my fellow Florida State University grad Sara Blakely, who founded Spanx in 2000 and revolutionized the women's shapewear market. She became a billionaire in 2012 at age forty-one when the value of Spanx reached $1.2 billion. And look at Julie Aigner-Clark, a stay-at-home mom who created Baby Einstein, a series of educational videos for babies and toddlers and disrupted the children's educational media market.

A friend shared with me that when she applied to a doctoral program twenty years ago at the university where she had earned straight As when she got her master's degree, her mother asked her, "How can *you* do that? That's what your uncle is doing."

Hmmm. The first American woman to earn a PhD was Helen Magill White in 1877. In 2021, in the United States alone, 27,069 women earned doctorates—47 percent of all PhD graduates that year.

That friend set out to achieve something unexpected—in this case, it had never occurred to her mother that a woman, let alone her own daughter, could aspire to having a doctorate. And this exchange happened in the late 1990s, not the 1940s, when the glamorous Hollywood actress Hedy Lamarr coinvented a groundbreaking technology involving radio signals that could make the location of torpedoes undetectable.

Lamarr wasn't credited with the invention at the time, but by the 1990s, its underlying principles became important for the development of Bluetooth and GPS, and she was honored for it.

Lamarr is a powerful example of how—and why—women should give themselves permission to be more than what others expect. As Ava DuVernay so very well states it, "Ignore the glass ceiling and do the work. If you're focusing on the glass ceiling, focusing on what you don't have, focusing on the limitations, then you will be limited."

Gender roles are certainly changing, but lingering cultural expectations and discrimination can still stifle the ambitions of women who aspire to succeed in or even disrupt fields once considered men's work. The same goes for their ambitions to fill leadership positions once reserved for men. At the same time, some men are discouraged from choosing fields like nursing and daycare, once the domain of women. In both cases, it could be more challenging to find mentors and champions who will embrace you along the way.

What that means is that future female disruptors have to blaze their own trails, with grit, courage, and the permission of nobody but themselves. Still, as I often say, nobody does this life alone. Some suggestions:

Find a mentor, even if it's difficult. Of the fifty companies on CNBC's 2023 Disruptor 50 list, thirteen had female founders. Maybe one of them has time for a conversation with you.

Advocate for yourself. Promote your accomplishments and keep a keen eye open for opportunities to grow.

Find a network. Even if you don't expect or want to disrupt an industry, networking is an important business tool that can help you achieve your goals. Get into a group of entrepreneurs that can share leadership advice and opportunities.

Take risks, even if your backup singers have warned you to limit your ambitions to the sure things. Every successful person has tons of stories to tell and even brag about their biggest failures. Failure equals learning, and learning equals growth.

Promote your unique perspective. That's how disruptors like Coco Chanel turned their ideas into marketable profit-makers. Showcase your innovation. Let everyone know how your idea is better than the status quo.

Plan for dealing with gender and other biases in the workplace—and everywhere. You'll run into plenty of it on your way to the top. Challenge traditional gender roles. Remain resilient, and always have a plan.

Be persistent. Failure is part of the journey. Work through it.

Be open to learning. Know the trends. Do lots of research. Learn technology. Be aware of your competition. Stay ahead of the curve.

Sell yourself as a leader who is already standing in the spotlight, even if you're not there yet. Continually tweak your personal brand so others see you as ready for the top tier. Then live that brand every day and sell it to everyone you meet. Be consistent. Sell yourself as a leader, even if you're still working your way up.

Ambition is a powerful emotion. Ambition without apology is even better. But equally strong are loyalty and trust in the words and wisdom of those who might have lovingly tried to manage your expectations for your life so you wouldn't be hurt or disappointed when your oversized dreams fell through. Still, reaching the top of your field or the pinnacle of your career is something that those backup singers might have assumed you could never do because they believed *they* could never do it. They would never have dreamed of achieving their personal permission mission. Things were different for them when they were your age.

To move toward fulfilling your goals, you might have to be a disruptor of your chorus of backup singers. Give yourself permission to elevate the ones who are singing from the same songbook as you are, and do your best to dismiss the ones who are stuck singing the oldies that went out of style with their outdated ideas about who can achieve what in this world.

Chapter 38

Permission to Unmute

> We realize the importance of our voices only when we are silenced.
>
> **—Malala Yousafzai**

I have a friend, Eleanor, who is smart, experienced, thoughtful, and painfully shy. She absolutely suffers from the confidence gap that we explored earlier. She knows she has solutions to problems and ideas that could be helpful and answers to questions, but she can't bring herself to offer those pearls when she's part of a group. One-on-one, she seems happy to add her two cents, but otherwise, she won't. She feels intimidated. What if she's wrong and makes a fool of herself?

For example, when Eleanor is at her book club meeting—it's usually around eight women from the neighborhood—she contributes by offering to open another bottle of wine or cut the cake someone made. She never comments on the novel, even though she read it, and stays quiet even if she has some insight that the others are overlooking.

Once, when one of the neighbors pulled her aside to ask if she had read the book, Eleanor admitted that she didn't feel comfortable sharing her opinions in a group. The neighbor, trying to be helpful, responded, "Just speak up. It'll be fine."

That wouldn't have been my response. It's easy to tell someone that they "just" need to speak up. It's way harder to do it if you learned during your childhood and teen years, as Eleanor did, that children "are meant to be seen, not heard" and "should speak only when spoken to."

Eleanor knows she isn't a child anymore, but her backup singers don't. Their voices are as loud as ever. "You don't know as much as they do." "They're not interested in what you have to say." "Let the grown-ups talk."

It's not always easy to speak up, even when it's your turn to speak. When I was a professor of communications at a community college early in my career, I approached a student who never spoke in my seminar class, even though class participation was worth 20 percent of each student's grade. The young woman said she was afraid to speak, so she had to work up to it. Plus, her classmates were so quick to offer their opinions that she didn't know how to wedge herself into the conversation.

It wasn't the kind of class where students had to raise their hands and wait for me to call on them. I always encouraged more of a free-for-all discussion, and most of the participants, although not all of them, were pretty courteous about not interrupting. So I negotiated a plan with the silent student: She was to give me a signal when she had something to say, and I would be the one to interrupt.

That's literally all it took: someone to acknowledge that she had something valuable to contribute and make way for her to share her thoughts.

Nobody does this life alone, remember?

Figuring out who or what can help you make your voice heard could be rewarding. Consider how impactful you might be if you added your ideas, wisdom, and personality to a discussion at a staff meeting, a seminar, or even a book club meeting or cocktail party. Your idea might spark ideas in others. What you say could be exactly what the others need to hear.

A great example is an East Coast city council member who was elected to replace another official who resigned half a year before the regular election. At his first council meeting, the newcomer listened and observed and said very little. At the second one, though, as his colleagues debated a proposed budget that included scarcely any funding to help hundreds of city residents who had suddenly lost their jobs due to downsizing, he asked his counterparts to pause and consider how those unemployed constituents' loss of income might affect the city. Everyone hushed to listen. He had a point.

When you choose not to speak up, whether what you have to say is mundane or profound, you deny the others in the room the opportunity to consider another valid viewpoint. You rob them of the chance to consider a perspective that could bring far-reaching change. And you cheat yourself out of the satisfaction of knowing that you truly bring value to any conversation you participate in.

Plus, you deserve to have your voice heard. You deserve to have a say in what's going on around the table; if you didn't, you wouldn't have been invited to sit down. Give yourself permission to have your moment. Let everyone hear what you have to say.

Again, though, for some that's easy to say and hard to do. Take Valerie, who enjoys hanging out with her boisterous friend group even though she is a bit shy. She's that friend who listens to everything and rarely contributes to the conversation, but when she does, her viewpoint is spot-on.

At one dinner, the group, absent one friend, excitedly planned a surprise birthday party for their missing pal. They spent half an hour checking their schedules and came up with a date that worked for everyone.

"Does anyone know the birthday girl's schedule?" Valerie interjected. "All of this planning will be for nothing if she's out of town that evening."

The group fell silent. Nobody else had thought that far ahead.

Your decision to speak up might not be quite that impactful every time, although it could be if you are ever moved to confront someone powerful or interject your opinion in a discussion about a critical situation.

It might be helpful to identify the reasons why you are hesitant or even fearful of speaking up. Public speaking, of course, is something most people fear a little or a lot; in fact, on various lists of the top ten things people are afraid of, public speaking often ranks number one.

That, of course, is an acquired skill that begins, like most journeys, with a good plan, serious prep, a lot of baby steps, and grit. The same is true for speaking to a small group, or even to your boss or family member when you have something difficult to discuss or a big favor to ask.

For women, social conditioning is often behind the reluctance to speak our minds. Research indicates that society's expectations persuade us to keep our mouths closed in an effort to avoid being judged as too aggressive or emotional or too full of ourselves—stereotypes that can undermine a woman's authority or credibility. Gender bias kicks in another heaping serving of hesitation and is often behind the interruptions and challenges women put up with as they try to make points that are at least as equally valid as those of their male counterparts.

Sounds like your backup singers are hard at work, telling you they wouldn't say that if they were you!

A 2011 study in *Administrative Science Quarterly* found that women who tended to speak up in meetings often were perceived by colleagues as less likable and competent than men who did the same thing. Another theory, this one in the book *Men and Women of the Corporation* by R. M. Kanter, suggests that when a woman is surrounded by men at work and has few female colleagues, she feels speaking up is more of a risk and is less likely to do it. Some even feel they don't deserve to be there and have no right to add to the conversation.

And some people—women and men—are just plain shy. That can be genetic, neurological, or learned, according to the experts. And, in my view, it's something you can use to your advantage when you're able to muster up the courage to offer your perspective or wisdom, especially in a professional setting.

Both Valerie and the city council member only spoke once, but everybody wanted to hear from them. When you seldom talk at meetings, your input can be especially impactful. It turns out that people tend to value things that are rare—including the input of someone who infrequently offers it. Plus, they are likely to believe that the introvert has spent time listening instead of speaking, so the comments that eventually come out are perceived as thoughtful. Being quiet, it seems, is to many a sign of wisdom. The actor Bob Newhart, famous for his shy, unassuming personality, embraced it. "I am a minimalist. I like saying the most with the least," he once said. The writer Susan Cain agreed, saying in a TED Talk: "I like to think before I speak (softly)," and "There's zero correlation between being the best talker and having the best ideas."

Both of them gave themselves permission to be quiet when they wanted to.

You can do that, too, or give yourself permission to speak up.

If you wish to be more outspoken but feel the pull of potential negative consequences, do what I do: Make a plan. Start with one small step forward in the direction of the spotlight that's waiting for you.

Brainstorm ways you might find opportunities to speak up. Write down some things you would like to say on those occasions. Do some research so you can back up your opinions with facts, and even science, and anticipate questions that others might ask once you speak up. Rehearse your answers.

Then, give yourself permission to at least try. If you chicken out, that's OK; you'll find another opportunity, and then another and another. Each time, it will be easier, especially if you continue to plan and prep so you're ready for anything once you get going.

Once you find your voice—and hush the backup singers who told you long ago that you didn't have anything worth saying—your world will get bigger. And you will touch, help, heal, inform, and encourage so many people along the way that you'll be the one inspiring others who are afraid to speak up, just like you used to be.

Chapter 39

Permission to Stand Up

> Never doubt that a small group of thoughtful, committed citizens can change the world; indeed, it's the only thing that ever has.
>
> **—Margaret Mead**

Few things are truer than the notion that we stand on the shoulders of those who came before us to slay the obstacles that tried to hold them back. Without the efforts of those involved in the early civil rights and feminist movements, for example, women in particular would not be in positions of authority and influence in the numbers we are today.

We have so many trailblazers to thank for giving themselves permission to take a bold stand, often at great risk and consequence to themselves, so that those who followed could live freer, happier, more abundant lives.

Just a few shout-outs here to Anna Pauline "Pauli" Murray, who, years before Rosa Parks refused to give up her seat on a bus to a white passenger, was arrested in 1940 for daring to sit in the whites-only section of a Virginia bus; to Malala Yousafzai, the fifteen-year-old Pakistani who was shot by the Taliban in 2012 for advocating for education for girls; to Tarana Burke, founder of the #MeToo movement, which brought international attention to survivors of sexual violence and harassment; and to Susan B. Anthony, a leading figure in the women's suffrage movement, who was arrested in 1872 for voting during a time when it was illegal for women to vote, and who used her trial as a platform for women's rights.

All of these heroes took a stand and took a giant step toward the center stage of their own lives. They distinguished themselves from their backup singers. They gave themselves permission to do great things.

Add your own favorites to this list of women who made big, bold moves out of principle; it's easy to find them. And then, add your own name and see how it looks; feel how it feels.

Do you give yourself permission to take a stand in support of something you believe in deeply or against something you strongly object to? Or do you wait for someone else to stand in your place? Do you let the offense slide because you don't feel you can do anything about it? Do you give in to a fear of consequences and stay silent, even when you know or even suspect that your voice could make a difference?

Who told you to keep your opinions to yourself?

Imagine a world where Clara Barton, a pioneering nurse who fearlessly brought medical supplies and aid directly to Civil War battlefields, had shied away from challenging the chaos and suffering with organized care? Where Supreme Court Justice Ruth Bader Ginsburg had not had the grit to fight for gender equality and women's rights?

While writing this book, I had the incredible honor of interviewing the legendary Dionne Warwick (yes, that Dionne Warwick!). And y'all—she is everything you think she is and somehow even more: elegant, sharp, and grounded in who she is and what she stands for. And perhaps most important, she is absolutely unafraid to speak the truth when it matters.

She shared a story with me that is permission in action.

Back in the 1990s, at the height of gangsta rap, she was really bothered by the way women were being described in the music. So, she did something bold. Really bold.

She invited some of the most influential rappers of the time, Snoop Dogg and Suge Knight, to name a couple, to her home at 7 a.m. for a conversation. No press. No entourage.

When they arrived, she began by asking them to call her a bitch.

They froze. Because they couldn't. They wouldn't. And that was the whole point.

"They just looked shocked," she shared with me, "which showed they had the respect for me that I demanded. I told them, I don't see anybody walking around here with four legs and a tail."

She wasn't trying to embarrass or shame them; she was making a point. A powerful one. If they couldn't say it to *her*, why say it about *any* woman? She wanted to open their eyes. These were artists shaping culture, and her grandbabies were listening. And one day, these artists will get married, and their little girls will ask them if they really said those things about women, and they will have to admit the truth.

She reminded them: You don't *need* the B-word to be powerful. And by the time the conversation ended, they got it. They really did. They thanked her.

And after that day, rap lyrics started to change, even if only a little. That day was not about confrontation, but about holding up a mirror with love and truth. It was not about calling people out; it was about calling them in to do better. "It was an understanding of the minds, and it was a wonderful day." She spoke from her heart and they listened. "It was how I felt personally."

This wasn't just about lyrics. It was about love. About legacy. Dionne stood not just as an artist and icon, but as a mother, a grandmother, and a woman who knew her worth. She didn't wait for permission. She gave herself permission to speak the truth, with clarity and compassion.

Snoop has since shared that he was genuinely shaken by the experience because it forced him to look in the mirror and reevaluate.

At the end of our conversation, I had to ask her what she thinks about some of today's rap lyrics and the messages some women rappers are putting out into the world.

She paused, and I could hear a smile as she said, "It might be time for another meeting."

Whether or not you agree with their positions or the way these women gave voice to them, can you admire their grit and courage? Do you wish you were willing to take a bold action on behalf of your deeply held values the way they did?

On a much smaller, more private level, have you ever wished you had the guts to tell your boss "no" when she demanded that you do something you truly objected to, in the name of profits? Have you ever beat yourself up after you neglected to stand up for a friend who was being teased or bullied? Do you ever feel that you missed an opportunity to make a needed change at work or in your community?

Have you ever kicked yourself after agreeing to throw the entire office holiday lunch or bake two hundred brownies for a fundraiser the day before your family vacation?

Do you ever wish you had permission to speak up and take a stand, even if others might disagree with you or even punish you for it?

You could have permission to do any or all of that, if you would give it to yourself.

A fact of life is that silence doesn't sell. You can hope and wish for and expect change, but it never comes until someone is willing to speak up or stand up. I can compare this to a salesperson who has a wonderful product to sell, a perfect sales presentation, and a very interested customer.

The sale rarely happens unless that salesperson asks for it.

So if you want to right a wrong, defend your rights, or even get something you need, speak up. Stand up. Ask for what you want, need, or deserve. Two things that are not on that list: staying silent and asking someone else for permission.

Dolores Huerta didn't ask anyone but herself for permission when she partnered with Cesar Chavez to found the United Farm Workers union. Her motto: "Sí, se puede," or "Yes, you can."

Megastar Taylor Swift took a bold stand when she sued former radio DJ David Mueller for sexual assault, accusing him of groping her under her skirt during a meet-and-greet photo op. When Mueller denied it and sued her for $3 million, Swift didn't back down—she countersued for just

$1. During the trial, she declared, "I'm not going to let you or your client make me feel like this is my fault." The jury ruled in her favor, sending a powerful message to sexual assault survivors everywhere: You *can* stand up, speak out, and seek justice. Taylor gave herself permission to stand up for herself.

You can, too.

It might be scary, though. The fear of backlash is a powerful censor.

That didn't stop Misty Copeland, who retired in 2025 after twenty-five years with the American Ballet Theater, where she was the first Black ballerina to become principal dancer. Her groundbreaking achievement—hard-won with enormous grit on the part of the dancer—paved the way for greater recognition and opportunities for dancers of color in ballet companies all over the world.

It didn't stop film director Kathryn Bigelow from becoming the first woman to win the Academy Award for best director in 2010, for *The Hurt Locker*, after being told countless times that women "don't" direct war films. Her four fellow nominees were all men.

These women didn't just succeed. They rewrote the rulebook.

Those who disagree with you might shun you socially or even professionally. You could become a victim of "cancel culture" or social media shaming. It's possible that you'll jeopardize your job or a friendship, which maybe you're not willing to do. You might suffer from what communications researchers call the "spiral of silence" if you assume your views are in the minority, so you keep them to yourself. Or you simply might wish to avoid conflict.

Deciding to leave it alone is a valid choice and one that only you can make. But if you feel sorry later that you didn't say or do something to right a wrong, speak up for someone not as strong, or push for a change that moves your soul, perhaps it's time to realize that you don't need permission from anyone but yourself to take a stand.

If you feel afraid to speak up or stand up, you're not alone. Experiencing fear before acting courageously is a human—and very common—feeling for all of the reasons listed above.

Embrace it. Your fear is less likely to control you if you look it right in the eye. Acknowledge it.

Then, consider whether your desire or need to take a stand is greater than your fear. That is the point when you reach your permission mission: when the mission is more important than the fear or whatever is keeping you from achieving it.

Next, take an inventory of your backup singers. Seriously, who told you to keep quiet? Who told you not to rock the boat? Who told you she wouldn't do that if she were you? When your role models taught you those lessons, did they have the same circumstances as you? The same passions? The same philosophies and experiences? Probably not. They lived in a different time. They had different priorities.

Give yourself permission to quiet those backup singers.

Focus on your mission, not on what others would do or are doing. Focus on the good you can do instead of fretting about the risk. Do you want to speak up and assume the role of activist or leader or spokesperson? Do you want to write an opinion column for the local newspaper that calls out the city council for a bad decision? Is that more important to you than staying safely shrouded in your diplomatic cocoon, where if you don't say anything, you won't lose anything?

I'm not saying you shouldn't consider the potential consequences of your decision. That's always part of the planning process whenever you're weighing the pros and cons of a big decision like taking a stand. As you consider the consequences, however, assess the worst-case scenario, how likely that is to happen, and whether you believe you could accept it. Then, consider the best-case scenario. Is that outcome more compelling than a decision to play it safe?

Still not sure if you should take a stand and let everyone know what it is? Start small. Instead of making a big speech to make your position known, work behind the scenes in a way that will benefit your cause without making you the face of it. Taking even small steps toward your goal eventually will help you reach it. Give yourself permission to take it slow. Give yourself permission to stay in the background if you feel that will help satisfy your need to take a stand.

And ask for help. Build a support system. Find people who share your views. Social support can be an effective buffer against fear and anxiety. And there's power in numbers. Working behind the scenes with a group of people can move your cause forward just as much as putting yourself front and center with a lone voice. Even participating in a charity race is a way for you to raise money and awareness for a good cause.

This applies to taking a stand for yourself as well as for others and for causes. Do you give yourself permission to put your foot down at home with your partner or children or parents when they insist that you engage in behavior that collides with your values? Do you allow yourself to override their wishes and decisions when you truly want to do something a different way or not do it at all? Do you stick up for yourself when others put you down or ridicule you in an effort to get their way? Are you fed up enough with the way someone treats you or someone you care about to do something about it?

Those scenarios are just as important as the ones that catapulted the women at the beginning of this chapter into superhero status. So whether your ambition is to be brave enough to effect societal change no matter what the cost or to finally stand up to a self-centered colleague, consider who needs to give you permission to take action: only you.

And consider this truism from historian and author Laurel Thatcher Ulrich: "Well-behaved women seldom make history."

Chapter 40

Permission to Resist Pressure

> When a woman finally learns that pleasing the world is impossible, she becomes free to learn how to please herself.

—Glennon Doyle

Deciding for yourself takes grit, bravery, and permission, especially when your backup singers are wailing from the chorus to remind you that their opinions are important, too.

Whether it's subtle or loud, pressure from those backup singers, including the ones who are still in your life today, can get in the way of what you truly want to do. Family, friends, coworkers, or even strangers pressure you to do what they think is best for you. But here's the truth: You are the one living your life. You get to decide what matters most to you.

Giving yourself permission to go after your goals—especially when others don't agree—can feel like an uphill battle. But that doesn't mean you're wrong. Sometimes people push you to stay the same because it's more comfortable for them. Or they want you to choose a path they would've chosen. Or they're afraid you'll fail. But their fear isn't your future.

Think about the moments when you've said "yes" to something just because it was expected. How did it feel? Probably not great. Now imagine saying "yes" to something because you believe in it. That's the real freedom—give yourself permission to do that.

Psychologists have long studied why we give in to pressure. One major reason is our deeply ingrained need to belong. As social creatures, humans are wired to avoid rejection because isolation once meant danger in our evolutionary past. Studies show that social pressure activates brain regions linked to pain, making rejection feel physically uncomfortable. This neurological basis helps explain why saying "no," especially to close friends or family, can feel so difficult.

We learned in an earlier chapter that Social Learning Theory explains how, especially when young, we model behavior based on what those around us do and say. We learn conformity because it often means safety, acceptance, and predictability. However, research also shows that cultivating self-awareness and practicing assertiveness can help us resist undue pressure. Techniques like pausing before responding, evaluating whether a request aligns with personal values, and rehearsing "no" statements have been shown to strengthen personal boundaries. Standing up to pressure often requires grit—the combination of passion and perseverance toward long-term goals. Grit helps you maintain your course when others try to sway you, giving you the stamina to say "no" to pressure that doesn't align with your true desires. In fact, grit is often the defining factor separating those who give in to pressure and those who break free to pursue their own paths.

Simone Biles, the most decorated gymnast in history, withdrew from several of her events at the Tokyo Olympics in 2021, citing mental health concerns related to something called the "twisties"—a sort of mental block that affects a gymnast's sense of where she is, a condition Biles has described as "lost in air." Loads of people tried to talk her out of that decision, but she made herself a priority.

And look at Toni Stone, who in the 1950s faced intense pressure to give up her dream of playing professional baseball. As the first woman to join the Negro Leagues—she played for men's teams—she was told repeatedly by coaches, teammates, and society that baseball was no place for a woman, that she should abandon the sport and pursue a more "appropriate" career like teaching or domestic work. But she gave herself permission to break barriers and follow her passion, becoming a symbol of courage and determination.

Finally, Harper Lee wrote *To Kill a Mockingbird* when she was thirty-one, supported by friends who encouraged her to quit her job and pursue writing. The book, published in 1960, addressed racial injustice and won the Pulitzer Prize in 1961; today it is regarded as a literary classic. As is common when a novice novelist strikes gold on her first try, Lee felt intense pressure from publishers and the public to write another novel. She didn't do it. She chose a private life over public demand. She often said she "said all she had to say" in *Mockingbird*, and that was enough.

Harper's story is a reminder that sometimes, pressure isn't just about being told *not* to do something—it can also be about being pushed *to* do something that isn't right for you. Standing firm in those moments takes grit, self-awareness, and the courage to say "no" to the expectations others set for you.

These inspirational women, like all of us, felt waves of guilt, doubt, judgment, and fear along the way to achieving their personal permission missions, which took an enormous amount of grit and a true belief that only they could give themselves the permission they needed to take one step forward, and then another and another, toward the spotlight.

When I decided to go to graduate school, I felt that same familiar pull to conform. It wasn't overt pressure necessarily, but I knew that some people around me wanted me to stick with a traditional path (i.e., get a job) that felt safe. But I had to step off that track. I had to give myself permission to chart my own course.

Sometimes pressure comes wrapped in opportunity: a job, a favor, a promise. It might come from someone who benefits when you say "yes"—or because they think it's for your own good. Still, it may clash with what you want.

Giving in to pressure might feel safe. It can ease conflict and give you a sense of belonging. But following someone else's script often leaves you unfulfilled—or worse, leads you away from your true self.

It's important to recognize that when you give in to pressure, it's almost like you're asking others for permission to live your life. You're handing over your power and letting someone else decide what you should do. True permission comes from within—you don't need anyone else to approve your dreams or choices. Giving yourself that permission means reclaiming your voice and your right to define your own path.

Do you want this dream or desire to do something more than you want the comfort of conformity? Is your passion stronger than the need to appease others?

Don't say "yes" just because it's expected. Pause, reflect, and then give yourself permission to choose your path—regardless of the pressures you're feeling from backup singers, living or long gone.

Chapter 41

Permission to Have Ageless Ambition

> I never think about age. Maybe that's the ticket.
>
> **—Iris Apfel**

You can't turn back the clock, but you can wind it up again—if you give yourself permission.

When she was seventy, Joan MacDonald had high blood pressure, high cholesterol, and acid reflux, and she was pondering what kind of life she wanted as she lived out her golden years. She decided to replace her multiple medications with long walks, yoga, and weightlifting. Since then, she has lost sixty pounds and excess body fat, gained strength and muscle, and started sharing her progress on social media. On her 78th birthday in 2024, she posted on Instagram: "I've made it to 78 years, and I'm fitter than ever."

Her decision to swap her sedentary lifestyle for an active one didn't happen overnight, and neither did her physical transformation. Still, MacDonald told *Shape* magazine in 2024, "Even though you can't turn back the clock, you can wind it up again."

MacDonald didn't turn her life upside down because someone pressured her to, even though her daughter, a fitness coach and powerlifter, encouraged and helped her all along the way. She did it, she told the magazine, because she decided she didn't want to spend the rest of her life popping pills. "I didn't want that life for myself," she said.

This silver-haired fitness influencer isn't the only one who called on grit to find success later in life. Colonel Harland Sanders opened the first Kentucky Fried Chicken store when he was sixty-two and sold the company when he was seventy-three. Laura Ingalls Wilder published her first book at sixty-five. Marathon runner Fauja Singh ran his first race at eighty-nine and became the first centenarian to complete a marathon at one hundred.

They took their sweet time climbing to the top of the ladder, never giving in to pressure to hurry up—or to slow down as they aged.

Then there's Anna Mary Robertson Moses, better known as Grandma Moses. She didn't pick up a paintbrush until her late seventies, when arthritis made embroidery painful. Yet her rustic, nostalgic paintings caught public attention: In 1940, at around eighty, her work began appearing in galleries, eventually selling for thousands. One painting, *Sugaring Off*, later sold for $1.2 million—and she painted into her nineties.

"Painting's not important," she said at the time. "The important thing is to keep busy. Life is what we make it—always has been, always will be."

At age fifty, Wally Funk, a trailblazing aviator from the Mercury 13 program—an informal, privately funded effort in the early 1960s to test whether women could qualify for spaceflight—finally fulfilled her dreams of space travel decades later. In July 2021, aged eighty-two, she became the oldest person to fly to space aboard Blue Origin's New Shepard—her lifelong passion realized long after her youth.

Not all of these stories of permission at any age are about artistry or exploration. Take Jim Owen, a retired Wall Street manager who, at seventy, decided to fix his chronic back pain and regain vitality. Starting with thirty-minute daily walks, he built up to strength training three times per week. By eighty-four, he'd lost thirty-five pounds, eased his pain, and even won gold medals at the San Diego Senior Games—all while inspiring others through a book and documentaries. He emphasizes three simple rules: Start slow, stay consistent, and lean on community. Or even my friend, Linda, who, after a successful career as a journalist, decided to pursue medicine in her mid-forties. Enrolling in medical school at forty-six, she overcame the challenges of returning to intense study after years away from school. She graduated with honors and became a practicing family physician, proving that making a major career change is not reserved for the young.

It's reserved for those who give themselves permission to do it.

With age comes many changes, and menopause, too, has a permission component. For too long, women were taught to hide or minimize their menopausal symptoms—to "push through" the hot flashes, mood swings, and fatigue quietly, often feeling isolated or dismissed. Giving yourself permission to be yourself during menopause—mood swings and all—means rejecting that silence and shame. It means prioritizing your well-being and embracing this transition as a natural and powerful stage of life.

In fact, menopause can be a turning point—an opportunity to set new boundaries, slow down, and listen deeply to what your body and mind need. It's a chance to advocate for better healthcare, to explore new interests, and to honor yourself without apology. This phase is not an end to vitality or purpose, but a gateway to renewed freedom and authenticity. Like Joan MacDonald and others who have embraced change later in life, you can give yourself permission to claim this stage as your own.

Here's something interesting: In Chinese medicine, menopause is called "second spring." It's considered a time for women to reorient and turn their energy toward something new.

Research supports the power of engaging in meaningful activities as we age. Staying mentally, physically, and socially active can help preserve cognitive function, reduce the risk of dementia, and promote emotional well-being. For example, studies show that lifelong learning and social engagement stimulate the brain, contributing to better memory and problem-solving skills. Physically, even gentle activities like walking and gardening boost heart health and longevity. And emotionally purposeful activity combats loneliness and depression by fostering a sense of connection and meaning.

When I was living in Vienna, Austria, I loved going to breakfast at a little place called Vollpension. It's a warm and welcoming café employing retirees known as "Omas" and "Opas" ("grandmas" and "grandpas" in English) to cook and bake. They each bring their family recipes and serve them up with love. But this hidden gem is more than just a place for amazing pastries—it's a mission. By employing seniors, the café helps them stay active and connected, and it also aids in fighting against poverty and isolation in older adults. Of course, finding the energy and motivation to pursue new interests later in life can feel daunting. Experts recommend starting small and building gradually, focusing on activities you truly enjoy to maintain commitment and passion. Combining social interaction with your pursuits—such as joining clubs or volunteer groups—can multiply benefits for brain health and happiness. Maintaining a balanced routine that includes rest helps sustain energy over time. And setting realistic, achievable goals with regular celebrations of progress reinforces motivation and grit.

It's not a contest. Give yourself permission to take your pursuits at your own pace.

You might worry you're too late to start something new or feel hesitant about beginning again. But growth often starts from humble beginnings. Give yourself permission to try, even if you have to be a beginner once more.

Ask yourself: Is this worth starting now—even if you feel behind? Are you willing to embrace being new at something?

You don't need the world's permission or your adult children's or the backup singers you've been lugging around with you since you were a kid. Call upon your grit and dive in to yourself. At seventy, eighty-two, ninety-five, or one hundred—you can start now. Your age is not a limit. It is never too late. You're right on time.

Chapter 42

Permission to Pause

> Through the sacred art of pausing, we develop the capacity to stop hiding, to stop running away from our experience. We begin to trust in our natural intelligence, in our naturally wise heart, in our capacity to open to whatever arises.
>
> **—Tara Brach**

Alysa Liu, who at age thirteen became the youngest-ever US women's figure skating champion in 2019, stunned the skating world and America during the 2025 World Figure Skating Championships when she became the first American woman to win a world title since 2006.

It was a surprise because three years earlier, at age sixteen, the 2022 Olympic bronze medalist had announced her retirement from competitive skating. She said she was tired of skating, that it had started to feel like a job. She said she wanted to see what life held beyond the ice rink.

Liu's passion for the sport didn't wane, however, when she walked away from it. So she came back, well-trained and ready to win, and she did; she won Olympic gold at age nineteen with a breathtakingly beautiful and technically advanced performance that drew rave reviews with words like "remarkable" and "unbelievable."

She even stunned herself. "I'm not going to lie, this is an insane story," Liu told NBC Sports after her victory. "I don't know how I came back to be world champion."

And then, "I'm so happy."

Liu is far from the only person who chose to end a pursuit and then changed her mind and came back, or who stayed on far beyond when critics said it was over. Like Liu, many athletes have hung up their skates or sneakers and then decided that they weren't finished yet.

They took control of their destinies by deciding for themselves when they were finished and not letting others dictate their futures.

If you have ever held yourself to a decision you made but later reconsidered, ask yourself: Who told you that you can't change your mind? Who told you that you're too old/out of practice to make a comeback? Who told you that you can't take a break or that once you say you quit, nobody will accept you if you perk back up?

Look at actor Robert Downey Jr. He left the public eye in the early 2000s to deal with his addictions, leading Hollywood to consider him uninsurable and the media to label him a has-been. He reemerged in 2008 with his blockbuster hit *Iron Man*, which resolidified him as a top-tier actor and launched the Marvel Cinematic Universe. Uber-famous media personality and taboo-breaking sex therapist Dr. Ruth Westheimer retired from full-time media work in the 1990s and picked it back up shortly after with a shift to podcasting and cultural commentary. US Supreme Court Justice Sandra Day O'Connor, the first woman appointed to the country's highest court, left the bench in 2006 at age seventy-five after twenty-five years. Instead of fading from public life, she founded a nonprofit organization that uses digital games to teach children about government and civics. Cindy Eckert, who sold her company Sprout Pharmaceuticals for $1 billion after developing the drug Addyi—some call it "female Viagra"—bought it back two years later after the firm that had acquired it allegedly mismanaged sales. Not only did Eckert get her company back, she paid nothing for it and got to keep the $1 billion she reaped from the original sale.

That's quite a second chance.

In each case, the mission of the "comeback kid" was greater than his or her fear. They didn't know if they would be accepted or shunned upon their return. They were OK with that—more OK than they would have been if they had never tried and looked back with regret. They gave themselves permission to take a risk, which is scary for anyone, because they decided that fear of an uncertain or negative consequence was less important to them than the potential for success and their desire to pick up where they left off.

Actor/producer/director/playwright Tyler Perry made a different kind of comeback after his first play, which he financed in 1992 using his $12,000 life savings, bombed. Only thirty people showed up over the weekend that *I Know I've Been Changed* opened in Atlanta. Perry wound up living out of his car for a short time afterward.

But he wasn't finished. He later said he believed in the message of the play, which focused on faith and child abuse. He rewrote it several times and put it back in the theater in Atlanta in 1998 to sold-out audiences. Today, of course, Perry presides over a billion-dollar entertainment empire.

Maybe you know someone who retired young and later decided she wasn't finished contributing. Or perhaps you have quit a job and then returned to it, or left a relationship and rekindled it later? An increasing number of millennial women are taking what researchers call the "power pause" to shift their attention to their babies and young children. Later, a majority of them return to their careers. The point is: It's up to you and no one else—not your critics, your colleagues, your advisors, or your backup singers—to decide for yourself when to stop and when to keep going, even if you need a break in between the two.

These are huge decisions. Most of us don't announce to the public that we're leaving a job that made us famous. Most of us aren't star athletes or movie stars or Supreme Court justices. But our decisions are just as important to us as theirs are to them. So those decisions have to be ours and ours alone. We have to give ourselves permission to make the choice that's right for us, even if it will inconvenience others or stop them from benefitting if we leave a position that they were profiting from.

It's up to us to decide if we want to finish what we started or if we're ready to throw in the towel. The examples above prove that the second act can be the one that propels us to greatness. They show that sometimes we're not quite ready to fulfill our destinies on someone else's timetable. They're a lesson in both humility and bravery. Most importantly, they highlight the importance of following your own dreams, your own gut, and not living the rest of your life with a decision that you are no longer happy with.

Give yourself permission to be great, no matter the timeline. You can pause. You can come back again and again. Reinvent yourself. Don't quit until you achieve your personal permission mission.

I'm not saying a comeback works out for every single person or every single time. I know one young woman who took a stand at work and quit when a colleague was fired over a personality clash with the boss. She later regretted her decision to leave a well-paying position that she loved, and she returned to ask for her job back. The answer was "no."

At least she tried. Alysa Liu had no guarantees of a flawless performance at the 2025 Olympics, even though it turned out that way. Robert Downey Jr. might have faced disdain and mistrust from the Hollywood types who were fed up with his behavior. If you leave the workforce to raise your family, it's possible your field will have advanced too far during your absence for you to fit into it anymore, and you'll need to change course. But when you look back at your accomplishments, you will count "going for it" as one of them. If you don't try, you will always wonder if you could have made it.

Often, the backup singers in our chorus are not just people from our past, but those who surround us now, whispering or shouting in our ears to do what they want us to do instead of what our intuition is telling us is right. In the end, they are only advisors, and their reasons for wanting you to stay or go, very often, are based on why it's right for them, not you. You don't have to do what they say.

Do you need a break to reflect and redirect?

Have you accomplished what you set out to do? Are you ready to move on to something completely different? If the answer to any or all of those questions is "yes," hit the pause button. And if you change your mind, come on back, no matter who is telling you you're finished.

Only you can decide that.

Chapter 43

Permission to Make Some Noise

> Letting others know the value you can—and want—to bring isn't a boastful or conceited action . . . it's a courageous action that will enable you to honor your potential more fully and expand your ability to make the difference you want. So get over yourself. Toot, toot.
>
> **—Margie Warrell**

The familiar quotation "It ain't bragging if it's true" is attributed by various sources to either boxing great Muhammad Ali or legendary performer Will Rogers, both who, during their lifetimes, had an awful lot to brag about.

But bragging, like proclaiming greatness, as Ali did again and again, can be considered crass and is sometimes looked at as a smokescreen that insecure people use to convince others of their value.

The thing about Ali's famous quote—"I am the greatest!"—that interests me is the second half of it, which is less quoted. "I am the greatest!" he famously said, before adding, "I said that even before I knew I was."

That second sentence reveals how convinced he was of his own value, worth, and abilities. He was bursting with self-confidence and felt secure in his skills and athleticism. With win after win in the boxing ring, he had plenty of evidence to back his claim up. And even before he emerged as a champion, he believed he could and would. Other celebrities brag, too: "I created the blueprint for influencers," Kim Kardashian has said. 1990s pop icon Madonna, in a 2012 interview with *The Advocate*, noted, "I opened doors for women in the music industry that they never even knew were closed." *Rolling Stone* quoted tennis phenomenon Serena Williams bragging, "I think I'm the greatest player to ever play the game." Way back in 1588, England's first Queen Elizabeth boasted, "I have the heart and stomach of a king, and of a king of England, too."

All of those claims are arguably true, and good on them for overriding any backup singers who might have tried their best to take them down a notch. It's not bragging, after all, if it's true, right?

Still, I tend to view boastful statements as over the top and almost always unnecessary. Most of us don't talk about ourselves in such grandiose terms. Instead, we swing too far to the other side, overdoing humility and avoiding any appearance of tooting our own horns—probably because our parents, grandparents, and teachers taught us that it's impolite to boast.

How about this: we all give ourselves permission to find a happy medium between over-the-top boasting and staying silent when it comes to our accomplishments. Usually, I have observed, most of us overrate the humble, believing that if we talk about ourselves in a positive way at all, we're bragging.

Self-promotion is an important part of success and a critical component of a powerful personal brand. In my book, *Sell Yourself: How to Create, Live, and Sell a Powerful Personal Brand,* I offer an argument for tooting your own horn. My premise: If you don't let others know what you're good at, how will they know if you're good at something they need help with? How will they know you're the right person for the job? How will they know you want or deserve the promotion? How will they know to choose you when they need an assistant or a partner? If you don't show others your superpower, why would they choose you over others for the projects, friendships, and jobs *you* want?

If you simply let your work and your personality speak for themselves, they rarely speak loud enough. You have to show and tell. It is entirely possible to promote yourself in a way that is gracious and humble. Self-promotion does not have to come off as conceited or egotistic or braggadocious. The key is to have evidence to support any claim you make about your qualifications, characteristics, or competence.

A professor at the University of Maryland School of Public Health, Stephen Thomas, is often quoted in the media. His social media pages are full of videos of himself with others who work on the public health projects he manages. Nobody would ever call him conceited, though, because he doesn't necessarily sing his own praises or take all the credit for the success of his projects. He points to the impact his work is having and introduces the teams he works with.

He calls this "gracious self-promotion." He shows pride in his work, graciously, on behalf of the people his actions benefit.

I love that, and I encourage you to practice it. It's that happy medium between bragging and hiding your superpowers. It's a way to let others know that you're doing valuable work and making a difference. It shows you have the confidence to promote your passions, your team, your friends, and your colleagues without shining the spotlight only on yourself.

The professor's strategy pays off in grants for his research, publicity for people who need assistance, and a continuing platform for publicizing the projects that are important to him. Everyone gets that he's awesome, but nobody would ever call him a braggart.

My own backup singers are quite clear on this point: They don't want me to be associated with bragging. I have chosen not to kick them out of my chorus because I believe that I can sell my value to others without turning up the volume as high as a Kardashian. I feel confident that I can talk about myself, my work, and my worth without stealing anyone else's thunder or making myself appear better than I am.

It's OK for you to believe the opposite, that you want to promote yourself in an extreme way. Maybe the field you're in calls for it, like the sports world or entertainment.

But if you're leaning all the way to the other end of the scale—where you don't talk about yourself at all for fear that you'll come off as boastful, consider why you're doing that. Consider who told you to never talk about yourself—why?

You're certainly not the only one who learned this kind of social modesty as a kid (I'm from the South, remember?). In fact, sociologists and communications experts have discovered that many people withhold any positive talk about themselves because society tells us to. Society seems to prize humility, and society's norms, for sure, are among our backup singers.

In Erving Goffman's well-regarded book, *The Presentation of Self in Everyday Life,* he likened how we interact with others socially to acting on a stage, an apt comparison that fits the metaphor I've used throughout this book. He coined the term "impression management" to explain how we use our behavior and words to try to control how others view us. I call that "personal branding."

Research results are split when it comes to whether bragging about yourself is helpful or harmful. Some researchers have found that while overt self-promotion can backfire and lead others to view us negatively, straight-up boasting can, indeed, convince some to perceive we are competent. The humblebrag, on the other hand, is less effective, although engaging in it on social media appears to lead to more favorable reviews than boasting.

That said, one report noted that self-promotion can lead others to consider you untrustworthy or manipulative.

Interestingly, a study in *Psychology Today* showed that just like many people fear the negative social consequences of bragging, some are instead afraid of the potential positive consequences. That fear can lead people to downplay their accomplishments because bragging about themselves might set high expectations that they're afraid they can't live up to.

Not surprisingly, others have linked a reluctance to brag to personal insecurities, while some studies show that those who brag, especially if they exaggerate, suffer from the same and are seeking validation or trying to convince others that they're as good or better than everyone else.

Validation, as we discussed, is a form of permission. Their backup singers must have really done a number on them.

To brag or not to brag? It's your choice to make, of course, and not the choice of the voices from your past who are telling you that you can't or shouldn't speak positively about yourself. It is completely up to you. But just because you choose to share your light with the world does not mean that others need to dim theirs. I choose to believe there is room for us all.

To fulfill your personal permission mission, the choice has to be yours.

Chapter 44

Permission to Celebrate Each Step Forward

> All it takes is ONE moment of courage, ONE step forward, ONE decision, to change your life.
>
> **—Mel Robbins**

Who doesn't love a party? Why don't we throw more of them?

As we reach the end of the book, it's time to take stock of how far you have come. And it's time to celebrate every single step you have taken so far toward your ultimate goal—your personal permission mission.

How many steps have you taken so far toward your own center stage, where the spotlight is waiting to welcome you and give you space to become the star of your own personal show—your life?

Like the vocalists in the documentary I mentioned earlier, *20 Feet from Stardom*, maybe you have twenty steps to go before you reach your personal permission mission—or at least one of the missions you identified earlier in the book. Or perhaps you have one hundred more steps to go, or just one. Maybe you haven't started walking yet, and that's OK. Give the lessons about grit, trust, fear, and permission time to marinate. You'll get there.

Along the way, I want to encourage you to celebrate every single step. Every inch of progress you make toward your goal is a reason to celebrate. Don't save the party for the end!

At the online shoe store Zappos, employees celebrate all the time. The digital retailer has, at times, given employees $50 gift cards to award to any colleague who did an especially good job at something. Managers recognize "heroes" among the staff by throwing mini indoor parades for them and awarding them special parking spaces. And all who work there get balloons, cards, and email announcements for their birthdays and anniversaries. It's a company that banks on a fun corporate culture, and key to that culture is celebrating small wins. I'm happy to say that one of the core values at my consulting firm, Orange Leaf Consulting, is that we take fun seriously.

But not everybody celebrates the small stuff. Research shows that we're often too preoccupied with the negatives to even notice mini victories. And as a culture, we're wired to focus on large accomplishments, like graduations and promotions, more than on life's tiny triumphs, like meeting a tight deadline or making it to the gym four times this week.

Plus, some people, notably perfectionists, tend to undervalue good results as opposed to stellar ones. Celebrating the small wins, perfectionists suppose, could encourage mediocrity, according to one study.

Think about it: Have you ever thrown a party for a child who came in second? Or who won the trophy for most improved rather than the one for most valuable player?

Think about it again: Why not? Second place is not nothing. It's an achievement, just not the biggest one. Yet celebrating it might just boost that kid's confidence and motivate her to win bigger next time. Then you can throw an even bigger party. Progress, in my book, is something to celebrate.

So next time you give yourself permission to take a baby step forward toward achieving one of your goals, share your joy with others. Getting one step closer to your dream come true is a milestone along the way to your success. And as Stanford University professor of biology and neurology Robert Sapolsky found in his research on pleasure, celebrating small achievements doses us with the feel-good hormone dopamine.

Small celebrations can keep us pressing forward when a goal seems complicated or far-off. Recognizing our accomplishments and progress on the way to a milestone can ward off burnout and alleviate stress, researchers say. It keeps our momentum going. It keeps us optimistic so we don't give up.

Celebrating, like permission, is a choice. Your choice. You can choose whether to congratulate yourself for the baby steps you took today toward achieving a future goal, or you can choose to beat yourself up because you didn't take more.

The mega-bestselling author Rhonda Byrne, who wrote *The Secret* and several other books about positive thinking and the law of attraction, said it well: "It is possible to be happy and joyful most of the time. You are free to choose worry or to choose joy, and whatever you choose will attract the same kind back to you. Worry attracts more worry. Joy attracts more joy."

It's a choice.

What better way to choose joy and attract more of it than to celebrate your small wins?

Research in psychology, neuroscience, and organizational behavior bears out that recognizing progress—even a little bit—is an effective strategy for staying motivated, feeling a sense of well-being, and becoming resilient. Viewing incremental achievements as substantial, it seems, has very little downside.

In their book *The Progress Principle: Using Small Wins to Ignite Joy, Engagement, and Creativity at Work*, Harvard business professor Teresa Amabile and her developmental psychologist husband, Steven Kramer, suggest that supporting progress at work "is the number one thing that leaders can do to keep workers engaged and happy at work."

In an article about the book for the American Management Association, the authors wrote that employees, when they described their best days at work, cited progress, not breakthroughs, as the catalyst for a good day. "They were usually small, incremental steps forward," they wrote. "Yet these 'small wins' often had huge effects."

They gave the example of a software engineer who cited his greatest "win" one day as smashing a bug "that's been frustrating me for almost a calendar week. That may not be an event to you, but I live a very drab life, so I'm all hyped." He said he was "rejoicing" over the moment.

We can all take a cue from the bug-smasher. Why wait to finish a big project to celebrate when we can pat ourselves on the back for the progress we made today? Why reserve your joy for when you achieve your ultimate goal when smiling about a tiny step forward will make you happy now and motivate you to go a little farther tomorrow?

It's something to celebrate when you take one step forward toward fulfilling your personal permission mission. So celebrate it.

Let's try it:

- Did you give yourself permission rather than asking or waiting for permission from someone else? What did you give yourself permission for? Celebrate it!
- Did you realize that your passion for what you want, need, or deserve exceeds your fear of trying? What do you have so much passion for that your fears seem in second place? Call a friend and share the good news!
- Did you in-power yourself to step into the spotlight on the stage of your own life and trust your own voice more than the voices of the past? What was the circumstance that led you to override a backup singer who told you that you couldn't or shouldn't do something? How did it make you feel when you did it anyway? Have a five-minute dance party!
- And a big one: Did you take a step forward toward your goal? Which goal? How many steps? Aren't you proud of yourself? Buy yourself a fancy coffee!

Give yourself permission to celebrate the small wins you achieve every day. Take a moment to congratulate yourself for staying on brand all day. Do a little dance after you cook a complicated dish for dinner, even if everybody else treats the accomplishment like you do it every day. Take yourself out to lunch for scoring half-price tickets to the concert you thought you couldn't afford to attend. Scream a happy scream when you realize that your accomplishment has surpassed the achievements of the backup singer who told you that you would never master that exact thing. Go ahead and laugh out loud when it occurs to you that there's a reason that backup singer never made it out of the chorus.

In short, celebrate progress. We do it with birthdays: a cake and balloons every year. We make a big deal out of graduations, which really are just a step toward our first day at our first job and our first paycheck. Let's start celebrating all three.

Most important, perhaps, is to consider it a milestone worth celebrating each time you give yourself permission to do something or acquire something that you've always wanted but have denied yourself because you didn't feel you deserved it or you believed there was no way you could ever achieve it. Even if that permission doesn't complete your mission, be proud of yourself for at least trying.

Celebrate the ordinary moments that lead up to the extraordinary ones. The simple act of acknowledging your accomplishment will help motivate you to take the next step, and then the next.

Author and motivational speaker Brené Brown, in her book, *The Gifts of Imperfection*, makes the point: "Joy comes to us in ordinary moments. We risk missing out when we get too busy chasing the extraordinary."

In fact, how about considering your ordinary achievements, especially if they're first-time successes, as extraordinary? Celebrate them with a smile, a nod to yourself, a quick text to your best friend—or a great big party.

At a friend's fiftieth birthday party, his wife took the stage to gush about how much she enjoys being married to him. She told the story about an evening when my friend brought home a bottle of expensive champagne for the two of them to share.

"What's the occasion?" she asked him.

"It's Tuesday," he said.

Just another Tuesday, but plenty of reasons to celebrate. As you put the principles and inspirations from this book into practice over the next days, weeks, and months, look for opportunities to celebrate. Sell yourself on the fact that you deserve to reward and congratulate yourself every single day. Make it part of your brand: *I celebrate everything.*

You've already taken the first step toward your own stardom: You gave yourself permission to pick up this book and read it all the way through. That's huge. Seriously—pat yourself on the back. Scroll your favorite shopping site. Call your bestie. Do a happy dance in your kitchen. Celebrate *you*.

Now take another step. A bold one. Because you're worth it. You deserve the success you're dreaming of, and I want you to pay close attention to me: You have everything inside you right now to make it happen. Your grit. Your voice. Your own permission.

So go. Stand in your spotlight. It's been waiting for you.

Take One Step Forward

Your responses to the prompts below will help you take one step forward toward the spotlight of your life and help you fulfill your personal permission mission.

What is the latest small step you took toward achieving your personal permission mission?

Think of a way you can celebrate taking that step.

What is the next small step forward for you?

Write down one thing you will no longer apologize for. Practice saying it unapologetically.

Identify one bold "yes" you're ready to give yourself. Schedule it on your calendar this week.

Choose one dream that has been on hold. Break it into three small steps and commit to the first.

Celebrate one win from today—big or small—by writing it down or sharing it with someone you trust.

Create a ritual for weekly reflection: What steps did I take? What held me back? What's my next move?

Write a final affirmation that ties it all together. Example: "I trust my voice. I give myself permission."

Visualize: Write your affirmation so you can see it every day. This is your Permission Mission Mantra.

Practice: Create a weekly ritual of celebration. Each Sunday, write down three wins—no matter how small—and say aloud, "These steps are proof of my progress."

Take Action: Celebrate your progress—big or small. Choose one small win to honor today. Then commit to your next step, because permission without action is just potential.

EPILOGUE

What Kind of Backup Singer Are You?

> Words do not live in dictionaries, they live in the mind.
>
> **—Virginia Woolf**

I know I don't have to tell you that words matter. Kind words matter and so do cruel words. I don't have to tell you because you remember both of those from your childhood. The words that others in your life said to you when you were young have become part of who you are now that you're grown, for better or for worse.

You know the sting of a criticism that perhaps has just enough truth in it that you believe it about yourself to this day. You understand that when someone you love and trust characterizes you in an unflattering or unfair way, you carry that with you, and it affects your ability to trust your own judgment.

Yes, words matter.

Which words are you saying to the young people in your life?

You, dear friend, are the backup singer that those impressionable kids will remember years from now whenever they consider taking a risk or trying something new. They will remember you and your words when they really, really want to go for something but they're not so sure they should, or are capable, or can handle it—because in one moment on one day way back when, you said they probably shouldn't or can't.

You might even have uttered the dreaded, "I wouldn't do that if I were you."

Can I remind you that you're not them, just as this was true for the adult who said it to you when you were a kid? But you took it to heart, didn't you? You thought if this grown-up, with all of her education and experience and wisdom and intelligence, wouldn't do it if she were me, maybe I shouldn't do it, either.

What kind of backup singer do you want to be? You have to decide *right now,* because right now is when you're speaking the words you say to the kids and even to the adults who trust and rely on you to tell it like it is.

Do you want to limit these children, students, young neighbors, interns, employees, and friends for the rest of their lives?

I'll answer for you: Of course not. So watch your words, starting now. Be mindful that the people you're speaking them to will play them over and over again like an old, scratched-up vinyl album that repeats the same thing again and again, and they will never, ever forget them.

Start thinking of yourself as a backup singer for others—not the star of their shows, but the steady voice in the background, the one who helps carry the melody, the rhythm, the soul of someone's life song. The words you say today, the tone you set, the encouragement or criticism you offer—they don't just vanish into thin air. They echo. They echo for years. Sometimes, for a lifetime.

Again, what kind of backup singer do you want to be?

If you're careless or harsh, if your words carry judgment like, "You'll never be able to do that," "You're not smart enough," or "You're not as talented as you think you are." Or worse, if you silently pass on your own doubts disguised as advice—"You can't do that," "You shouldn't try," "I would never do a thing like that"—you are planting seeds in that young person's mind. Those seeds will grow into beliefs about who they are and what they can be. Those seeds become weeds, blocking confidence, clouding dreams, muting voices.

These words don't just shape a kid's day, or even a year—they become the soundtrack playing in her memory long after you're gone. You, the backup singer, become an inner voice, guiding or misguiding choices, self-worth, and worldview.

That's powerful. Use your power for good.

Remember the old saying, "Sticks and stones may break my bones, but words will never hurt me"? It's wrong. Words *do* hurt. They hurt more deeply, more quietly, and more permanently.

Words are not just temporary; they are seeds planted in fertile ground. Even when the planter is long gone, the people you have sown them with water those seeds daily, giving everlasting life to either doubt or hope, depending on what you said.

Psychologists show that negative feedback and criticism in childhood can create self-fulfilling prophecies, limiting potential and increasing anxiety and depression later in life. Our inner voice—the one we hear when we're alone—echoes what others said to us long ago.

You know this. You read this book. And you're living with your own backup singers.

When we tell a child, "You're not good enough," that weight just gets heavier as adulthood approaches. When we limit people with our own fears, they learn to doubt themselves. When we frame the world as a place where failure means rejection, they might stop trying altogether.

Here's the hopeful news: Just as words can wound, they can also heal. They can inspire. They can build a resilient, loving inner voice that a person can carry through life's hardest moments.

Consider Aibileen from the Oscar-nominated movie *The Help*. Every day, she tells Mae Mobley, "You is kind. You is smart. You is important." Not "You're a good girl" or "You're pretty." Those words—kind, smart, important—build the toddler's identity in ways that shape her confidence and sense of worth. Aibileen's voice becomes a backup singer in Mae Mobley's life, singing a steady, positive refrain that drowns out negativity.

Imagine if we all spoke like Aibileen. Imagine the strength, the resilience, the courage we'd be helping to cultivate.

And some kids are more prone to your influence than others. Sometimes, life thrusts children out of their safe spaces too soon. When a parent dies young or is absent, a child might become her own backup singer—taking on the role of the parent, the protector, the encourager, or sometimes, the critic.

For these kids, the internal backup singer isn't just background noise; it's survival. It can be nurturing or harsh. If it's harsh, they carry not only the loss of a parent but also a relentless inner critic shaped by early trauma. Understanding this helps us realize how important our words can be for *all* children, especially those who have had to grow up faster than they should.

And think about how your words may differ depending on whether you are speaking to a girl or a boy.

Culturally, we often sing different songs to boys and girls. Girls get told they're pretty. Boys get told they're smart. Girls are praised for appearance, boys for achievement.

This shaping matters. When girls grow up hearing "You're pretty," they might tie their worth to looks. When boys grow up hearing "You're smart," they might tie theirs to performance. Both are incomplete scripts. Both are limiting.

What if instead, we sang songs of kindness, curiosity, creativity, and strength for everyone? What if we said, "You are valuable because you are *you*, regardless of how you look or how fast you succeed?" The world would be richer for it.

You get to choose the kind of backup singer you want to be. You get to practice mindfulness about your words—the power you have in each conversation to shape someone's future.

Every day, you give yourself permission to lift someone up, to boost her self-confidence, to help her in-power herself with self-worth and permission. Or the opposite.

You choose.

I want to be a voice people carry forward. Friends and clients tell me I'm like a bobblehead sitting on their shoulder—a small, steady cheerleader they hear when they need it most, even if I'm not physically there. That brings me so much joy. That's the magic of being a backup singer: You can be a positive influence long after the moment has passed.

Take body image, for example. Casual comments about weight, looks, or ability can be devastating. "You're too fat" or "You'll never be good at math" plants insecurity in young minds, shaping self-doubt for decades.

Instead, you could say: "You're strong," "You have so much potential," "I believe in your ability to learn and grow." These are seeds worth planting.

Your role as a backup singer is not just temporary. It's not about momentary praise or criticism. It's about helping to build someone's lifelong soundtrack.

The choices you make in your conversations today—especially with young people—are an opportunity to do something extraordinary: to power someone's journey forward with kindness, confidence, and courage.

The choice is yours. Will you sing a song that lifts, encourages, and empowers? Or one that limits, judges, and casts a shadow over potential?

Be mindful. Be kind. Be the voice that someone carries forever. Be the backup singer who nudges the people you meet into the spotlight on the stage of their lives.

Whether you realize it or not, whether you want it or not, you are—or soon will be—a backup singer for the rest of someone's life. Give yourself permission to change their soundtrack forever.

Endnotes

PART 1

Chapter 1

"You are not" Dunaway, Faye. "You are not an extra in somebody else's film." AZ Quotes. Accessed August 30, 2025. https://www.azquotes.com/quote/1246818.

Chapter 2

Researchers call this: McAdams, Dan P. "'First We Invented Stories, Then They Changed Us': The Evolution of Narrative Identity." *ESIC* 3, no. 1 (2019). https://web.ics.purdue.edu/~drkelly/McAdamsFirstWeStoriesThenTheyChangedUs2019.pdf.

the 2013 documentary: *20 Feet from Stardom*. Directed by M. Neville. Los Angeles, CA: Tremolo Productions and Gil Friesen Productions, 2013.

Chapter 3

"Many of us": Dalla-Camina, Megan. "From 'Good Girl' to Authentic Leader." *Real Women* (blog). *Psychology Today*. May 9, 2025. https://www.psychologytoday.com/us/blog/real-women/202505/from-good-girl-to-authentic-leader.

In my book: McGovern, Cindy. *Every Job is a Sales Job: How to Use the Art of Selling to Win at Work*. McGraw-Hill Education, 2019.

Psychological and sociocultural: Gerdeman, Dina. "How Gender Stereotypes Kill a Woman's Self-Confidence." Harvard Business School. February 25, 2019. https://www.library.hbs.edu/working-knowledge/how-gender-stereotypes-less-than-br-greater-than-kill-a-woman-s-less-than-br-greater-than-self-confidence.

Imposter syndrome: Harvey, Joan C. and Cynthia Katz. *If I'm So Successful, Why Do I Feel Like a Fake?: The Imposter Phenomenon*. St. Martin's Press, 1985.

Good Girl Syndrome: Fezler, William and Eleanor S. Field. *The GoodGirl Syndrome: How Women Are Programmed to Fail in a Man's World and How to Stop It*. MacMillan, 1985.

women can face: Brescoll, Victoria L. "Who Takes the Floor and Why: Gender,

Power, and Volubility in Organizations." *Administrative Science Quarterly* 56, no. 4 (2012): 622–641. https://doi.org/10.1177/0001839212439994/.

women were paid: Fry, Richard and Carolina Aragão. "Gender Pay Gap in U.S. Has Narrowed Slightly over 2 Decades." Pew Research Center. March 4, 2025. https://www.pewresearch.org/short-reads/2025/03/04/gender-pay-gap-in-us-has-narrowed-slightly-over-2-decades/#:~:text=The%20gender%20gap%20in%20pay,81%25%20as%20much%20as%20men.

Chapter 4

"Some rules are": Fowler, Therese Anne. *Souvenir.* Ballantine Books, 2008.

A 1963 law: Carmel California. "Fun Facts About Carmel." Accessed August 30, 2025. https://www.carmelcalifornia.com/fun-facts-about-carmel/.

City of Carmel-By-The-Sea. "Chapter 8.44 Permits for Wearing Certain Shoes." Code Publishing. March 31, 2025. https://www.codepublishing.com/CA/CarmelbytheSea/html/Carmel08/Carmel0844.html.

Tiernan, Meaghan Clark. "The Outrageous 1962 Law That Carmel Still Hasn't Abolished." SFGATE. April 12, 2025. https://www.sfgate.com/centralcoast/article/weird-awful-california-laws-restricting-dress-20263621.php.

those boxes lead: Whelpley, Heather. *An Overachiever's Guide to Breaking the Rules: How to Let Go of Perfect and Live Your Truth.* Wise Ink, 2020.

Chapter 5

"Power's not given": *Life Is But a Dream.* Directed by Ed Burke and Beyoncé Knowles. Encino, CA: Parkwood Entertainment, 2013.

Chapter 6

"Grit is living": TED. "Grit: The Power of Passion and Perseverance | Angela Dee Duckworth | TED." YouTube video, 6:12. May 9, 2013. https://youtu.be/H14bBuluwB8?si=nZPTXMbjdtICaNi1.

beloved Disney character: Seif, S. and S. Winston. "Dumbo and the Magic Feather: A Great Metaphor for Anxiety Reduction Techniques." JSA Psychotherapy. February 27, 2017. https://jsapsychotherapy.com/dumbo-and-the-magic-feather-a-great-metaphor-for-anxiety-reduction-techniques/.

PART 2

Chapter 7

"Tell me, what": Oliver, Mary. "Poem 133: The Summer Day." In *New and Selected Poems*. Beacon Street, 1992.

Consider Walt Disney: Gillett, Rachel. "How Walt Disney, Oprah Winfrey, and 19 Other Successful People Rebounded After Getting Fired." *Inc.* October 7, 2015. https://www.inc.com/business-insider/21-successful-people-who-rebounded-after-getting-fired.html.

Chapter 8

"The minute you": Dowd, Maureen. "The minute you settle for less than you deserve, you get even less than you settled for." Brainy Quote. Accessed August 31, 2025. https://www.brainyquote.com/quotes/maureen_dowd_391359.

"I can't even": Faris, Anna, host. "Gwyneth Paltrow." Anna Fair Is Unqualified (podcast). March 22, 2021. Accessed December 22, 2025. https://unqualified.com/episodes/gwyneth-paltrow/?utm_source=chatgpt.com.

depicted women as: Wood, Julia T. "Chapter 9: Gendered Media: The Influence of Media on Views of Gender." In *Gendered Lives: Communication, Gender, and Culture*, 231–244. NYU Reprinted from Wadsworth Publishing, 1994. https://pages.nyu.edu/jackson/causes.of.gender.inequality/Readings/Wood%20-%20Gendered%20Media%20-%2094.pdf.

"SeeHer": SeeHer. "Our Mission." Accessed September 17, 2025. https://www.seeher.com/about/.

overcome the entertainment: Geena Davis Institute. "Home Page." Accessed August 31, 2025. https://geenadavisinstitute.org.

pledged to collaborate: Lee, Chantelle. "Nicole Kidman on the 'Radical Honesty' of *Babygirl* and Her Female Director Pledge." *Time.* February 25, 2025. https://time.com/7225495/nicole-kidman-women-of-the-year-interview/.

just 26.7 percent: Cocca, Carolyn. *Superwomen: Gender, Power, and Representation*. Bloomsbury, 2016.

Engage in self-reflection: Sutton, Anna. "Measuring the Effects of Self-Awareness: Construction of the Self-Awareness Outcomes Questionnaire." *Europe's Journal of Psychology* 12, no. 4 (2016): 645–658. https://doi.org/10.5964/ejop.v12i4.1178.

Practice self-compassion: Neff, K. D. and Pommier, E. "The Relationship Between Self-Compassion and Other-Focused Concern Among College Undergraduates, Community Adults, and Practicing Meditators." *Self and Identity 12*, no. 2 (2013): 160–176. https://doi.org/10.1080/15298868.2011.649546.

Set boundaries: Nash, Jo. "How to Set Healthy Boundaries & Build Positive Relationships." PositivePsychology.com. January 5, 2018. https://positivepsychology.com/great-self-care-setting-healthy-boundaries/.

Stop comparing: Festinger, Leon. "A Theory of Social Comparison Processes." *Human Relations* 7, no. 2 (1954): 117–140. https://doi.org/10.1177/001872675400700202.

Chapter 9

"If you want": Morrison, Toni. "If you want to fly, you have to give up everything that weighs you down." Goodreads. Accessed September 22, 2025. https://www.goodreads.com/quotes/10758622-if-you-want-to-fly-you-have-to-give-up.

"You are the": Rohn, Jim. *The Jim Rohn Guide to Personal Development.* Success Enterprises, 2014.

"Sometimes, it ain't": Macasero, Michael. "'Don't Be an A**hole to People, Cause You Never Know Who the F**k You May Be Talking To'—LeBron James' Advice on Treating People Correctly on the Journey to Success, Says His Mother Raised Him the Right Way." Sportskeeda. Last modified November 8, 2022. https://www.sportskeeda.com/basketball/news-don-t-a-hole-people-cause-never-know-f-k-may-talking-to-lebron-james-advice-treating-people-correctly-journey-success-says-mother-raised-right-way?utm_source=chatgpt.com.

clients often felt: Schwartz, Richard C. *Internal Family Systems Therapy.* Guilford Press, 1997.

Upholding the traditions: Brown, Brené. *Atlas of the Heart: Mapping Meaningful Connection and the Language of Human Experience.* Random House, 2021.

allowing others to: Galindo, Linda. *The 85% Solution: How Personal Accountability Guarantees Success—No Nonsense, No Excuses.* Jossey-Bass, 2009.

Chapter 10

"When we deny": Brown, Brené. "Own Our History. Change the Story." June 18, 2015. https://brenebrown.com/articles/2015/06/18/own-our-history-change-the-story/.

"I felt . . . that": S., Pangambam. "Full Transcript: Natalie Portman Harvard Commencement Speech 2015." The Singju Post. April 6, 2019. https://singjupost.com/full-transcript-natalie-portman-harvard-commencement-speech-2015/.

"It makes me": Selleck, Emily. "Selena Gomez Feels 'Sick' Thinking About Her Past Negative Self-Talk: 'I Had My Rock Bottom.'" *Page Six.* March 14, 2024. https://pagesix.com/2024/03/14/entertainment/selena-gomez-feels-sick-thinking-about-her-past-negative-self-talk/.

going over those: Evans, Patricia. *The Verbal Abusive Relationship, Expanded Third Edition: How to Recognize It and How to Respond.* Adams Media, 2010.

Looking-Glass Self: Cooley, Charles Horton. *Human Nature and the Social Order.* Charles Scribner's Sons, 1902.

question in 2015: Stampler, Laura. "Here's What Happens When Women Decide to Call Themselves Beautiful." *Time.* April 7, 2015. https://time.com/3773858/dove-choose-beautiful-average-door/.

"I really needed": Lima, Jamie Kern. "Jamie Kern Lima | WORTHY." *Goss Magazine.* September 21, 2025. https://gossclub.com/jamie-kern-lima-worthy/?utm_source=chatgpt.com.

Chapter 11

"It took me": Steffenauer, Kami. "Incalculable but Invisible: Why Georgetown Should Erect a Statue of Madeleine Albright." The Georgetown Voice. March 21, 2023. https://georgetownvoice.com/2023/03/21/erect-a-statue-of-madeleine-albright/.

many people feel: Brummelman, Eddie, Sander Thomaes, Meike Slagt, et al. "My Child Redeems My Broken Dreams: On Parents Transferring Their Unfulfilled Ambitions onto Their Child." *PLoS One* 8, no. 6 (2013): e653360. https://doi.org/10.1371/journal.pone.0065360.

"Would you tell": Carroll, Lewis. "Chapter 6: Pig and Pepper." In *Alice's Adventures in Wonderland*, 82–100. Macmillan, 1865.

"If you can": Clear, James. *Atomic Habits: An Easy & Proven Way to Build Good Habits & Break Bad Ones.* Avery, 2018.

Chapter 12

"If you obey": Hepburn, Katharine. "If you obey all the rules, you miss all the fun." AZ Quotes. Accessed August 31, 2025. https://www.azquotes.com/quote/130410.

"Sir, you're doing": Oscars. "Julia Roberts Wins Best Actress | 73rd Oscars (2001)." YouTube video, 5:04. April 25, 2008. https://youtu.be/ZV0YbYEC-U7A?si=buYJB-j9Y9l_4WmT.

Social Learning Theory: Sutton, Jeremy. "What Is Bandura's Social Learning Theory? 3 Examples." PositivePsychology.com. May 17, 2021. https://positivepsychology.com/social-learning-theory-bandura/.

saw a difference: Zou, Xi and Krishna Savani. "Descriptive Norms for Me, Injunctive Norms for You: Using Norms to Explain the Risk Gap." *Judgment and Decision Making* 14, no. 6 (2019): 644–648. https://pdfs.semanticscholar.org/ae46/776d34ec303af01f93ba69da88dca04b76dd.pdf.

"My mom said": Markie. "Cher on Dateline with Jane Pauly (1996) 4K." YouTube video, 13:10. April 9, 2023. https://youtu.be/PKUL18U1J28?si=sUN-DoXi39f9MbqYS.

One BuzzFeed user: Capobianco, Molly. "People Are Sharing the Most Utterly Ridiculous Rule That They Ever Had to Follow at Work, and Wow, Most of These Bosses Should Be Fired." BuzzFeed. March 14, 2023. https://www.buzzfeed.com/mollycapobianco/worst-workplace-rules.

Chapter 13

"I've never seen": Gilbert, Elizabeth. "Dear Ones: Yesterday I Wrote on Twitter, 'I've never seen any life transformation that didn't begin with the person in question finally getting tired of their own bullshit.'" May 7, 2014. https://www.elizabethgilbert.com/dear-ones-yesterday-i-wrote-on-twitter-ive-never-seen-any-life-transformati/.

Prince Harry and: Davies, Caroline. "Prince Harry: We Had 'No Other Option' Than to Stand Down as Royals." *The Guardian*. January 19, 2020. https://www.theguardian.com/uk-news/2020/jan/19/harry-and-meghan-in-netflix-sights-says-streaming-firm-chief.

Scobie, Omid and Carolyn Durand. "Finding Freedom Book: Meghan Gave Up Her Entire Life for Harry and His Family." *The Times*. August 24, 2020. https://www.thetimes.com/article/finding-freedom-book-meghan-markle-prince-harry-srbkwxvz6.

PART 3

"The world hates": Zarowitz, Barbara. "The World Hates Change, Yet It Is the Only Thing That Has Brought Progress." –Charles Kettering, 1959." *Journal of the American College of Clinical Pharmacy* 3, no. 8 (2020): 1403–1404. https://doi.org/10.1002/jac5.1333.

Chapter 14

"All too often": Blakely, Sara. "All too often we are taught that 'fear' is a bad thing." Facebook, April 15, 2019. https://www.facebook.com/sarablakely/photos/all-too-often-we-are-taught-that-fear-is-a-bad-thing-but-sometimes-the-presence-/779633425752446/?locale=ms_MY.

"It was my": Streisand, Barbara. *My Name is Barbara.* Viking, 2023.

"I thought I": TEDx Talks. "Standing Up to Fear | David Nihill | TEDManchester." YouTube video, 15:49. March 8, 2019. https://youtu.be/r2gEpWKOQ1Y?si=P7jlEBCQwUvMhroY.

Adele, has openly: PerformanceAnxiety.com. "How Adele Manages Her Stage Fright." Last modified June 24, 2024. https://performanceanxiety.com/adele-stage-fright/.

reportedly declined at: Genard, Gary. 2014. "Abraham Lincoln and Stage Fright: How to Overcome Fear of Public Speaking." *Speak for Success!* (blog). *The Genard Method.* August 3, 2014. https://www.genardmethod.com/blog/abraham-lincoln-and-stage-fright-how-to-overcome-fear-of-public-speaking#:~:text=Following%20the%20Cooper%20Union%20talk,was%20a%20lawyer%2C%20after%20all.

Mean World Syndrome: Perera, Ayesh. "Cultivation Theory in Media." Simply Psychology. Last modified September 7, 2023. https://www.simplypsychology.org/cultivation-theory.html?utm_source=chatgpt.com.

the more fear: Wake, Sean, Jolie Wormwood, and Ajay B. Satpute. "The Influence of Fear on Risk Taking: A Meta-Analysis." *Cognition and Emotion* 34, no. 6 (2020): 1143–1159. https://doi.org/10.1080/02699931.2020.1731428.

Chronic fear can: Rosenberg, Jaime. "The Effects of Chronic Fear on a Person's Health." AJMC. November 11, 2017. https://www.ajmc.com/view/the-effects-of-chronic-fear-on-a-persons-health.

that exposure therapy: Catanese, Lisa. "Exposure Therapy: What Is It and How

Can It Help?" Harvard Health Publishing. July 15, 2024. https://www.health.harvard.edu/mind-and-mood/exposure-therapy-what-is-it-and-how-can-it-help.

Chapter 15

"the obnoxious roommate": Huffington, Arianna. "Do you ever feel like you have imposter syndrome, that feeling of phoniness in people who believe that they are not intelligent, capable or creative despite evidence of high achievement." LinkedIn, 2018. https://www.linkedin.com/posts/ariannahuffington_this-is-how-you-get-rid-of-imposter-syndrome-activity-6413080757694132224-6Loa?utm_source=share&utm_medium=member_desktop&rcm=ACoAACrb8T4BfExlW2vl1u8IP1dHaZq5Ui5tK2g.

"When are they": Gross, Terry, host. "Tom Hanks Says Self-Doubt Is 'A High-Wire Act That We All Walk.'" Fresh Air (podcast). April 26, 2016. Accessed August 31, 2025. https://www.npr.org/2016/08/29/491800907/tom-hanks-says-self-doubt-is-a-high-wire-act-that-we-all-walk.

"never goes away": Impostor Syndrome Institute. "Unpacking Michelle Obama's Imposter Syndrome." Accessed August 31, 2025. https://impostorsyndrome.com/article-featured/unpacking-michelle-obamas-impostor-syndrome/.

"I have written": Angelou, Maya. "I have written 11 books but each time I think 'Uh-oh, they're going to find out now.'" BBC. April 25, 2016. https://www.bbc.com/news/magazine-36082469.

"imposter phenomenon": Clance, Pauline Rose and Suzanne Ament Imes. "The Imposter Phenomenon in High Achieving Women: Dynamics and Therapeutic Intervention." *Psychotherapy: Theory, Research & Practice* 15, no. 3 (1978): 241–247. https://psycnet.apa.org/doi/10.1037/h0086006.

"First of all": Banks, Emma. "Gillian Anderson Has Some Very Relatable Thoughts on Imposter Syndrome." *InStyle*. April 1, 2025. https://www.instyle.com/gillian-anderson-eleanor-roosevelt-self-doubt-11706929.

imposter syndrome is: Young, Dr. Valerie. "What If I Really Am an Imposter?" Impostor Syndrome Institute. Accessed August 31, 2025. https://impostorsyndrome.com/articles/what-if-i-really-am-an-impostor/.

Chapter 16

"I definitely think": Ditrolio, Megan. "What Reese Witherspoon Wants You to Remember About Failure." *Marie Claire*. September 21, 2018. https://www.

marieclaire.com/celebrity/a23340335/reese-witherspoon-crate-and-barrel/.

"started to black": Clarendon, Dan. "'The Streak Is Over!': Remembering Susan Lucci's Overdue Daytime Emmy Win, 25 Years Later." *TV Insider*. May 21, 2024. https://www.tvinsider.com/1136802/susan-lucci-1999-daytime-emmy-award-win/.

"Every time I": Go Red for Women. "Prioritizing Care for Others, Women Often Neglect Their Own Health." Accessed August 31, 2025. https://www.goredforwomen.org/en/beyond-the-table/stories/women-often-neglect-their-own-health.

rejected by thirty: Shukla, Girish. "Meet the Author Who Turned Rejection into a Bestselling Phenomenon." *Times Now News*. Last modified February 21, 2025. https://www.timesnownews.com/lifestyle/books/features/meet-the-author-who-turned-rejection-into-a-bestselling-phenomenon-article-118436543?utm_source=chatgpt.com.

rejected by thirty-seven: Gilchrist, Karen. "Media Icon Arianna Huffington Faced 37 Rejections Before Kick-Starting Her Career." CNBC Make It. June 25, 2019. https://www.cnbc.com/2019/06/25/huffington-post-founder-faced-rejection-before-kick-starting-career.html?utm_source=chatgpt.com.

failed four times: WOWSA. "WOWSA Advisory Board's Decision on Diana Nyad's 2013 Cuba to Florida Swim." Open Water Swimming. September 9, 2023. https://www.openwaterswimming.com/wowsa-advisory-boards-decision-on-diana-nyads-2013-cuba-to-florida-swim/.

"Try again": Beckett, Samuel. *Worstward Ho*. Grove Press Inc., 1983.

"Grit is having": Duckworth, Angela. *Grit: The Power of Passion and Perseverance*. Scribner, 2016.

trying again after: Edmondson, Amy C. 2023. "Framing Failure for Learning and Innovation." *Executive Education* (blog). Harvard Business School. December 21, 2023. https://www.exed.hbs.edu/blog/framing-failure-for-learning-innovation?utm_source=chatgpt.com.

scientist at 3M: Post-it. "History Timeline: Post-it® Notes." Accessed August 31, 2025. https://www.post-it.com/3M/en_US/post-it/contact-us/about-us/.

Learning from others: Towry, Kristy. "Researchers Urge: Learn from (Someone Else's) Experience." Emory Goizueta Business School. October 29, 2020. https://goizueta.emory.edu/research-spotlight/

researchers-urge-learn-someone-elses-experience.

"Insanity is doing": Einstein, Albert. "Insanity is doing the same thing, over and over again, but expecting different results." QuoteFancy. Accessed August 31, 2025. https://quotefancy.com/quote/35/Albert-Einstein-Insanity-is-doing-the-same-thing-over-and-over-again-but-expecting.

It's not a: Sheldon, Kennon M., Richard Ryan, and Harry T. Reis. "What Makes for a Good Day? Competence and Autonomy in the Day and in the Person." *Personality and Social Psychology Bulletin* 22, no. 12 (1996): 1270–1279. https://selfdeterminationtheory.org/SDT/documents/1996_SheldonRyanReis.pdf.

women are prone: Tinsley, Catherine H. and Robin J. Ely. "What Most People Get Wrong About Men and Women." *Harvard Business Review*, May–June 2018. https://hbr.org/2018/05/what-most-people-get-wrong-about-men-and-women.

Driving Instructors Association. "Study Reveals the Different Reaction Each Gender Has to Failure." March 10, 2022. https://www.driving.org/study-reveals-the-different-reaction-each-gender-has-to-failure/?utm_source=chatgpt.com.

Szulanski, Gabriel and Sidney Winter. "Getting It Right the Second Time." *Harvard Business Review*, January 2002. https://hbr.org/2002/01/getting-it-right-the-second-time.

Chapter 17

"Some people believe": Landers, Ann. "Some people believe holding on and hanging in there are signs of great strength." Goodreads. Accessed December 22, 2025. https://www.goodreads.com/quotes/17642-some-people-believe-holding-on-and-hanging-in-there-are.

she wanted to: Winfrey, Oprah, host. "Super Soul Special: Julianna Margulies." Oprah's Super Soul (podcast). April 24, 2024. Accessed August 31, 2025. https://www.oprah.com/own-podcasts/super-soul-special-julianna-margulies.

Mobil credit card: Raggio, Eva. "A Woman Left Her Abusive Husband in Dallas and Went on to Become Tina Turner." *Dallas Observer.* May 24, 2023. https://www.dallasobserver.com/music/a-reminder-that-tina-turner-left-her-abuser-ike-at-the-statler-hotel-in-dallas-16659314/?utm_source=chatgpt.com.

raising her children: UNICEF. "Audrey Hepburn: UNICEF Goodwill Ambassador from 1988 to 1993." Accessed August 31, 2025. https://www.unicef.org/goodwill-ambassadors/audrey-hepburn?utm_source=chatgpt.com.

Florence Nightingale rejected: History.com Editors. "Florence Nightingale." *HISTORY.* Last modified May 28, 2025. https://www.history.com/articles/florence-nightingale.

divorced her husband: WAMS and The New York Historical Story. "Life Story: Edith Wharton (1862–1937). Accessed August 31, 2025. https://wams.nyhistory.org/industry-and-empire/labor-and-industry/edith-wharton/.

hard for women: Mehrotra, Shinjini. "The Cages You Live In: Understanding Social Conditioning." Shinjinim. Accessed August 31, 2025. https://shinjinim.com/2021/09/29/the-cages-you-live-in-understanding-social-conditioning/?utm_source=chatgpt.com.

"sunk cost fallacy": Pilat, Dan and Dr. Sekoul Krastev. "Why Are We Likely to Continue with an Investment Even if It Would Be Rational to Give It Up?" The Decision Lab. Accessed August 31, 2025. https://thedecisionlab.com/biases/the-sunk-cost-fallacy.

Ann Russell Miller: Orrell, Harriet. "The US Socialite Who Gave It All Up to Become a Carmelite Nun." BBC. June 8, 2021. https://www.bbc.com/news/world-us-canada-57399288.

Her son, Mark: Ibid.

At her farewell: Ibid.

walking away reinforces: Grand Rising Staff. "The Importance of Addressing Toxic Relationships in Mental Health Care." *Grand Rising Behavioral Health* (blog). February 23, 2025. https://www.grandrisingbehavioralhealth.com/blog/the-importance-of-addressing-toxic-relationships-in-mental-health-care?utm_source=chatgpt.com.

Chapter 18

"Don't be afraid": Scott, Kendra. "Don't be afraid to ask for help." Brainy Quote. Accessed August 31, 2025. https://www.brainyquote.com/quotes/kendra_scott_1215179?utm_source=chatgpt.com.

Eshita Kabra-Davies: Prevett, Hannah. "Clothes for Rent? Men Didn't Get It, So I Raised Money from Women." *The Times.* March 7, 2025. https://www.thetimes.com/business-money/entrepreneurs/article/clothes-for-rent-men-didnt-get-it-so-i-raised-money-from-women-g23t2tkdv.

saying "yes" to: De Witte, Melissa. "Asking for Help Is Hard, but People

Want to Help More Than We Realize, Stanford Scholar Says." *Stanford Report* (blog). *Stanford University*. September 8, 2022. https://news.stanford.edu/stories/2022/09/asking-help-hard-people-want-help-realize.

"The majority of": Zhao, Xuan and Nicholas Epley. "Surprisingly Happy to Have Helped: Underestimating Prosociality Creates a Misplaced Barrier to Asking for Help." *Psychological Science* 33, no. 10 (2022): 1708–1731. https://doi.org/10.1177/09567976221097615.

"As a girl": Summers, Juanna, host. "Rapper Flavor Flav on Why He Decided to Sponsor the U.S. Women's Water Polo Team." All Things Considered (podcast). August 4, 2024. Accessed August 31, 2025. https://www.npr.org/2024/08/04/nx-s1-5061526/rapper-flavor-flav-on-why-he-decided-to-sponsor-the-u-s-womens-water-polo-team.

convince "any man": Petit, Stephanie. "Kevin Hart Gave Tiffany Haddish Money When She Was Homeless and Living in Her Car." *People*. January 30, 2018. https://people.com/movies/kevin-hart-gave-tiffany-haddish-money-homeless/.

Chapter 19

"Your new life": Wiest, Brianna. *The Mountain Is You: Transforming Self-Sabotage into Self-Mastery*. Thought Catalog Books, 2020.

"You're saying 'no'": Stott, Nikkley, host. "The Grief No One Talks About When You Change Your Body | Ep. 252." The Macro Hour (podcast). April 21, 2025. Accessed August 31, 2025. https://www.themacrohour.com/2109644/episodes/17013142-the-grief-no-one-talks-about-when-you-change-your-body-ep-252.

"The more you keep": Ibid.

PART 4

Chapter 20

"There is always": Steinem, Gloria. "Gloria Steinem—Happy 80th Birthday and Thank You!" Suites Culturelles. March 28, 2014. https://suitesculturelles.wordpress.com/tag/gloria-steinem/?utm_source=chatgpt.com.

"When I write": Vonnegut, Kurt. *Conversations with Kurt Vonnegut*. University

Press of Mississippi, 1988.

"I am no": Mazur, Gail. "Michelangelo: To Giovanni Da Pistoia When the Author Was Painting the Vault of the Sistine Chapel." Poetry Foundation. Accessed August 31, 2025. https://www.poetryfoundation.org/poems/57328/michaelangelo-to-giovanni-da-pistoia-when-the-author-was-painting-the-vault-of-the-sistine-chapel.

lack of confidence: Davis, Becke Martin. "What Would Agatha Christie Say?" Helping Writers Become Authors. January 20, 2012. https://www.helpingwritersbecomeauthors.com/what-would-agatha-say/.

"You gain strength": Franklin D. Roosevelt Library & Museum. "Eleanor Roosevelt Biography." Accessed August 31, 2025. https://www.fdrlibrary.org/er-biography.

"The worst enemy": Plath, Sylvia. *The Unabridged Journals of Sylvia Plath*. Vintage, 2000.

"If you hear": Van Gogh, Vincent. *The Letters of Vincent van Gogh*. Penguin Classics, 1998.

think in two: Kahneman, Daniel. *Thinking, Fast and Slow*. Farrar, Straus, and Giroux, 2011.

Chapter 21

"If you think": Gracious Quotes. "Top 39 Mary Kay Ash Quotes (LEADERSHIP). November 30, 2023. https://graciousquotes.com/mary-kay-ash/?utm_source=chatgpt.com.

"Everybody said, 'Nobody": Oches, Sam. "How Candace Nelson Achieved Sweet Success." NRN. October 2, 2024. https://www.nrn.com/casual-dining/how-candace-nelson-achieved-sweet-success?utm_source=chatgpt.com.

Chapter 22

"You have been": Hay, Louise. *You Can Heal Your Life*. Hay House, 1984.

seventh-grade boys: Dodd, Johnny. "Aly Raisman Says Abuse by Team Doctor Began When She Was 15: 'It's Horrific What I Went Through.'" *People*. November 13, 2017. https://people.com/sports/aly-raisman-abuse-team-doctor-began-when-she-was-15/.

first black supermodel: Castilla, Amira. "The Complex Life of Donyale Luna, the First Black Supermodel." *The Root*. September 15, 2023. https://www.theroot.com/the-complex-life-of-donyale-luna-the-first-black-super-1850842057?utm_source=chatgpt.com.

as socially "maladjusted": Medhurst, Eleanor. "The Miraculous Masculinity of Gladys Bentley." Dressing Dykes. June 4, 2021. https://dressingdykes.com/2021/06/04/the-miraculous-masculinity-of-gladys-bentley/?utm_source=chatgpt.com.

one time denied: De Beauvoir, Simone. *The Second Sex*. Vintage International, 2011.

"This question made": Pilley, Max. "Billie Eilish Says She's 'Never Really Felt Very Beautiful': 'Being a Woman is Hard.'" NME. April 14, 2025. https://www.nme.com/news/music/billie-eilish-says-shes-never-really-felt-very-beautiful-being-a-woman-is-hard-3854853.

came to terms: Muñoz, Jacob. "The Powerful, Complicated Legacy of Betty Fridan's 'The Feminine Mystique.'" *Smithsonian Magazine*, February 4, 2021.

"one of the": Beck, Aaron T., A. John Rush, Brian F. Shaw, and Gary Emery. *Cognitive Therapy of Depression*. The Guilford Press, 1987.

Chapter 23

"Love yourself first": Ball, Lucille. "Love yourself first and everything else falls into line." Brainy Quote. Accessed October 8, 2025. https://www.brainyquote.com/quotes/lucille_ball_127076.

when a neighbor's: Alcott, Louisa May. *Little Women*. Roberts Brothers, 1868.

"in Mandarin Chinese": Green, L. "Self, Selfish, Selfish!" *VIVANT Magazine*, October 1, 2018. https://www.vivantmagazine.com/selfish-selfish-selfish/.

Edward VIII, who: HISTORY.com Editors. "Duke of Windsor Weds American Socialite Wallis Simpson." *HISTORY*. Last modified May 28, 2025. https://www.history.com/this-day-in-history/june-3/duke-of-windsor-weds.

"It's literally impossible": Villarreal, Yvonne. "Read the Stirring Monologue About Womanhood America Ferrera Delivers in 'Barbie.'" *Los Angeles Times*. July 23, 2023. https://www.latimes.com/entertainment-arts/movies/story/2023-07-23/barbie-america-ferrera-monologue.

when women practice: Angel Care, Inc. "The Importance of Self-Care for Caregivers." September 26, 2023. https://angelcareny.com/the-importance-of-self-care-for-caregivers/?utm_source=chatgpt.com.

Chapter 24

"The best and": Keller, Helen. "The best and most beautiful things in the world cannot be seen or even touched." Goodreads. Accessed September 23, 2025. https://www.goodreads.com/quotes/4900-the-best-and-most-beautiful-things-in-the-world-cannot.

she would rather: O'Dea, Eve. "The Woman's Picture: Garbo-Spotting." Eve on Film. June 1, 2024. https://www.eveonfilm.com/post/the-woman-s-picture-garbo-spotting.

reduce your stress: Calm's Editorial Team. "Can Smiling Make You Happier? 6 Benefits You Need to Know About." *Calm* (blog). May 12, 2025. https://www.calm.com/blog/benefits-of-smiling.

Smiling is contagious: Lewis, Dr. Guy M. "Benefits of Smiling: 8 Unbelievable Reasons to Smile More." *Dental Blog. Texas Center for Cosmetic Dentistry.* November 10, 2022. https://lovethatsmile.com/dental-articles/benefits-of-smiling-8-unbelievable-reasons-to-smile-more.

joy isn't simply: Moon, Tiffany. *Joy Prescriptions: How I Learned to Stop Chasing Perfection and Embrace Connection*. Legacy Lit, 2025.

Empathy-Altruism Hypothesis: Miyazono, Kengo and Kiichi Inarimori. "Empathy, Altruism, and Group Identification." *Frontiers in Psychology* 12 (2021). https://doi.org/10.3389/fpsyg.2021.749315.

Dixon, Travis. "Key Theory & Studies: The Empathy-Altruism Hypothesis (Batson et al. 1981 & 1982). IB Psychology. July 15, 2023. https://www.themantic-education.com/ibpsych/2023/07/15/key-theory-studies-the-empathy-altruism-hypothesis-batson-et-al-1981-1982/?utm_source=chatgpt.com.

crying at work: Weldon, Michele. "OK to Cry? Expressing Emotions and Vulnerability Is a New Wave at Work." *The Movement Blog. Take the Lead Women*. April 12, 2024. https://www.taketheleadwomen.com/blog/ok-to-cry-expressing-emotions-and-vulnerability-is-a-new-wave-at-work?utm_source=chatgpt.com.

"Any basketball questions": Golden State Warriors. "Steve Kerr Comments on the Tragic Shooting in Uvalde, Texas." YouTube video, 2:50. May 24, 2022.

https://youtu.be/vPvf5RgCU08?si=muQHROsVgV9TS95S.

"I'm so tired . . .": Ibid.

Walden starts to: *Courage Under Fire*. Directed by Edward Zwick. Los Angeles, CA: Davis Entertainment, Fox 2000 Pictures, Joseph M. Singer Entertainment, and 20th Century Fox, 1996.

"encouraged to develop": Barden, Donald W. *Here Come the Girls: A Celebration of Why Women Will Take over Global Leadership in 2028*. Independently Published, 2025.

the societal pressures: *The Mask You Live In*. Directed by Jennifer Siebel Newsom. Sacramento, CA: The Representation Project, 2015.

PART 5

Chapter 25

"There's no prerequisites": He, Grace. "62 Inspiring Women Empowerment Quotes for Work." *Quotes* (blog). *TeamBuilding.com*. Last modified February 13, 2025. https://teambuilding.com/blog/women-empowerment-quotes?utm_source=chatgpt.com.

"You're a black": McKinney, Jessica. "Tracee Ellis Ross Considers Cutting Apperance on 'Black-ish' Amid Anthony Anderson Pay Gap." Vibe. January 18, 2018. https://www.vibe.com/music/music-news/tracee-ellis-ross-gender-pay-gap-anthony-anderson-black-ish-560033/.

"Women belong in": Edge, Simon. "Battle of the Sexes: When Bobby Riggs Called Out Billie Jean King." *Express*. June 20, 2013. https://www.express.co.uk/sport/tennis/408768/Battle-of-the-sexes-When-Bobby-Riggs-called-out-Billie-Jean-King.

Engineer Robert Kearns: Crockett, Zachary. "The Epic, Decades-Long Battle Between Ford and a Small-Time Inventor." The Hustle. September 2, 2019. https://thehustle.co/windshield-wiper-inventor-robert-kearns.

7 percent compared: Exley, Christine L., Muriel Niederle, and Lise Vesterlund. "Knowing When to Ask: The Cost of Leaning In." *Journal of Political Economy* 128, no. 3 (2020): 816–854. https://www.journals.uchicago.edu/doi/10.1086/704616.

struggles of women: *Who Does She Think She Is?* Directed by Pamela Tanner Boll and Nancy Kennedy. Los Angeles, CA: Mystic Artists Films Productions, 2008.

Chapter 26

"I am no": Davis, Angela Y. "I am no longer accepting the things I cannot change." Goodreads. Accessed October 8, 2025. https://www.goodreads.com/quotes/7767240-i-am-no-longer-accepting-the-things-i-cannot-change.

"It is better": Dorner, Udi. "Ask Permission, Not Forgiveness." *Forbes*. July 12, 2023. https://www.forbes.com/councils/forbesbusinesscouncil/2023/07/12/ask-permission-not-forgiveness/.

Chapter 27

"Find out who": Parton, Dolly. "Find out who you are and do it on purpose." X, April 8, 2015. https://x.com/dollyparton/status/585890099583397888.

Chapter 28

"The whole point": Winfrey, Oprah. "What Oprah Knows for Sure About Finding the Courage to Follow Your Dreams." Oprah.com. Accessed August 31, 2025. https://www.oprah.com/spirit/what-oprah-knows-for-sure-about-finding-your-dreams.

the "Kotex girl,": Herndon, Meredith. "Lee Miller's Legacy: From Fashion Model to War Correspondent." *Smithsonian African Women's History Museum* (blog). *Smithsonian*. September 26, 2024. https://womenshistory.si.edu/blog/lee-millers-legacy-fashion-model-war-correspondent.

Putnam, Jennifer. "Lee Miller: Witness to the Concentration Camps and the Fall of the Third Reich." The National WWII Museum. March 28, 2024. https://www.nationalww2museum.org/war/articles/lee-miller-witness-concentration-camps-and-fall-third-reich.

NPR Staff. "Much More Than a Muse: Lee Miller and Man Ray." *NPR*. August 20, 2011. https://www.npr.org/2011/08/20/139766533/much-more-than-a-muse-lee-miller-and-man-ray.

wild fashion choices: Ciminelli, David. "Lady Gaga's Fashion Woes: Sometimes Style Overshadows Substance." *California Apparel News*. April 25, 2011. https://www.apparelnews.net/news/2011/apr/25/lady-gagas-fashion-woes-sometimes-style/.

"I don't think": Briese, Nicole. "The Real Reason Lady Gaga Toned Down Her

Look Will Make You Cheer." Brit + Co. September 23, 2017. https://www.brit.co/lady-gaga-style-evolution-netflix-documentary/.

a "comedy genius": Crouch, Ian. "Martha Stewart, Comedy Genius?" *The New Yorker*. November 17, 2016. https://www.newyorker.com/culture/culture-desk/martha-stewart-comedy-genius-snoop-dogg-potluck-dinner.

Chapter 29

"Stop comparing yourself": Liv. "'Walk Your Walk . . .' A Lesson About Comparison Inspired by Michelle Obama." Liv Your Life. March 31, 2020. https://livyourlife.ca/2020/03/31/walk-your-own-walk-a-lesson-about-comparison-inspired-by-michelle-obama/.

Demi Lovato grew: Ganz, Caren. "How Honest Can Demi Lovato Be?" *The New York Times*. Last modified April 6, 2021. https://www.nytimes.com/2021/03/16/arts/music/demi-lovato-interview.html.

"I have been": Clerk, Carol. *Madonna Style*. Omnibus Press, 2009.

"Our heroes are": Twain, Mark. *Mark Twain at Your Fingertips: A Book of Quotations*. Dover Publications, 2009.

"I was spending": Heid, Markham. "We Need to Talk About Kids and Smartphones." *Time*. Last modified October 10, 2017. https://time.com/4974863/kids-smartphones-depression/.

"The mental health": Murthy, Vivek H. "Surgeon General: Why I'm Calling for a Warning Label on Social Media Platforms." *The New York Times*. June 17, 2024. https://www.nytimes.com/2024/06/17/opinion/social-media-health-warning.html.

heavy social media: STRIPED. "Science Summary: The Impact of Social Media on Adolescent Health." Harvard T.H. Chan. Accessed August 31, 2025. https://hsph.harvard.edu/research/eating-disorders-striped/policy-translation/holding-social-media-platforms-accountable/science-summary-social-media-adolescent-health/.

More than 60: Schulz, Matt. "62% of Gen Zers Feel Pressured to Keep Up with the Joneses, as Many Overspend into Debt." LendingTree. Last modified March 18, 2024. https://www.lendingtree.com/debt-consolidation/overspending-survey/.

many of the: Fligstein, Neil, Pat Hastings, and Adam Goldstein. "Keeping Up with the Joneses: Inequality and Indebtedness, in the Era of the Housing Price Bubble, 1999–2007." University of California, August 2015. https://sociology.berkeley.edu/sites/default/files/faculty/fligstein/Keeping%20up%20with%20the%20Jones%203.1.pdf.

Social Comparison Theory: Festinger, Leon. "A Theory of Social Comparison Processes." Human Science. 1954. https://www.humanscience.org/docs/Festinger%20%281954%29%20A%20Theory%20of%20Social%20Comparison%20Processes.pdf.

Festinger, Leon. *A Theory of Cognitive Dissonance.* Stanford University Press, 1975.

"If you struggle": Robbins, Mel and Sawyer Robbins. *The Let Them Theory: A Life-Changing Tool That Millions of People Can't Stop Talking About.* Hay House, 2024.

Avoiding social media: STRIPED. "Science Summary: The Impact of Social Media on Adolescent Health." Harvard T.H. Chan. Accessed August 31, 2025. https://hsph.harvard.edu/research/eating-disorders-striped/policy-translation/holding-social-media-platforms-accountable/science-summary-social-media-adolescent-health/.

Chapter 30

"It takes years": Poehler, Amy. *Yes Please.* Dey Street, 2014.

"I say 'sorry'": Dunham, Lena. "Sorry, Not Sorry: My Apology Addiction." LinkedIn, May 25, 2016. https://www.linkedin.com/pulse/sorry-my-apology-addiction-lena-dunham/.

women reported that: Gupta, S. and Risen, J. L. "Why Women Apologize More Than Men: Gender Differences in Thresholds for Perceiving Offensive Behavior." *Psychological Science* 21, no. 11 (2010): 1649–1655. https://www.pittcorelab.com/uploads/1/1/5/5/115561629/why_women_apologize_more_than_men_10.pdf.

people who apologize: Young, Emma. "People Who Apologise a Lot Are Seen as More Warm and Sincere." The British Psychological Society. February 17, 2022. https://www.bps.org.uk/research-digest/people-who-apologise-lot-are-seen-more-warm-and-sincere.

women are conditioned: Schumann, Karina and Michael Ross. "Why Women Apologize More Than Men: Gender Differences in Thresholds for Perceiving

Offensive Behavior." *Psychological Science* 21, no. 11 (2010): 1649–55. https://doi.org/10.1177/0956797610384150.

"Men aren't actively": Ibid.

"I learned that": Koblin, John. "Ellen DeGeneres Returns to Show with Apology for Toxic Workplace." *The New York Times*. Last modified May 21, 2021. https://www.nytimes.com/2020/09/21/business/media/ellen-degeneres-show.html.

Chapter 31

"Forgiving isn't something": Picoult, Jodi. *The Storyteller*. Atria/Emily Bestler Books, 2013.

weight of your: Selva, Joaquin. "Why Shame and Guilt Are Functional for Mental Health." PositivePsychology.com. January 22, 2018. https://positivepsychology.com/shame-guilt/.

when we hurt: Boon, Susan D., Madelynn R. D. Stackhouse, and Hollman Lozano. "Reconsidering Forgiveness and Unforgiveness: A Call for a More Nuanced Understanding of Unforgiveness." *Social and Personality Psychology Compass* 19 (2015): e70047. https://doi.org/10.1111/spc3.70047.

Being forgiven actually: Tangney, June P., Angela L. Boone, and Rhonda L. Dearing. "Forgiving the Self: Conceptual Issues and Empirical Findings." In *Handbook of Forgiveness*, edited by Everett L. Worthington Jr., 143–158. Routledge, 2005.

when others won't: Ibid.

Toussaint, Loren, Everett L. Worthington Jr., and David R. Williams. "Forgiveness and Health: Scientific Evidence and Theories Relating Forgiveness to Better Health." In *Handbook of Forgiveness*, edited by Everett L. Worthington Jr. and N. Wade, 2nd ed., 203–214. Routledge, 2015.

That's because holding: Ibid.

impact that forgiveness: Johns Hopkins Medicine. "Forgiveness: Your Health Depends on It." Accessed August 31, 2025. https://www.hopkinsmedicine.org/health/wellness-and-prevention/forgiveness-your-health-depends-on-it.

"I went through": Groth, Leah. "The Important Self-Truth Jane Fonda Learned from Her Mother's Suicide." Prevention. September 19, 2018. https://www.prevention.com/health/mental-health/a23317858/jane-fonda-mother-suicide/.

OWN. "Jane Fonda on Learning to Forgive Yourself | Oprah's Master Class |

Oprah Winfrey Network." YouTube video, 2:04. January 9, 2012. https://youtu.be/raOVBwoGlD4?si=54WWcwQgl9sFgodL.

blaming others might: Golden, Bernard. "7 Consequences of Blaming Others for How We Manage Anger." *Overcoming Destructive Anger* (blog). *Psychology Today.* November 10, 2018. https://www.psychologytoday.com/us/blog/overcoming-destructive-anger/201811/7-consequences-blaming-others-how-we-manage-anger.

Chapter 32

"'No' is a": Anne Lamott Quotes. "'No' is a complete sentence." X, October 18, 2017. https://x.com/AnneLamottQuote/status/920657616707182592?utm_source=chatgpt.com.

Chapter 33

"Say yes, and": Winfrey, Oprah. "Tina Fey's Aha! Moment." *O, The Oprah Magazine*, June 2003. https://www.oprah.com/omagazine/tina-feys-aha-moment?utm_source=chatgpt.com.

"I would say": Rhimes, Shonda. "My Year of Saying Yes to Everything." TED video, 18:34. February 2016. https://www.ted.com/talks/shonda_rhimes_my_year_of_saying_yes_to_everything.

"A crazy thing": Ibid.

when we're generous: Grant, Adam. *Give and Take: Why Helping Others Drives Our Success*. Viking, 2013.

"Altruism, Happiness and": Post, Stephen G. "Altruism, Happiness, and Health: It's Good to Be Good." *International Journal of Behavioral Medicine* 12, no. 2 (2005): 66–77. https://doi.org/10.1207/s15327558ijbm1202_4.

credited his success: Adam, Grant, host. "Richard Branson on Saying Yes Now and Figuring It Out Later." ReThinking (podcast). June 18, 2024. Accessed August 31, 2025. https://www.ted.com/pages/richard-branson-on-saying-yes-now-and-figuring-it-out-later-transcript.

Chapter 34

"I always give": Winfrey, Oprah. "How Oprah Protects and Restores Her Energy Every Day." Oprah.com. Accessed August 31, 2025. https://www.oprah.com/ownyourhealth/how-oprah-relaxes-what-oprah-does-to-relax.

"Almost everything will": Pierce, Kristen Pedroli. "Almost Everything Will

Work Again if You Unplug It." The MRP Project. June 30, 2020. https://themrpproject.org/almost-everything-will-work-again-if-you-unplug-it/.

overworking can change: BMJ Group. "Long Working Hours May Alter Brain Structure, Preliminary Findings Suggest." Accessed August 31, 2025. https://bmjgroup.com/long-working-hours-may-alter-brain-structure-preliminary-findings-suggest/.

long working hours: Saunders, Tom. "85% of Workers 'Burnt Out and Exhausted.'" *The Times*. May 12, 2025. https://www.thetimes.com/business/companies-markets/article/85-percent-workforce-burnout-mental-health-reed-pvcqwt3l3?gaa_at=eafs&gaa_n=AWEtsqcUVmlc86GB9O92g9a-Kq3UVUa7RUN13zLI9PbI8LwhEA_okkCo4Psmjel104M8%3D&gaa_ts=694b0a2f&gaa_sig=oL9PzUSsTwHjn-yfoZxC05KqicMfu75UBy-o4BJiDT0-NPWBMXQzGdylSQ1petR_lvG-7bHKRhnA8GLN1eL-4hEg%3D%3D.

85 percent: Ibid.

women, especially those: American Heart Association. "Prioritizing Care for Others, Women Often Neglect Their Own Health." Go Red for Women. Last modified November 10, 2020. https://www.goredforwomen.org/en/beyond-the-table/stories/women-often-neglect-their-own-health.

55 percent of: Transamerica Institute. "Caregiving Is Risky Business for Family Caregivers." September 2017. https://www.transamericainstitute.org/research/publications/details/caregiving-is-risky-business-for-family-caregivers?utm_source=chatgpt.com.

you could be: Mieres, Dr. Jennifer. "Caregiver Burnout Can Hurt Your Heart." *Heart and Smiles* (blog). *Psychology Today*. July 2018. https://www.psychologytoday.com/us/blog/heart-smarts/201807/caregiver-burnout-can-hurt-your-heart.

American Heart Association. "Prioritizing Care for Others, Women Often Neglect Their Own Health." Go Red for Women. Last modified November 10, 2020. https://www.goredforwomen.org/en/beyond-the-table/stories/women-often-neglect-their-own-health.

a phenomenon trauma: Figley, C. R. "Compassion Fatigue as Secondary Traumatic Stress Disorder: An Overview." In *Compassion Fatigue: Coping with Secondary Traumatic Stress Disorder in Those Who Treat the Traumatized*, 1–20.

Brunner/Mazel, 1995.

Wikipedia contributors. "Compassion Fatigue." Wikipedia, The Free Encyclopedia. Last modified November 27, 2025. https://en.wikipedia.org/wiki/Compassion_fatigue.

"When we take": Hudson, Kate G. "The irony is that when we take care of ourselves first, we are in a much stronger place to take care of those we love." Goodreads. Accessed October 21, 2025. https://www.goodreads.com/quotes/7573171-the-irony-is-that-when-we-take-care-of-ourselves.

"Remember, if you": Levenson, Sam. *In One Era and Out the Other.* Simon & Schuster, 1973.

"Never expect people": Ziogas, George J. "Do You Treat Others Better Than You Treat Yourself?" Medium. March 12, 2022. https://georgejziogas.medium.com/do-you-treat-others-better-than-you-treat-yourself-1a81be2abc25.

Chapter 35

"If you feel": Carter, Alexandra. "If you feel like you're not worthy enough to ask for what you want, you've already got one foot in the water." LinkedIn, May 2025. https://www.linkedin.com/posts/alexandrabcarter_if-you-feel-like-youre-not-worthy-enough-activity-7329171512001785856-UMtl?utm_source=share&utm_medium=member_desktop&rcm=ACoAACrb8T4BfExl-W2vl1u8IP1dHaZq5Ui5tK2g.

each member of: Sager, Jessica. "Friends with Money! Jennifer Aniston, Courteney Cox, and the Rest of the Cast's Sky-High Salaries for the Series." *Parade.* January 1, 2025. https://parade.com/1212498/jessicasager/friends-cast-salaries/.

Warner Bros. made: Chmielewski, Dawn. "How 'Friends' Generated More Than $1.14 Billion for Its Stars and Creators." *Forbes*. Last modified May 28, 2021. https://www.forbes.com/sites/dawnchmielewski/2021/05/28/how-friends-generated-more-than-14-billion-for-its-stars-and-creators/.

Chapter 36

"You don't owe": Williams, Patrícia. "You Don't Owe Anyone Anything." Medium. November 3, 2020. https://medium.com/change-your-mind/you-dont-owe-anyone-anything-366695714339.

"carefully curated image": Thorpe, Vanessa. "Still Modern After All These Years … Marlene Dietrich's Ageless Charisma." *The Guardian.* November 25, 2017.

https://www.theguardian.com/film/2017/nov/26/marlene-dietrich-androgyny-sexuality-exhibitions.

"incorporate white lives": Malik, Sarah. "Why This Clip of Jana Wendt Interviewing Toni Morrison Has Gone Viral." *Voices* (blog). *SBS*. Last modified February 21, 2019. https://www.sbs.com.au/voices/article/why-this-clip-of-jana-wendt-interviewing-toni-morrison-has-gone-viral/9smkuemml.

Chapter 37

"We must reject": Pope, Karla. "65 Powerful Quotes from Women About Strength and Empowerment." *Good Housekeeping*. Last modified March 6, 2025. https://www.goodhousekeeping.com/life/g38335193/strong-women-quotes/.

"Nothing is more": Cerini, Marianna. "How Coco Chanel Changed the Course of Women's Fashion." *CNN Style* (blog). *CNN*. January 9, 2021. https://www.cnn.com/style/article/coco-chanel-fashion-50-years?utm_source=chatgpt.com.

Nellie Bly: Bly, Nellie. *Ten Days in a Mad-House*. 2019 eBook ed. Norman L. Munro, 1887. https://www.gutenberg.org/ebooks/59899.

engineer Mary Jackson: NASA. "From Hidden to Modern Figures." Accessed October 21, 2025. https://www.nasa.gov/from-hidden-to-modern-figures/.

"A woman is": Fuller, Thomas. *Gnomologia: Adagies and Proverbs; Wise Sentences and Witty Sayings, Ancient and Modern, Foreign and British*. B. Barker, 1732. https://archive.org/details/gnomologiaadagi00conggoog.

"People say for": Newman-Bremang, Kathleen. "Salt-N-Pepa Celebrate Hip-Hop Turning 50 & Talk Navigating the Genre's Misogyny." Refinery29. Last modified February 7, 2023. https://www.refinery29.com/en-us/2023/02/11286200/hip-hop-50-anniversary-salt-n-pepa-interview.

27,069 women earned: WIA Report. "After Four Years of Decline, the Number of Women Earning Research Doctorates Was up 10 Percent in 2022." February 14, 2024. https://wiareport.com/2024/02/after-four-years-of-decline-the-number-of-women-earning-research-doctorates-was-up-10-percent-in-2022/.

"Ignore the glass": Yee, Hannah-Rose. "Ava DuVernay's Powerful Message for Women Dealing with Rejection." *Stylist*. 2018. https://www.stylist.co.uk/people/ava-duvernay-sundance-film-festival-rejection-twitter-message-female-directors/239895.

thirteen had female: CNBC. "CNBC Reveals Eleventh Annual CNBC

Disruptor 50." May 9, 2023. https://www.cnbc.com/2023/05/09/cnbc-reveals-eleventh-annual-cnbc-disruptor-50.html.

Chapter 38

"We realize the": Yousafzai, Malala. "Malala Yousafzai: 16th Birthday Speech at the United Nations." Malala Fund. July 12, 2013. https://malala.org/news-and-voices/malala-un-speech.

public speaking often: National Social Anxiety Center. "Public Speaking Anxiety." Accessed October 21, 2025. https://nationalsocialanxietycenter.com/social-anxiety/public-speaking-anxiety/.

society's expectations persuade: Wimmer, Rishelle. "The Authority Gap: Why Women Are Still Taken Less Seriously Than Men. And What We Can Do About It." *SWE*, Spring 2023. https://swe.org/magazine/media-spring-23/.

women who tended: Brescoll, Victoria L. "Who Takes the Floor and Why: Gender, Power and Volubility in Organizations." *Administrative Science Quarterly* 56, no. 4 (2011): 622–641. https://web.mit.edu/curhan/www/docs/Articles/15341_Readings/Power/brescoll-2012-who-takes-the-floor-and-why-gender-power-and-volubility-in-organizations.pdf.

just plain shy: Keating, Sarah. "The Science Behind Why Some of Us Are Shy." BBC. June 5, 2019. https://www.bbc.com/future/article/20190604-the-science-behind-why-some-of-us-are-shy.

"I am a": Cain, Susan. "The Power of Introverts." TED, 18:47. February 2012. https://www.ted.com/talks/susan_cain_the_power_of_introverts.

Chapter 39

"Never doubt that": Mead, Margaret. "Never Doubt That a Small Group of Thoughtful, Committed Citizens Can Change the World: Indeed It's the Only Thing That Ever Has." National Museum of American History. Accessed September 1, 2025. https://americanhistory.si.edu/collections/object/nmah_1285394.

These were artists: Irvin, Jack. "Dionne Warwick Once Scolded Snoop Dogg and Tupac over Misogynistic Lyrics: 'We Got Out-Gangstered.'" Yahoo! Entertainment. January 3, 2023. https://www.yahoo.com/entertainment/dionne-warwick-once-scolded-snoop-224551963.html.

"Well-behaved women": AmRev360. "Well-Behaved Women Seldom Make History with Laurel Thatcher Ulrich." Museum of the American Revolution.

March 2022. https://www.amrevmuseum.org/amrev360-well-behaved-women-seldom-make-history-with-laurel-thatcher-ulrich.

Chapter 40

"When a woman": Doyle, Glenn. *Untamed.* The Dial Press, 2020.

social pressure activates: Weir, Kirsten. "The Pain of Social Rejection." *Monitor on Psychology* 43, no. 4 (2012): 50. https://www.apa.org/monitor/2012/04/rejection.

cultivating self-awareness: Gökbayrak, N. Simay PhD. "How to Be More Self-Aware and Why It's Important." PsychCentral. Last modified May 6, 2022. https://psychcentral.com/health/how-to-be-more-self-aware-and-why-its-important.

citing mental health: Caplan, Anna Lazarus. "Simone Biles Explains the Twisties—and How She Came Back for the Paris Olympics." *People.* July 30, 2024. https://people.com/simone-biles-explains-the-twisties-and-how-she-came-back-for-paris-olympics-8686088.

"said all she": Atler, Alexander. "Harper Lee, Author of 'To Kill a Mockingbird,' Is to Publish a Second Novel." *The New York Times*. February 3, 2015. https://www.nytimes.com/2015/02/04/books/harper-lee-author-of-to-kill-a-mockingbird-is-to-publish-a-new-novel.html.

Chapter 41

"I never think": Clifford, Catherine. "Irisi Apfel: 10 Life Lessons from a 96-Year-Old Who Is Probably Cooler Than You." CNBC Make It. Last modified July 23, 2021. https://www.cnbc.com/2018/03/29/10-life-lessons-from-96-year-old-iris-apfel.html.

"I've made it": Brar, Faith. "This 76-Year-Old Fitness Fanatic Is Defying Expectations on Every Level." *Shape.* Last modified May 27, 2024. https://www.shape.com/lifestyle/mind-and-body/joan-macdonald-73-year-old-fitness-fanatic.

"Even though you": Ibid.

"Painting's not important": AMBA. "Grandma Moses: Wise Words from a Master Retiree." *Get Amba* (blog). August 8, 2019. https://blog.getamba.com/grandma-moses-wise-words-from-a-master-retiree/.

lifelong learning and: Godman, Heidi. "Get Back Your Social Life to Boost

Thinking, Memory, and Health." *Mind & Mood* (blog). *Harvard Health Publishing, Harvard Medical School.* October 22, 2023. https://www.health.harvard.edu/mind-and-mood/get-back-your-social-life-to-boost-thinking-memory-and-health.

starting small and: FasterCapital. "Pursuing Hobbies and Passions Outside of Work." Accessed August 31, 2025. https://fastercapital.com/topics/pursuing-hobbies-and-passions-outside-of-work.html.

Chapter 42

"Through the sacred": Brach, Tara. "The Sacred Art of Pausing." Awakin.org. Accessed August 31, 2025. https://www.awakin.org/v2/read/view.php?tid=2231.

"I'm not going": Zaccardi, Nick. "Alysa Liu Is First U.S. Woman to Win Figure Skating World Title in 19 Years." NBC Sports. March 28, 2025. https://www.nbcsports.com/olympics/news/alysa-liu-wins-figure-skating-world-championships-2025.

Chapter 43

"Letting others know": Warrell, Margie. "Who Knows What You Know." April 10, 2012. https://margiewarrell.com/who-knows-what-you-know.

"I am the": Muhammad Ali Center. "In His Own Words." Accessed September 1, 2025. https://alicenter.org/meet-ali/in-his-own-words/.

"I opened doors": Karpel, Ari. "Our Exclusive Madonna Interview." *Advocate*. February 2, 2012. https://www.advocate.com/print-issue/cover-stories/2012/02/02/madonna-truth-she-never-left-you?utm_source=chatgpt.com.

"I have the": Roller, Sarah. "10 of Elizabeth I's Key Achievements." History Hit. November 7, 2022. https://www.historyhit.com/elizabeth-i-key-achievements/.

many people withhold: Whitbourne, Susan Krauss PhD. "Bragging: When Is It OK and When Is It Not OK?" *Fulfillment at Any Age* (blog). *Psychology Today*. July 28, 2012. https://www.psychologytoday.com/us/blog/fulfillment-at-any-age/201207/bragging-when-is-it-ok-and-when-is-it-not-ok?utm_source=chatgpt.com.

bragging about yourself: Mittan, Kyle. "Are You Good at What You Do? Bragging About It Could Make People Trust You Less." The University of Arizona News. July 20, 2022. https://news.arizona.edu/news/are-you-good-what-you-do-bragging-about-it-could-make-people-trust-you-less.

overt self-promotion: Sezer, Ovul, Francesca Gino, Michael I. Norton. "Humblebragging: A Distinct—and Ineffective—Self-Presentation Strategy." Working paper, Harvard Business School. 2015-2017. https://www.hbs.edu/ris/Publication%20Files/15-080_97293623-53aa-4df8-b967-38617e144fd9.pdf.

self-promotion can: Tal-Or, Nurit. "Direct and Indirect Self-Promotion in the Eyes of the Perceivers." *Social Influence* 5, no. 2 (2010): 87–100. https://doi.org/10.1080/15534510903306489.

afraid of the: Krueger, Joachim I. PhD. "Why Some People Are Afraid of Praise." *One Among Many* (blog). *Psychology Today.* March 11, 2022. https://www.psychologytoday.com/us/blog/one-among-many/202203/why-some-people-are-afraid-of-praise.

linked a reluctance: Wadley, Jared. "Don't Be Modest. It's OK to Brag." University of Michigan News. April 8, 2021. https://news.umich.edu/dont-be-modest-its-ok-to-brag/.

Chapter 44

"All it takes": Robbins, Mel. "You have the power to change your life." Instagram, March 3, 2021. https://www.instagram.com/p/CL-Vq1xFzOt/?utm_source=chatgpt.com.

given employees $50: Gainsford, Matt. "Zappos: A Case Study into Company Culture." Titus Talent Strategies. July 17, 2024. https://www.titustalent.com/insights/zappos-a-case-study-into-company-culture/.

Zappos Employee Wellness. "Recognition and Fun: How Zappos Demonstrates Core Values." *Zappos Insights* (blog). *Zappos.* Accessed September 1, 2025. https://www.zapposinsights.com/blog/recognition-and-fun-how-zappos-demonstrates-core-values/.

we're often too: McNally, Melanie A. Psy.D. "From Small Steps to Big Wins: The Importance of Celebrating." *Empower Your Mind* (blog). *Psychology Today.* June 12, 2024. https://www.psychologytoday.com/us/blog/empower-your-mind/202406/from-small-steps-to-big-wins-the-importance-of-celebrating?utm_source=chatgpt.com.

celebrating small achievements: Sapolsky, Robert. "Dopamine Jackpot! Sapolsky on the Science of Pleasure." FORA.tv video, 04: 59. July 6, 2022. https://leerburg.com/flix/player.php/2313/Dopamine_Jackpot_Sapolsky_on_the_Science_of_Pleasure?srsltid=AfmBOoqj4fNSuaEwNX9JdlnTfx7_uF02ly-

THX35r3upyna7BDiKcexlI.

Recognizing our accomplishments: McNally, Melanie A. Psy.D. "From Small Steps to Big Wins: The Importance of Celebrating." *Empower Your Mind* (blog). *Psychology Today.* June 12, 2024. https://www.psychologytoday.com/us/blog/empower-your-mind/202406/from-small-steps-to-big-wins-the-importance-of-celebrating?utm_ source=chatgpt.com.

that recognizing progress: Amabile, Teresa and Steven Kramer. *The Progress Principle: Using Small Wins to Ignite Joy, Engagement, and Creativity at Work.* Harvard Business Review, 2011.

"They were usually": Amabile, Teresa and Steven Kramer. "The Worth of Small Things: Teresa Amabile and Steven Kramer on the Progress Principle." American Management Association. Last modified March 24, 2020. https://www.amanet.org/articles/the-worth-of-small-wins-teresa-amabile-and-steven-kramer-on-the-progress-principle/.

negative feedback and: Ackerman, Courtney E. "Self-Fulfilling Prophecy in Psychology." Positive Psychology.com. May 1, 2018. https://positivepsychology.com/self-fulfilling-prophecy/.

About the Author

Dr. Cindy McGovern, known as the First Lady of Sales®, is an internationally acclaimed speaker, sales strategist, and bestselling author whose work redefines the way people think about selling, communication, and personal branding and influence. With a doctorate in organizational communication, she began her career as a college professor before trading the classroom for the real world, where she discovered a bigger mission.

Today, Dr. Cindy helps individuals and organizations understand that sales isn't a business skill; it's a life skill. Her work empowers individuals to advocate for themselves, communicate with confidence, and stop waiting for permission to go after what they want, at work and in life.

As founder and CEO of Orange Leaf Consulting and Academy, Dr. Cindy and her team partner with companies, teams, and leaders to create ethical, effective sales and communication strategies built on trust and real human connection. Her approach helps people learn how to sell themselves, their ideas, and their value, without the "ick" factor, proving that everyone sells every day, whether they realize it or not.

Dr. Cindy is the author of *Wall Street Journal* bestseller *Every Job Is a Sales Job: How to Use the Art of Selling to Win at Work* and *Sell Yourself: How to Create, Live, and Sell a Powerful Personal Brand*, which earned both the 2024 Book Excellence Award and the New York Big Book Award. Her writing blends research, straight talk, and practical tools that help readers discover what they're capable of and "in-powers" them to go after it.

A highly sought-after keynote speaker and workshop leader, Dr. Cindy delivers engaging, highly interactive presentations on sales, leadership, communication, and personal branding. Her sessions are known for equal parts insight, humor, and real talk. Through her work, she inspires others—especially women—to stop waiting for permission and start leading their lives on their own terms.

When she's not helping people to rethink sales and self-advocacy, Dr. Cindy lives in San Francisco with her husband and their dog, Biscuit. She loves to travel, thrives on laughter and great conversations, enjoys dinner with friends—and has a *slight* dark chocolate addiction. If there's food and fun on the menu, count her in.

For more information about Dr. Cindy McGovern or to inquire about speaking engagements, interviews, and events, visit www.DrCindy.com—and don't be surprised if food and travel come up along the way.

Index